DC COMICS PROUDLY PRESENTS

The UNTOLD LEGEND of the BAT MAN ™

Written by
LEN WEIN

Illustrated by
JIM APARO · JOHN BYRNE

TOR

A TOM DOHERTY ASSOCIATES BOOK
NEW YORK

This is a work of fiction. All the characters and events portrayed in this book are fictitious, and any resemblance to real people or events is purely coincidental.

THE UNTOLD LEGEND OF THE BATMAN

Interior design and production by Bob Rozakis, Jodi Saviuk and Alex Saviuk
Edited by Andrew Helfer

A Tor Book
Published by Tom Doherty Associates, LLC
175 Fifth Avenue
New York, NY 10010

www.tor.com

Tor® is a registered trademark of Tom Doherty Associates, LLC.

ISBN 0-812-52042-4
EAN 978-0-812-52042-2

First edition: August 1982

Printed in the United States of America

20   19   18   17   16   15   14   13   12   11

INTRODUCTION TO AN INTRODUCTION

In 1939 *Detective Comics* featured a story called "The Case of the Chemical Syndicate". The seemingly innocuous tale opened with a scene of Commissioner Gordon of Gotham City chatting with his friend, socialite Bruce Wayne. Later in the story a mysterious cloaked figure appeared who not only solved the case Gordon was working on, but also single-handedly brought the criminals to justice. He was called The Bat-Man. Little more was said to explain The Bat-Man's mysterious crusade against the criminal element of the world. His motives remained his own. The only other insight we received into his personality was his secret indentity. In the last panel of the story it was revealed that Bruce Wayne was The Bat-Man!

That was it. It wasn't much of a beginning. His predecessor, and soon to be close friend, Superman, had an entire page to tell of his beginnings, but The Bat-Man had to wait six more issues of *Detective Comics* before he was looked upon with enough regard to be given a history, and then only two pages worth. For almost nine years the stalker of human vermin remained as much an enigma to his faithful readers as he was to his notorious prey until editor Mort Weisinger commissioned writer Bill Finger to draft a full history of the cowled sleuth. It appeared as a single story in 1948, in *Batman* #47. By now The Batman had dropped the hyphen.

Had The Batman followed most of his costumed contemporaries to oblivion, that one story would probably have been enough. But The Batman proved that he was even tougher than the super-powered crime-busters of his time. Because of his vulnerability, he had only his wit and courage to shield him against the ruthless attacks from the soldiers of crime. Cut him and he would bleed. Shove the muzzle of a tommy-gun into his ribs and he was scared. It was, perhaps, this humanity which allowed The Batman not only to endure but also to flourish. His family of crime-fighters grew and he added some of the most infamous and, at the same time, the most unforgettable villains to his Rogues Gallery.

The time has come for a more lengthy retelling of The Batman Legend. But for those of you who expect to find no more than a rehashing of oft-told tales, you are in for a most surprising and pleasurable experience. Writer Len Wein has woven together the human histories of The Batman and his friends and foes into a brilliant psychological thriller which will keep you hooked right up to its shattering climax, when The Batman confronts his most deadly antagonist.

In page after well-crafted page, artists Jim Aparo and John Byrne follow the Darknight Detective through the back alleys and smokey after-hour hangouts of Gotham City's Underworld Figures. The tension of every panel is heightened by the drama of their fine layouts and foreboding shadows.

Besides the tribulations or our brooding hero, you will learn several little-known facts which Wein has cleverly peppered into this exciting yarn. Who, for example, were the first people to wear a Batman and Robin costume? The obvious answers are not necessarily the correct ones.

If you are looking for a book of facts about one of the most fascinating characters in fiction, this book is for you. If, instead, you have a hankering for a fast-paced thriller then...this is ALSO for you.

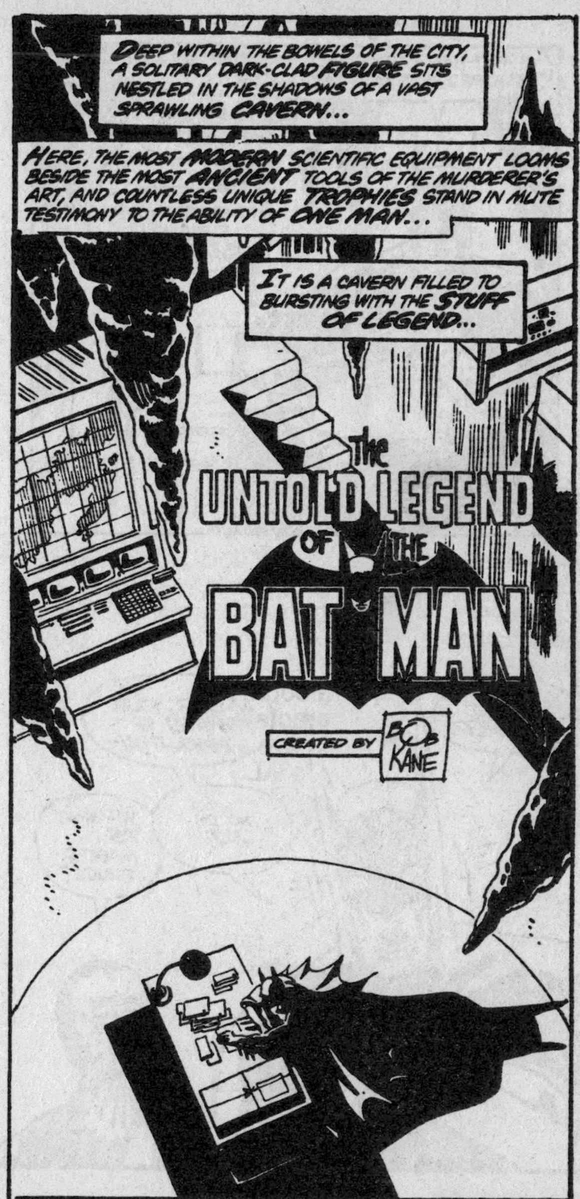
DEEP WITHIN THE BOWELS OF THE CITY, A SOLITARY DARK-CLAD FIGURE SITS NESTLED IN THE SHADOWS OF A VAST SPRAWLING CAVERN...
HERE, THE MOST MODERN SCIENTIFIC EQUIPMENT LOOMS BESIDE THE MOST ANCIENT TOOLS OF THE MURDERER'S ART, AND COUNTLESS UNIQUE TROPHIES STAND IN MUTE TESTIMONY TO THE ABILITY OF ONE MAN...
IT IS A CAVERN FILLED TO BURSTING WITH THE STUFF OF LEGEND...
THE UNTOLD LEGEND OF THE BATMAN
CREATED BY BOB KANE

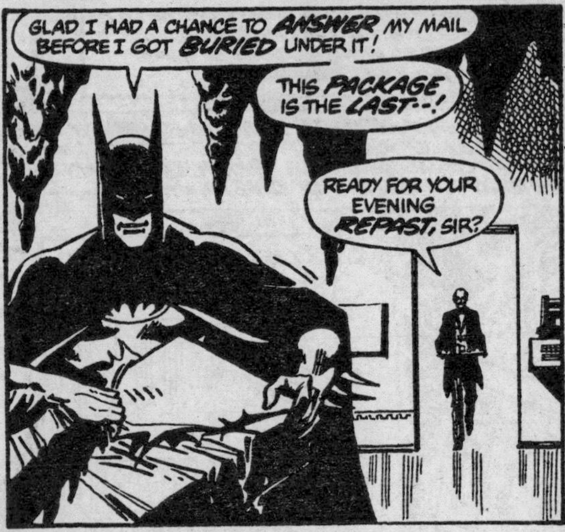
GLAD I HAD A CHANCE TO ANSWER MY MAIL BEFORE I GOT BURIED UNDER IT!
THIS PACKAGE IS THE LAST--!
READY FOR YOUR EVENING REPAST, SIR?

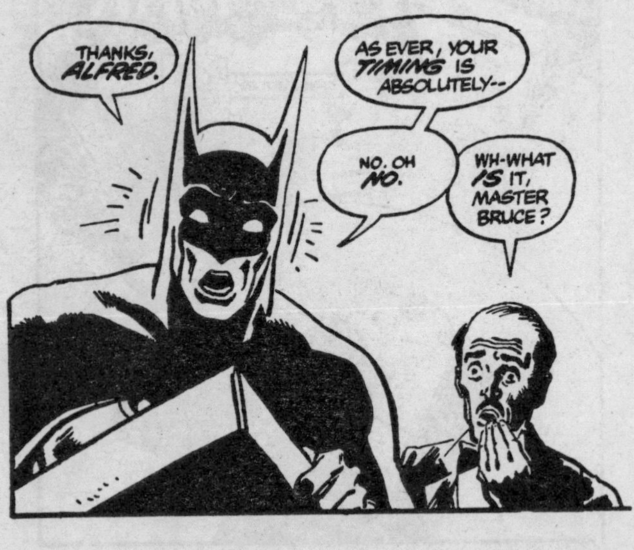
THANKS, ALFRED.
AS EVER, YOUR TIMING IS ABSOLUTELY--
NO. OH NO.
WH-WHAT IS IT, MASTER BRUCE?

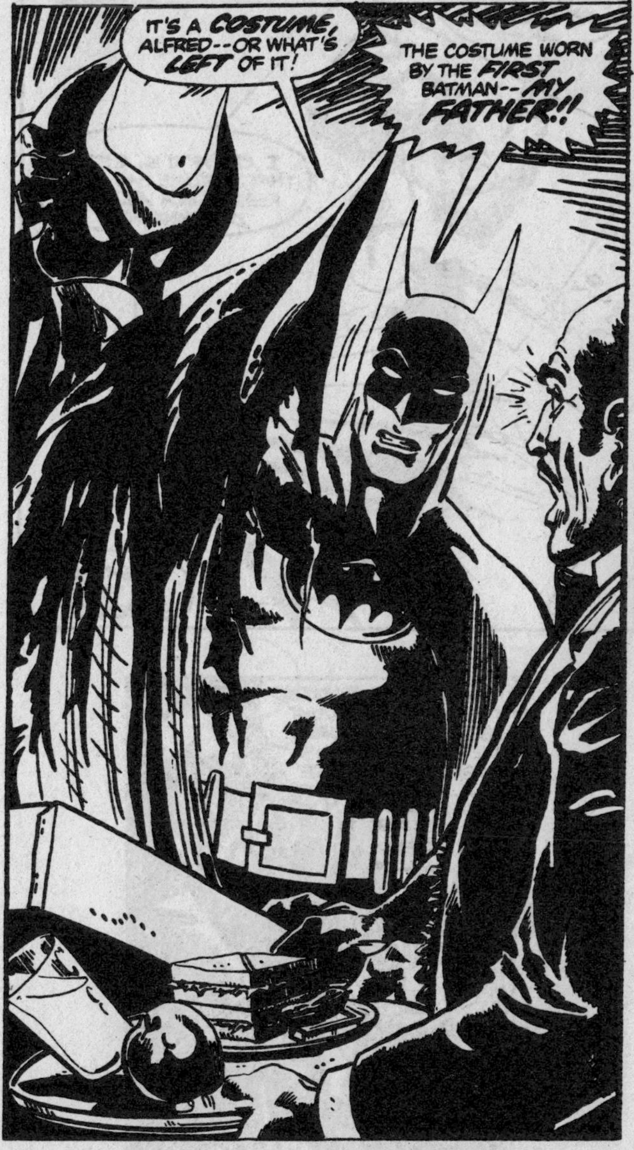
IT'S A COSTUME, ALFRED--OR WHAT'S LEFT OF IT!
THE COSTUME WORN BY THE FIRST BATMAN--MY FATHER!!

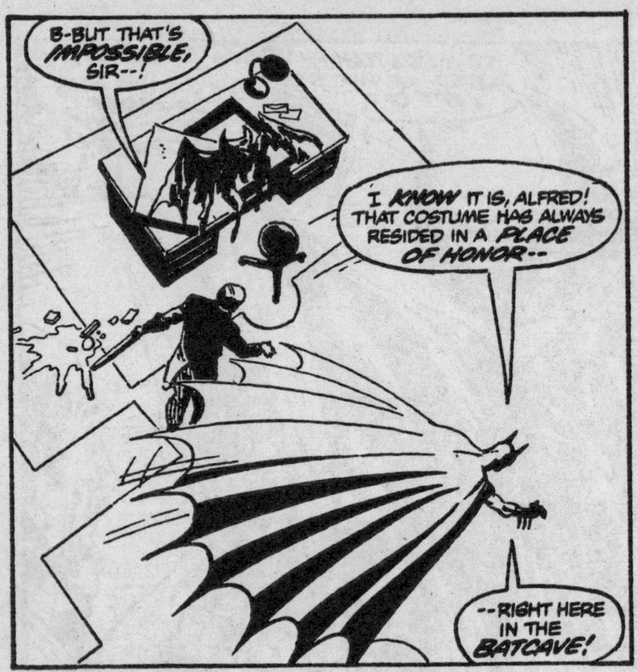
B-BUT THAT'S IMPOSSIBLE, SIR--!
I KNOW IT IS, ALFRED! THAT COSTUME HAS ALWAYS RESIDED IN A PLACE OF HONOR--
--RIGHT HERE IN THE BATCAVE!

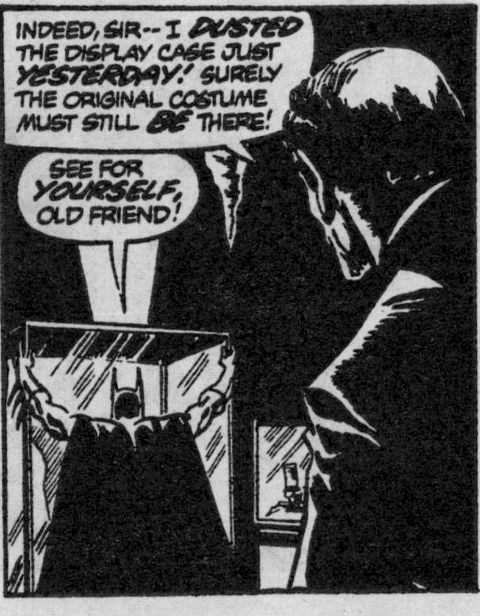
INDEED, SIR--I DUSTED THE DISPLAY CASE JUST YESTERDAY! SURELY THE ORIGINAL COSTUME MUST STILL BE THERE!
SEE FOR YOURSELF, OLD FRIEND!

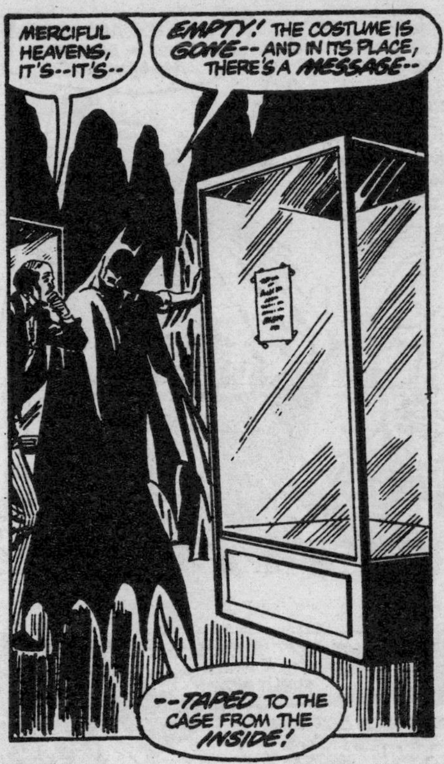
MERCIFUL HEAVENS, IT'S--IT'S--
EMPTY! THE COSTUME IS GONE-- AND IN ITS PLACE, THERE'S A MESSAGE--
--TAPED TO THE CASE FROM THE INSIDE!

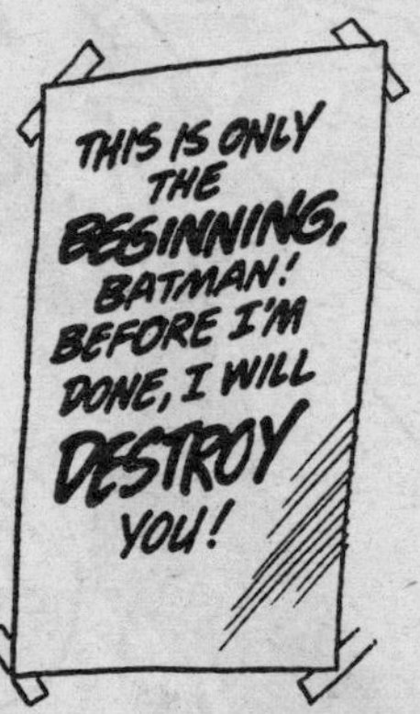
THIS IS ONLY THE BEGINNING, BATMAN! BEFORE I'M DONE, I WILL DESTROY YOU!

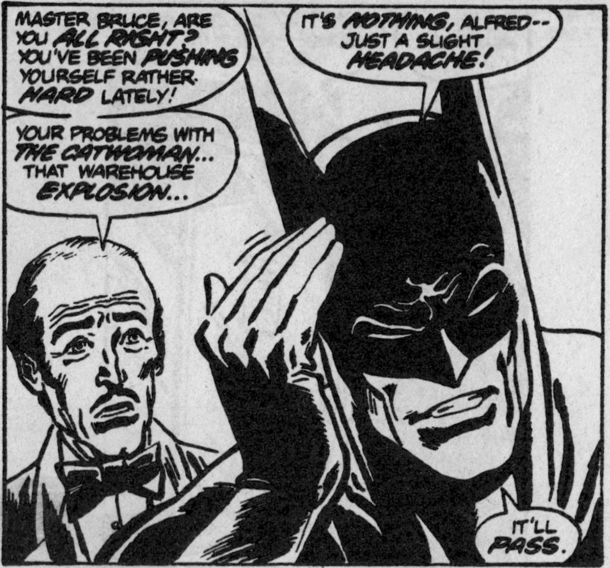
MASTER BRUCE, ARE YOU ALL RIGHT? YOU'VE BEEN PUSHING YOURSELF RATHER HARD LATELY!
YOUR PROBLEMS WITH THE CATWOMAN... THAT WAREHOUSE EXPLOSION...
IT'S NOTHING, ALFRED-- JUST A SLIGHT HEADACHE!
IT'LL PASS.

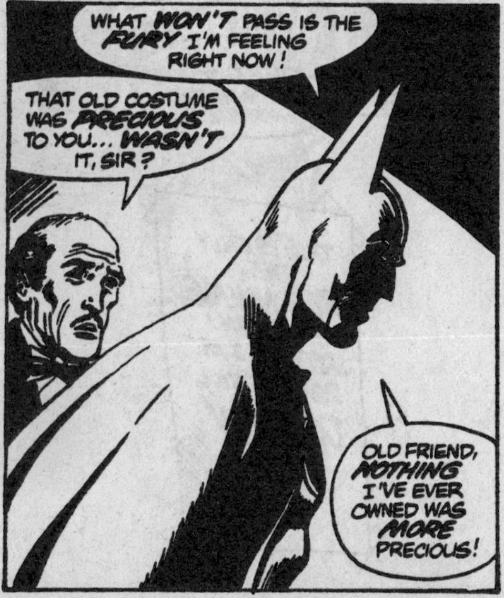
WHAT WON'T PASS IS THE FURY I'M FEELING RIGHT NOW!
THAT OLD COSTUME WAS PRECIOUS TO YOU... WASN'T IT, SIR?
OLD FRIEND, NOTHING I'VE EVER OWNED WAS MORE PRECIOUS!

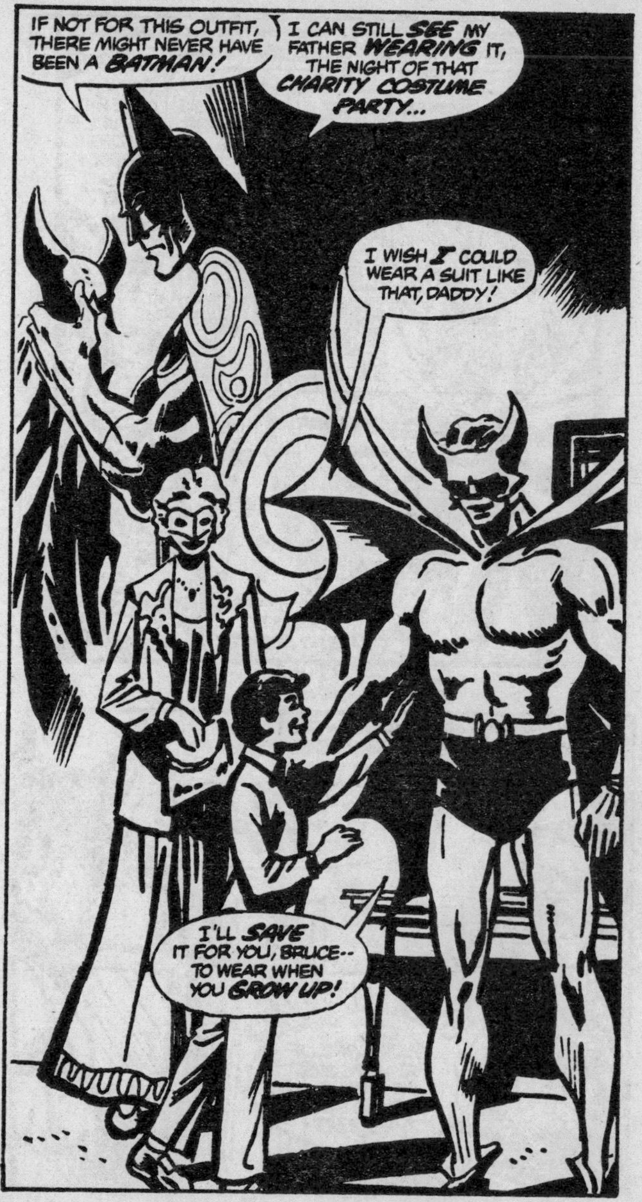
IF NOT FOR THIS OUTFIT, THERE MIGHT NEVER HAVE BEEN A BATMAN!
I CAN STILL SEE MY FATHER WEARING IT, THE NIGHT OF THAT CHARITY COSTUME PARTY...
I WISH I COULD WEAR A SUIT LIKE THAT, DADDY!
I'LL SAVE IT FOR YOU, BRUCE-- TO WEAR WHEN YOU GROW UP!

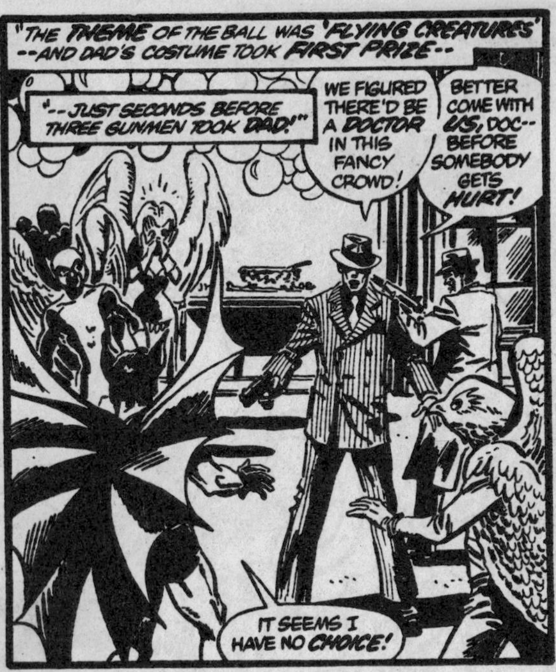
"THE THEME OF THE BALL WAS 'FLYING CREATURES' --AND DAD'S COSTUME TOOK FIRST PRIZE--
"--JUST SECONDS BEFORE THREE GUNMEN TOOK DAD!"
WE FIGURED THERE'D BE A DOCTOR IN THIS FANCY CROWD!
BETTER COME WITH US, DOC-- BEFORE SOMEBODY GETS HURT!
IT SEEMS I HAVE NO CHOICE!

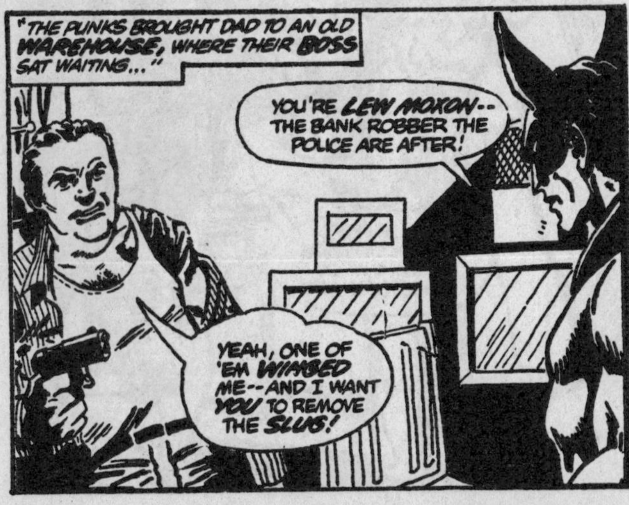
"THE PUNKS BROUGHT DAD TO AN OLD WAREHOUSE, WHERE THEIR BOSS SAT WAITING..."
YOU'RE LEW MOXON-- THE BANK ROBBER THE POLICE ARE AFTER!
YEAH, ONE OF 'EM WINGED ME--AND I WANT YOU TO REMOVE THE SLUG!

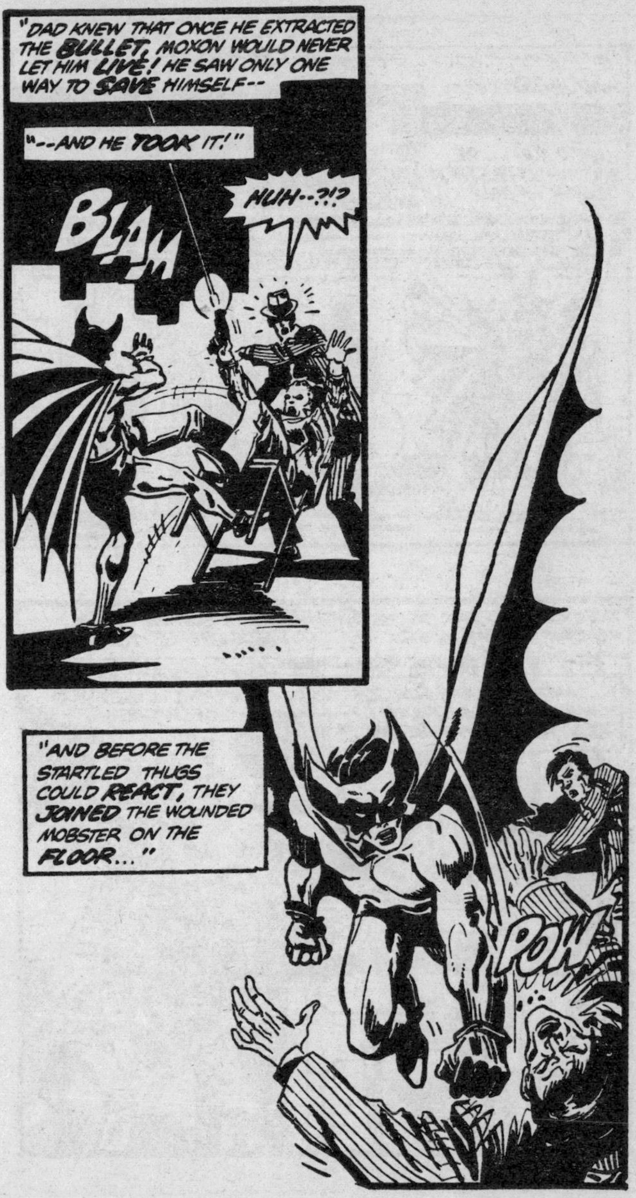

"DAD KNEW THAT ONCE HE EXTRACTED THE BULLET, MOXON WOULD NEVER LET HIM LIVE! HE SAW ONLY ONE WAY TO SAVE HIMSELF--
"--AND HE TOOK IT!"
BLAM
HUH--?!?
"AND BEFORE THE STARTLED THUGS COULD REACT, THEY JOINED THE WOUNDED MOBSTER ON THE FLOOR..."
POW

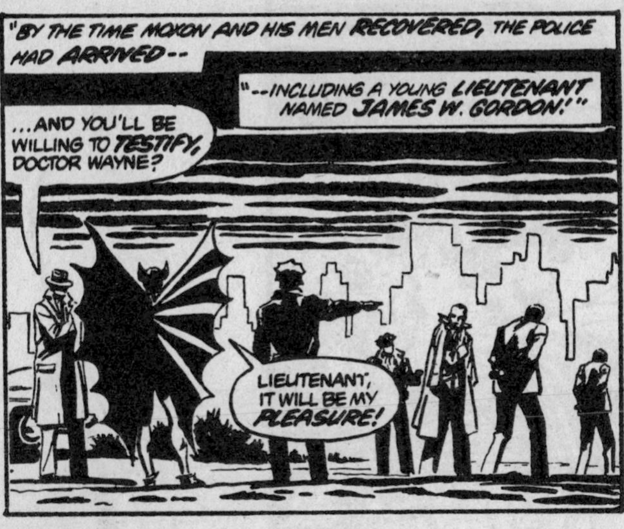
"BY THE TIME MOXON AND HIS MEN RECOVERED, THE POLICE HAD ARRIVED--
"--INCLUDING A YOUNG LIEUTENANT NAMED JAMES W. GORDON!"
...AND YOU'LL BE WILLING TO TESTIFY, DOCTOR WAYNE?
LIEUTENANT, IT WILL BE MY PLEASURE!

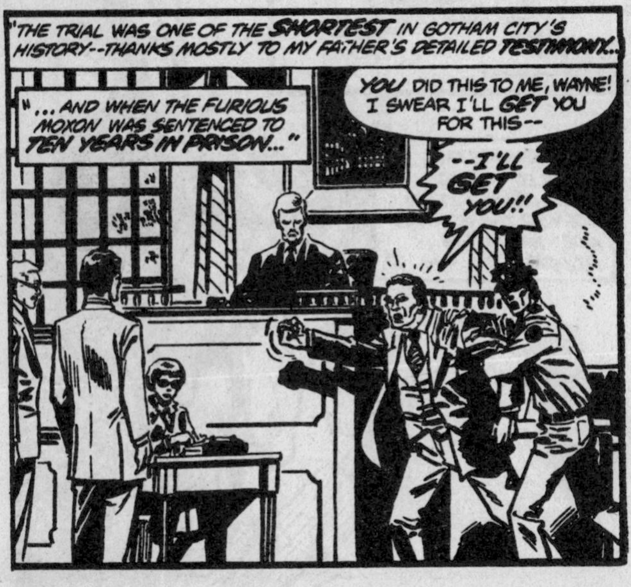
"THE TRIAL WAS ONE OF THE SHORTEST IN GOTHAM CITY'S HISTORY--THANKS MOSTLY TO MY FATHER'S DETAILED TESTIMONY...
"...AND WHEN THE FURIOUS MOXON WAS SENTENCED TO TEN YEARS IN PRISON..."
YOU DID THIS TO ME, WAYNE! I SWEAR I'LL GET YOU FOR THIS--
--I'LL GET YOU!!

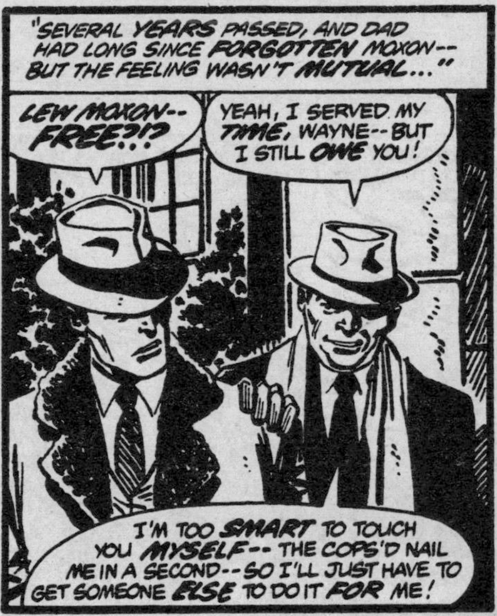
"SEVERAL YEARS PASSED, AND DAD HAD LONG SINCE FORGOTTEN MOXON-- BUT THE FEELING WASN'T MUTUAL..."
LEW MOXON-- FREE?!?
YEAH, I SERVED MY TIME, WAYNE-- BUT I STILL OWE YOU!
I'M TOO SMART TO TOUCH YOU MYSELF-- THE COPS'D NAIL ME IN A SECOND-- SO I'LL JUST HAVE TO GET SOMEONE ELSE TO DO IT FOR ME!

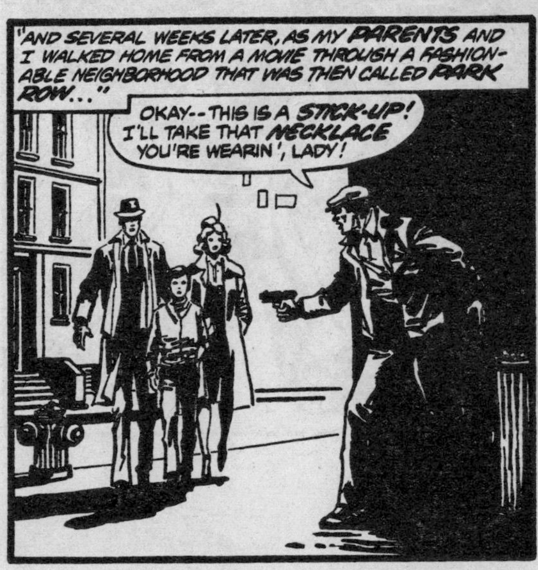
"AND SEVERAL WEEKS LATER, AS MY PARENTS AND I WALKED HOME FROM A MOVIE THROUGH A FASHION-ABLE NEIGHBORHOOD THAT WAS THEN CALLED PARK ROW..."
OKAY-- THIS IS A STICK-UP! I'LL TAKE THAT NECKLACE YOU'RE WEARIN', LADY!

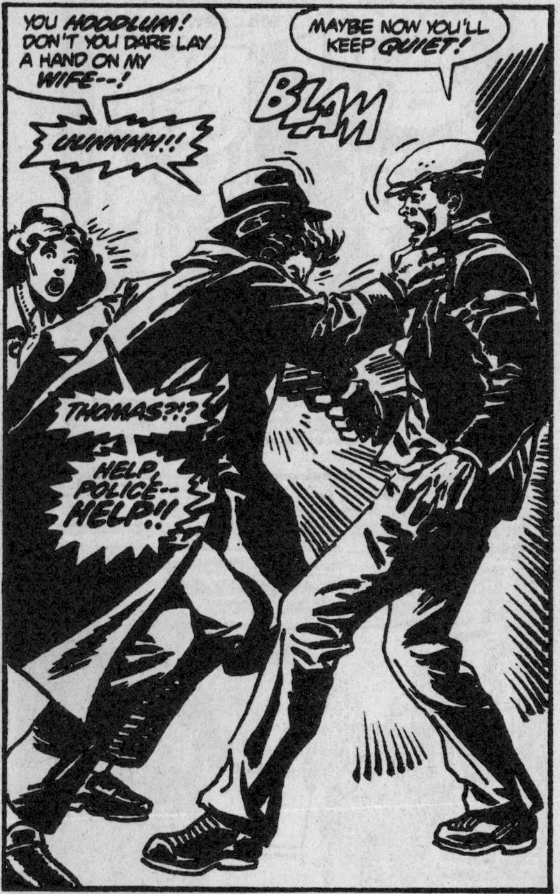
YOU HOODLUM! DON'T YOU DARE LAY A HAND ON MY WIFE--!
UUNNHH!!
MAYBE NOW YOU'LL KEEP QUIET!
BLAM
THOMAS?!?
HELP, POLICE-- HELP!!

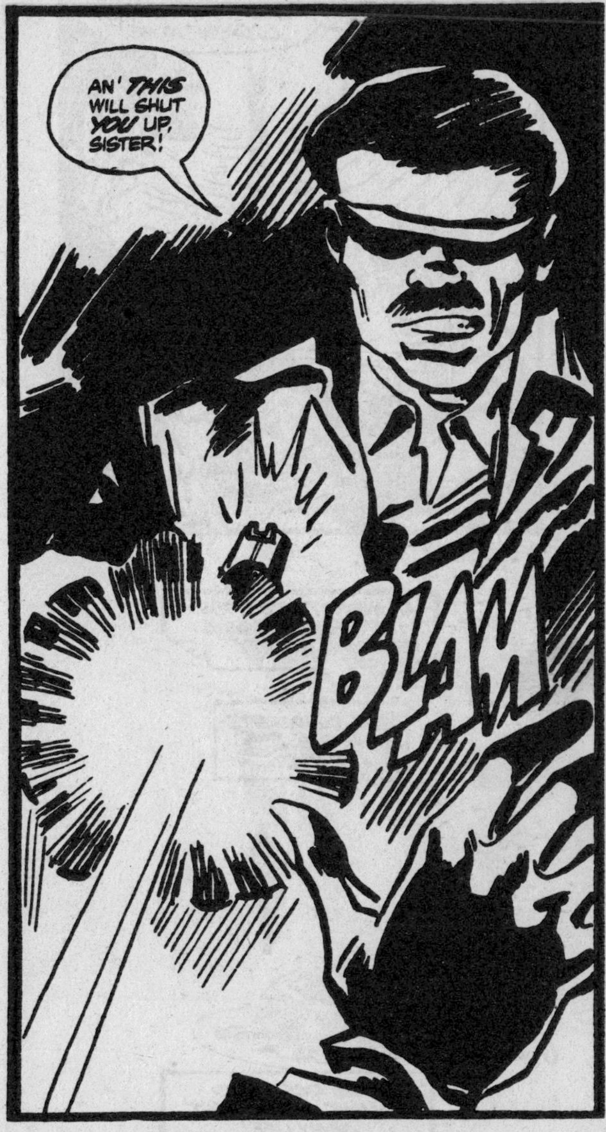
AN' THIS WILL SHUT YOU UP, SISTER!
BLAM

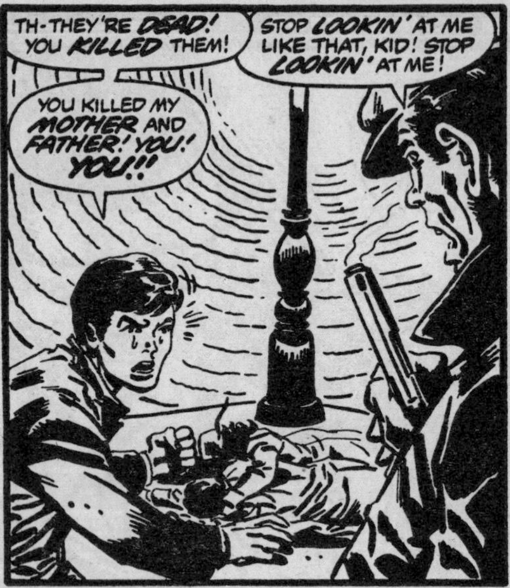
TH-THEY'RE DEAD! YOU KILLED THEM!
STOP LOOKIN' AT ME LIKE THAT, KID! STOP LOOKIN' AT ME!
YOU KILLED MY MOTHER AND FATHER! YOU! YOU!!

"AN INSTANT LATER, THE KILLER FLED, LEAVING ME BEHIND WITH MY GRIEF!

"THE MURDERER'S NAME WAS JOE CHILL...

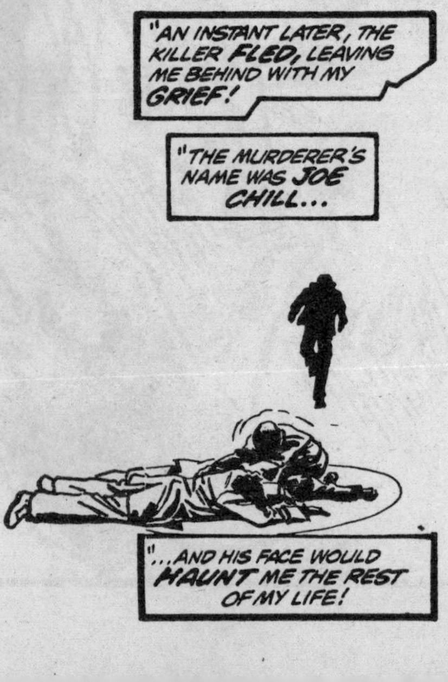

"...AND HIS FACE WOULD HAUNT ME THE REST OF MY LIFE!

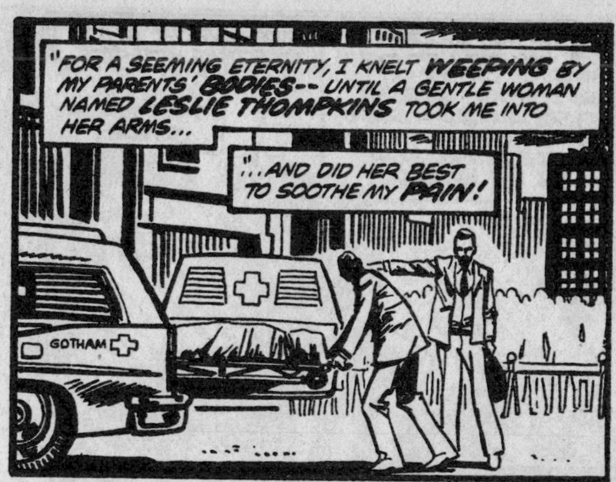
"FOR A SEEMING ETERNITY, I KNELT WEEPING BY MY PARENTS' BODIES-- UNTIL A GENTLE WOMAN NAMED LESLIE THOMPKINS TOOK ME INTO HER ARMS...
"...AND DID HER BEST TO SOOTHE MY PAIN!
GOTHAM

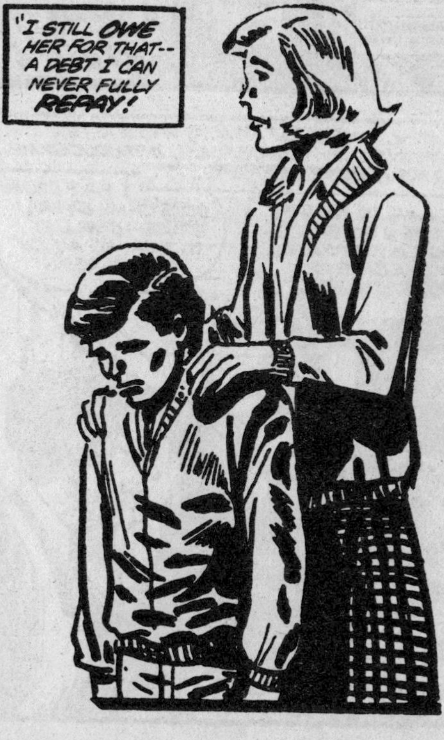
"I STILL OWE HER FOR THAT-- A DEBT I CAN NEVER FULLY REPAY!

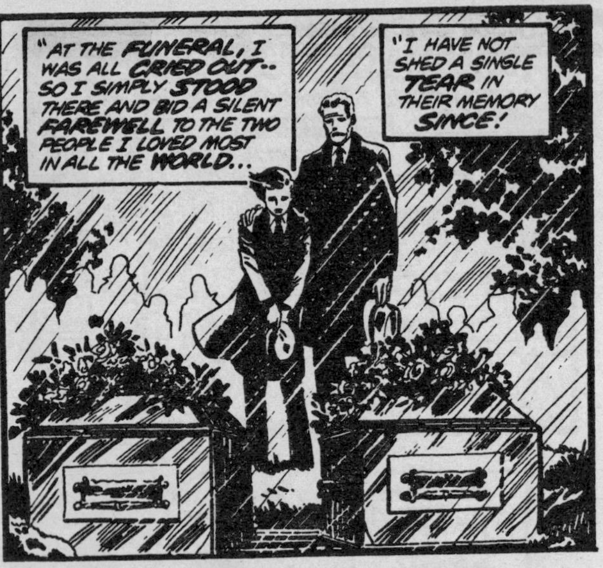
"AT THE FUNERAL, I WAS ALL CRIED OUT-- SO I SIMPLY STOOD THERE AND BID A SILENT FAREWELL TO THE TWO PEOPLE I LOVED MOST IN ALL THE WORLD...
"I HAVE NOT SHED A SINGLE TEAR IN THEIR MEMORY SINCE!

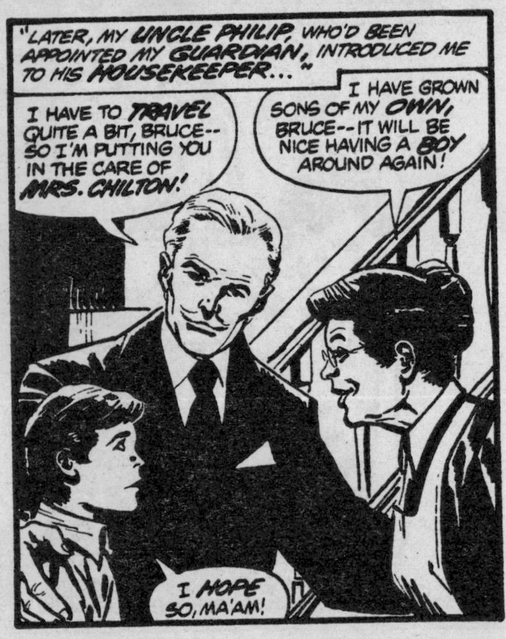
"LATER, MY UNCLE PHILIP, WHO'D BEEN APPOINTED MY GUARDIAN, INTRODUCED ME TO HIS HOUSEKEEPER..."
I HAVE TO TRAVEL QUITE A BIT, BRUCE-- SO I'M PUTTING YOU IN THE CARE OF MRS. CHILTON!
I HAVE GROWN SONS OF MY OWN, BRUCE--IT WILL BE NICE HAVING A BOY AROUND AGAIN!
I HOPE SO, MA'AM!

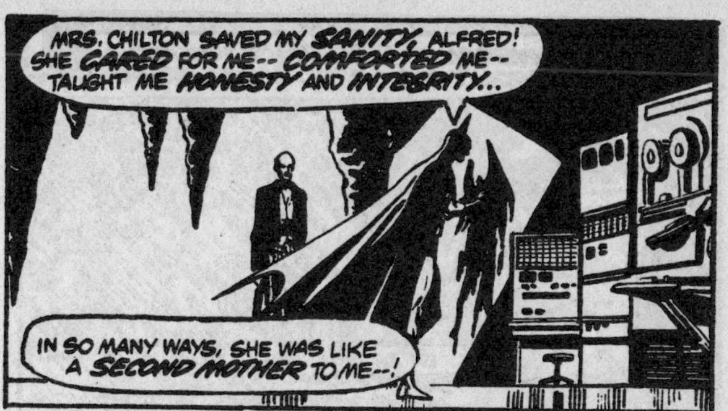
MRS. CHILTON SAVED MY SANITY, ALFRED! SHE CARED FOR ME-- COMFORTED ME-- TAUGHT ME HONESTY AND INTEGRITY...
IN SO MANY WAYS, SHE WAS LIKE A SECOND MOTHER TO ME--!

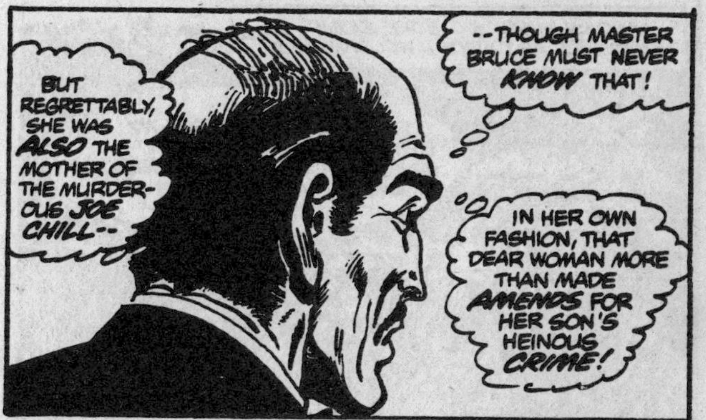
BUT REGRETTABLY, SHE WAS ALSO THE MOTHER OF THE MURDEROUS JOE CHILL--
--THOUGH MASTER BRUCE MUST NEVER KNOW THAT!
IN HER OWN FASHION, THAT DEAR WOMAN MORE THAN MADE AMENDS FOR HER SON'S HEINOUS CRIME!

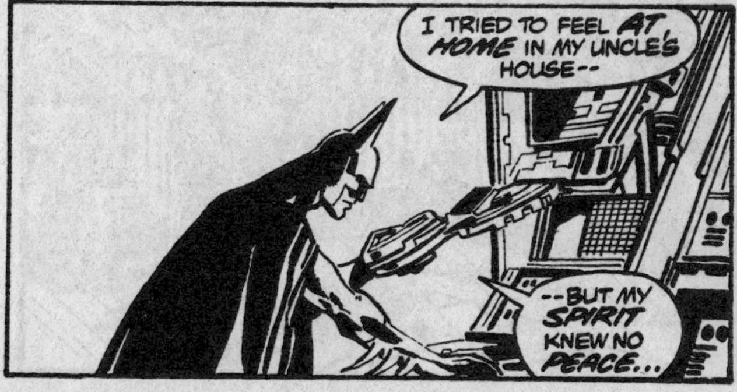
I TRIED TO FEEL AT HOME IN MY UNCLE'S HOUSE--
--BUT MY SPIRIT KNEW NO PEACE...

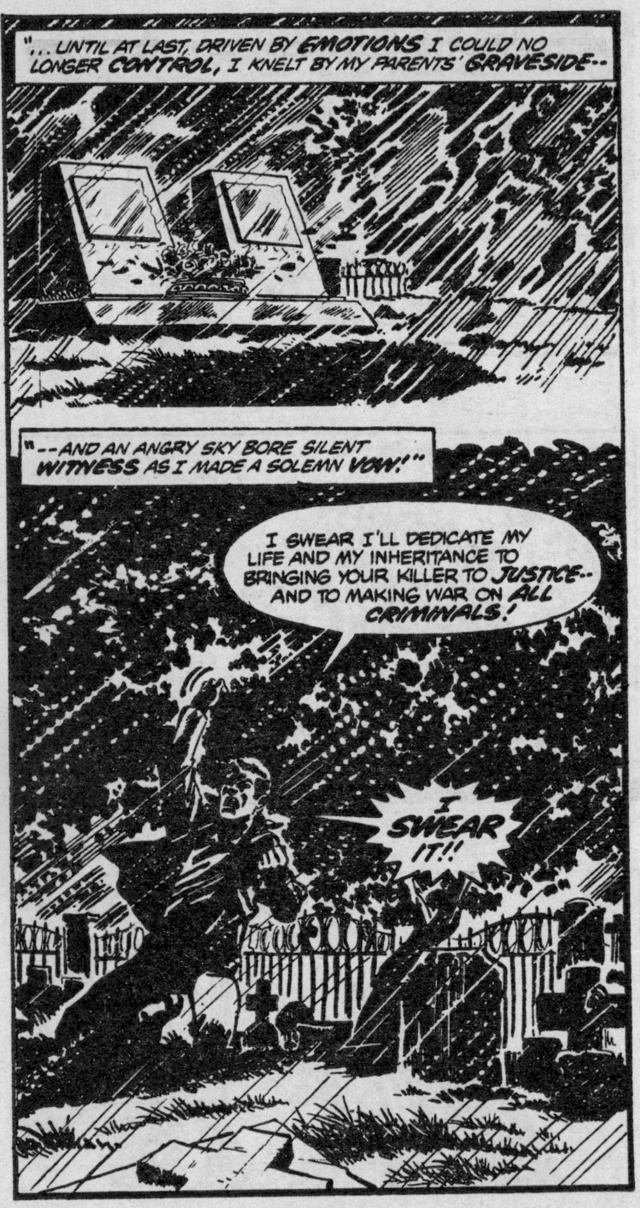
"...UNTIL AT LAST, DRIVEN BY EMOTIONS I COULD NO LONGER CONTROL, I KNELT BY MY PARENTS' GRAVESIDE--
"--AND AN ANGRY SKY BORE SILENT WITNESS AS I MADE A SOLEMN VOW!"
I SWEAR I'LL DEDICATE MY LIFE AND MY INHERITANCE TO BRINGING YOUR KILLER TO JUSTICE-- AND TO MAKING WAR ON ALL CRIMINALS!
I SWEAR IT!!

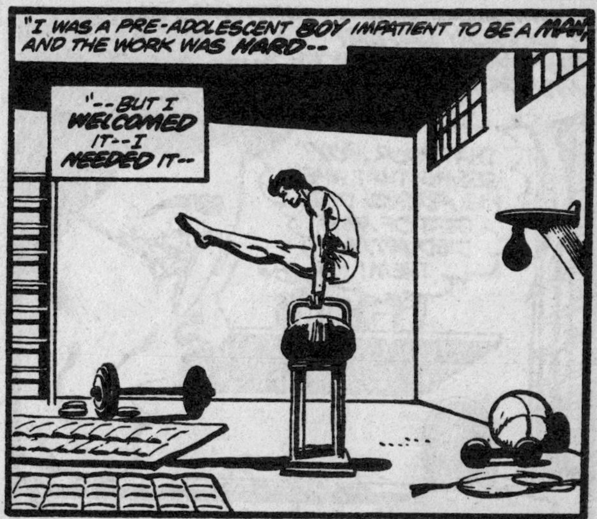
"I WAS A PRE-ADOLESCENT BOY IMPATIENT TO BE A MAN, AND THE WORK WAS HARD--
"--BUT I WELCOMED IT--I NEEDED IT--

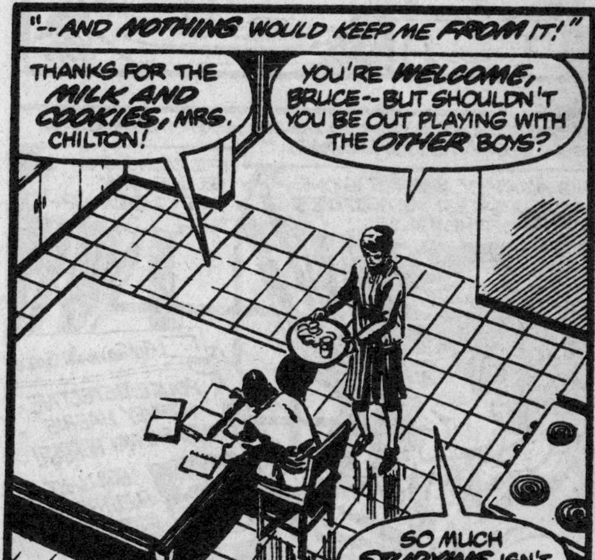
"--AND NOTHING WOULD KEEP ME FROM IT!"
THANKS FOR THE MILK AND COOKIES, MRS. CHILTON!
YOU'RE WELCOME, BRUCE--BUT SHOULDN'T YOU BE OUT PLAYING WITH THE OTHER BOYS?
SO MUCH STUDYING ISN'T GOOD FOR YOU!

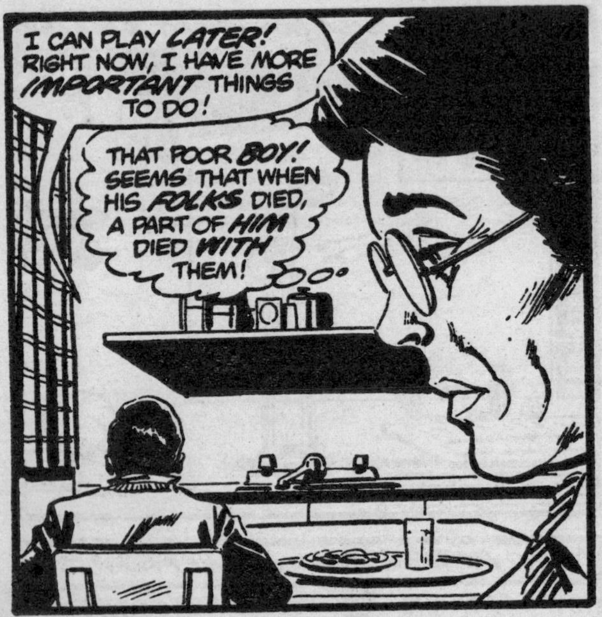
I CAN PLAY LATER! RIGHT NOW, I HAVE MORE IMPORTANT THINGS TO DO!
THAT POOR BOY! SEEMS THAT WHEN HIS FOLKS DIED, A PART OF HIM DIED WITH THEM!

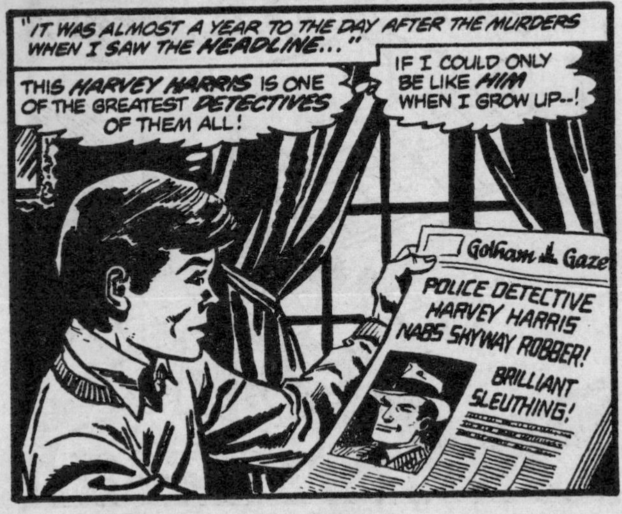
"IT WAS ALMOST A YEAR TO THE DAY AFTER THE MURDERS WHEN I SAW THE HEADLINE..."
THIS HARVEY HARRIS IS ONE OF THE GREATEST DETECTIVES OF THEM ALL!
IF I COULD ONLY BE LIKE HIM WHEN I GROW UP--!
Gotham Gaze
POLICE DETECTIVE HARVEY HARRIS NABS SKYWAY ROBBER!
BRILLIANT SLEUTHING!

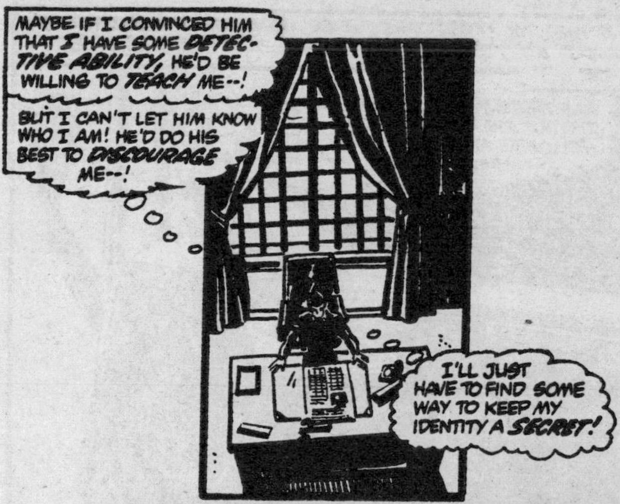
MAYBE IF I CONVINCED HIM THAT I HAVE SOME DETECTIVE ABILITY, HE'D BE WILLING TO TEACH ME--!
BUT I CAN'T LET HIM KNOW WHO I AM! HE'D DO HIS BEST TO DISCOURAGE ME--!
I'LL JUST HAVE TO FIND SOME WAY TO KEEP MY IDENTITY A SECRET!

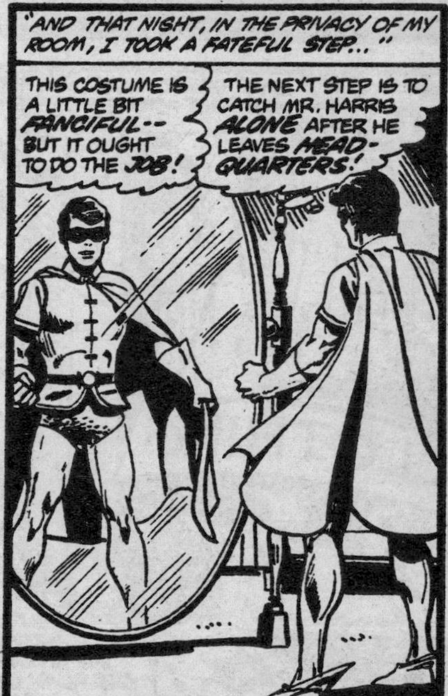
"AND THAT NIGHT, IN THE PRIVACY OF MY ROOM, I TOOK A FATEFUL STEP..."
THIS COSTUME IS A LITTLE BIT FANCIFUL-- BUT IT OUGHT TO DO THE JOB!
THE NEXT STEP IS TO CATCH MR. HARRIS ALONE AFTER HE LEAVES HEADQUARTERS!

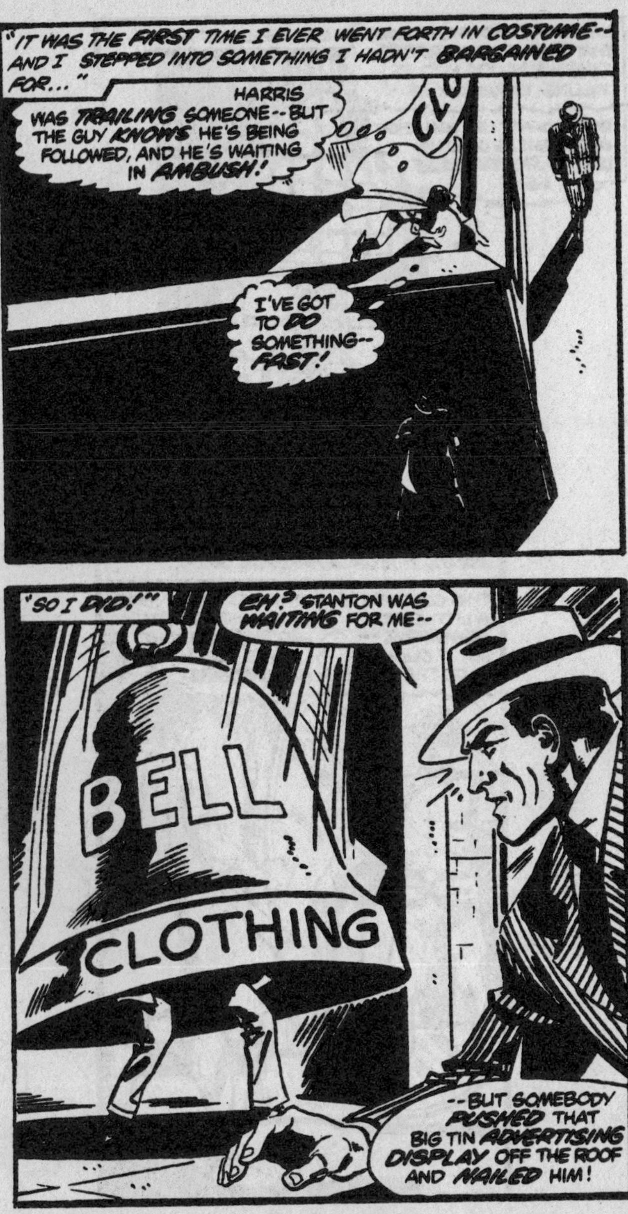
"IT WAS THE FIRST TIME I EVER WENT FORTH IN COSTUME-- AND I STEPPED INTO SOMETHING I HADN'T BARGAINED FOR..."
HARRIS WAS TRAILING SOMEONE--BUT THE GUY KNOWS HE'S BEING FOLLOWED, AND HE'S WAITING IN AMBUSH!
I'VE GOT TO DO SOMETHING-- FAST!
"SO I DID!"
EH? STANTON WAS WAITING FOR ME--
BELL
CLOTHING
--BUT SOMEBODY PUSHED THAT BIG TIN ADVERTISING DISPLAY OFF THE ROOF AND MAILED HIM!

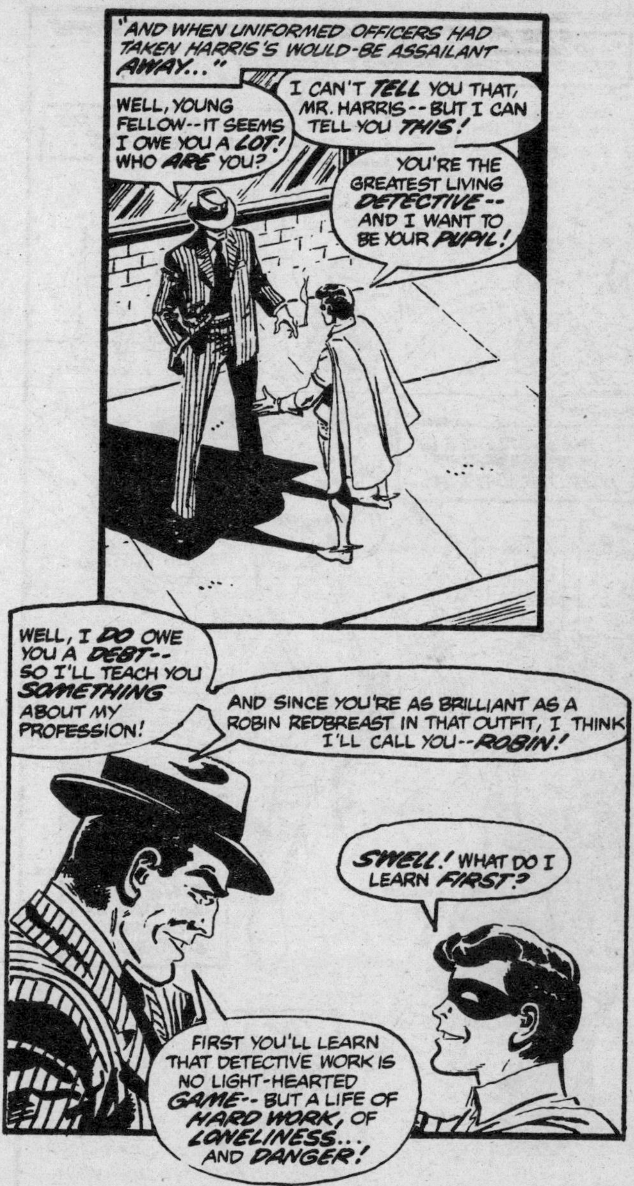
"AND WHEN UNIFORMED OFFICERS HAD TAKEN HARRIS'S WOULD-BE ASSAILANT AWAY..."
WELL, YOUNG FELLOW--IT SEEMS I OWE YOU A LOT! WHO ARE YOU?
I CAN'T TELL YOU THAT, MR. HARRIS--BUT I CAN TELL YOU THIS!
YOU'RE THE GREATEST LIVING DETECTIVE--AND I WANT TO BE YOUR PUPIL!
WELL, I DO OWE YOU A DEBT--SO I'LL TEACH YOU SOMETHING ABOUT MY PROFESSION!
AND SINCE YOU'RE AS BRILLIANT AS A ROBIN REDBREAST IN THAT OUTFIT, I THINK I'LL CALL YOU--ROBIN!
SWELL! WHAT DO I LEARN FIRST?
FIRST YOU'LL LEARN THAT DETECTIVE WORK IS NO LIGHT-HEARTED GAME--BUT A LIFE OF HARD WORK, OF LONELINESS... AND DANGER!

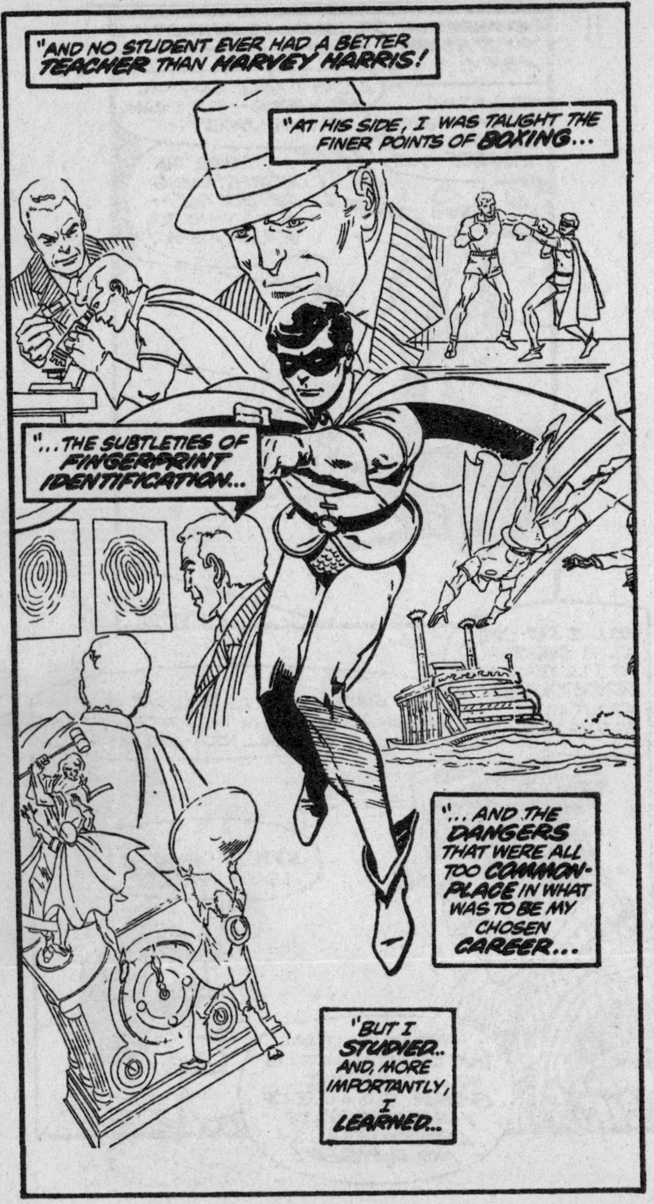
"AND NO STUDENT EVER HAD A BETTER TEACHER THAN HARVEY HARRIS!
"AT HIS SIDE, I WAS TAUGHT THE FINER POINTS OF BOXING...
"...THE SUBTLETIES OF FINGERPRINT IDENTIFICATION...
"...AND THE DANGERS THAT WERE ALL TOO COMMON-PLACE IN WHAT WAS TO BE MY CHOSEN CAREER...
"BUT I STUDIED... AND, MORE IMPORTANTLY, I LEARNED...

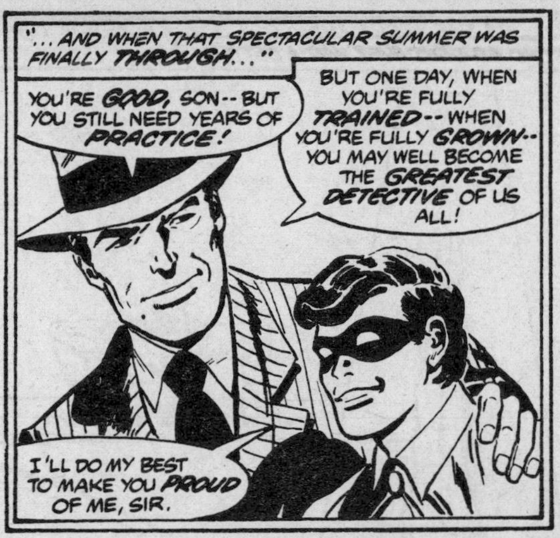
"... AND WHEN THAT SPECTACULAR SUMMER WAS FINALLY THROUGH..."
YOU'RE GOOD, SON--BUT YOU STILL NEED YEARS OF PRACTICE!
BUT ONE DAY, WHEN YOU'RE FULLY TRAINED--WHEN YOU'RE FULLY GROWN--YOU MAY WELL BECOME THE GREATEST DETECTIVE OF US ALL!
I'LL DO MY BEST TO MAKE YOU PROUD OF ME, SIR.

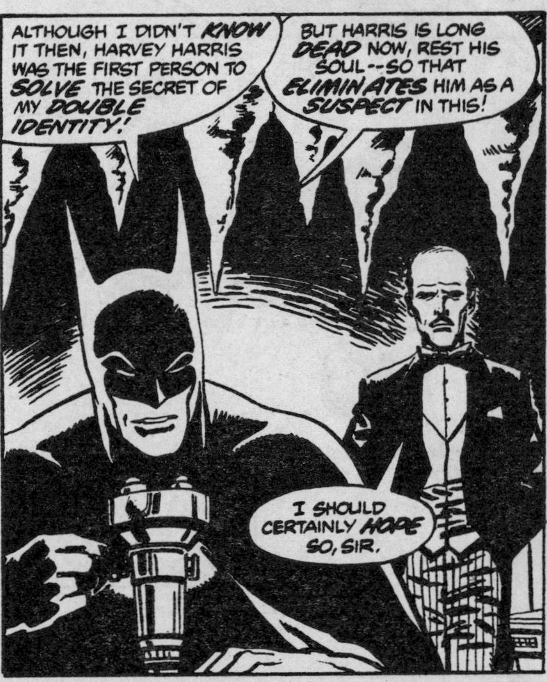
ALTHOUGH I DIDN'T KNOW IT THEN, HARVEY HARRIS WAS THE FIRST PERSON TO SOLVE THE SECRET OF MY DOUBLE IDENTITY!
BUT HARRIS IS LONG DEAD NOW, REST HIS SOUL--SO THAT ELIMINATES HIM AS A SUSPECT IN THIS!
I SHOULD CERTAINLY HOPE SO, SIR.

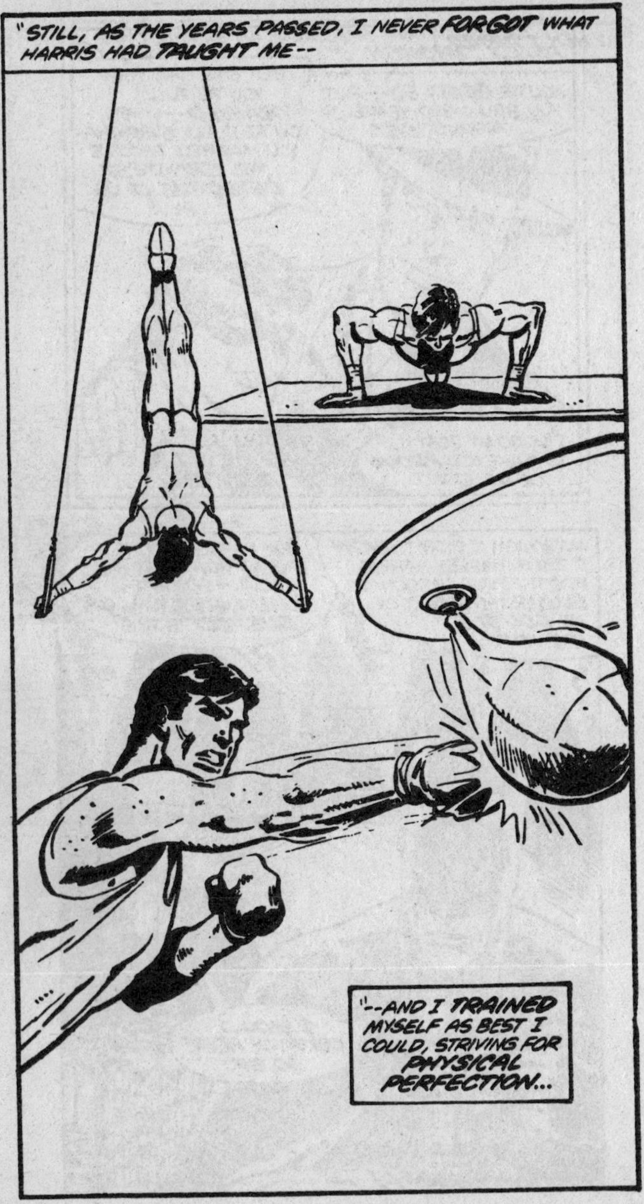
"STILL, AS THE YEARS PASSED, I NEVER FORGOT WHAT HARRIS HAD TAUGHT ME--
"--AND I TRAINED MYSELF AS BEST I COULD, STRIVING FOR PHYSICAL PERFECTION...

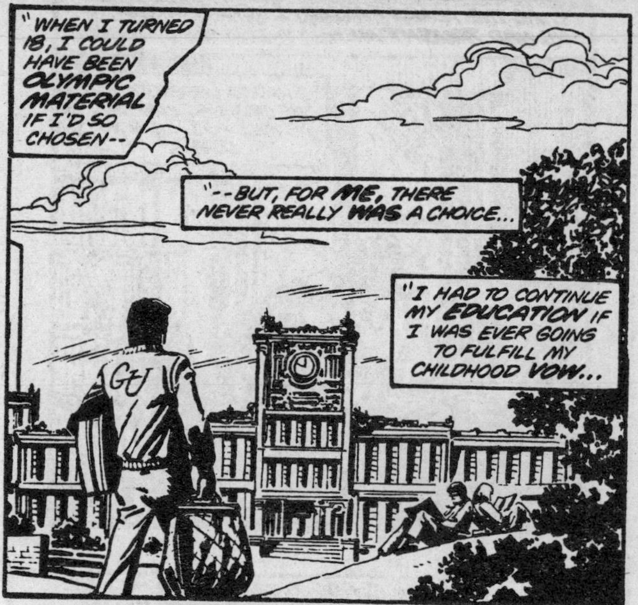
"WHEN I TURNED 18, I COULD HAVE BEEN OLYMPIC MATERIAL IF I'D SO CHOSEN--
"--BUT, FOR ME, THERE NEVER REALLY WAS A CHOICE...
"I HAD TO CONTINUE MY EDUCATION IF I WAS EVER GOING TO FULFILL MY CHILDHOOD VOW...
GU

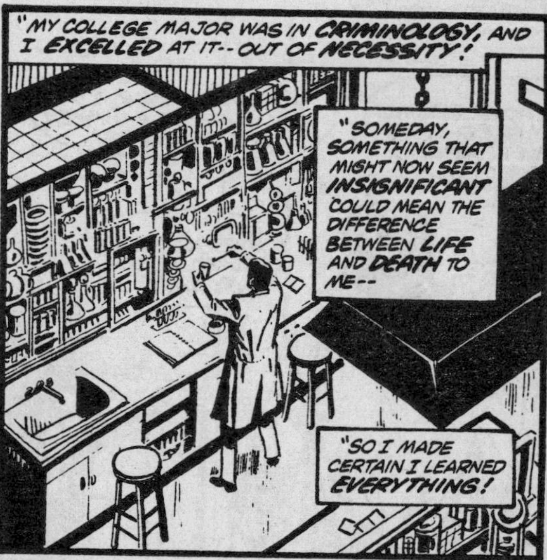
"MY COLLEGE MAJOR WAS IN CRIMINOLOGY, AND I EXCELLED AT IT--OUT OF NECESSITY!
"SOMEDAY, SOMETHING THAT MIGHT NOW SEEM INSIGNIFICANT COULD MEAN THE DIFFERENCE BETWEEN LIFE AND DEATH TO ME--
"SO I MADE CERTAIN I LEARNED EVERYTHING!

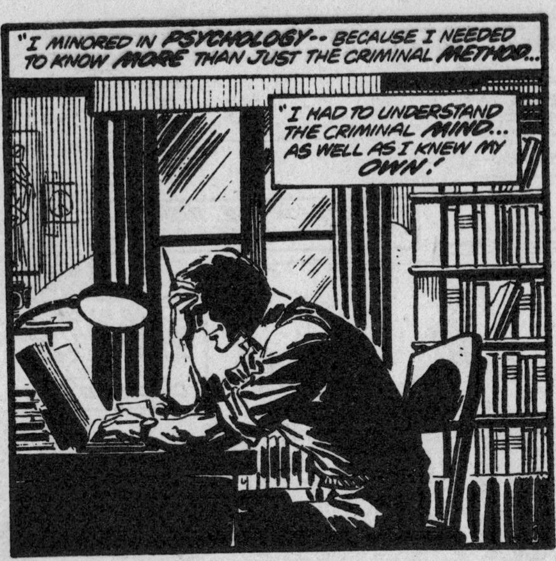
"I MINORED IN PSYCHOLOGY-- BECAUSE I NEEDED TO KNOW MORE THAN JUST THE CRIMINAL METHOD...
"I HAD TO UNDERSTAND THE CRIMINAL MIND... AS WELL AS I KNEW MY OWN!

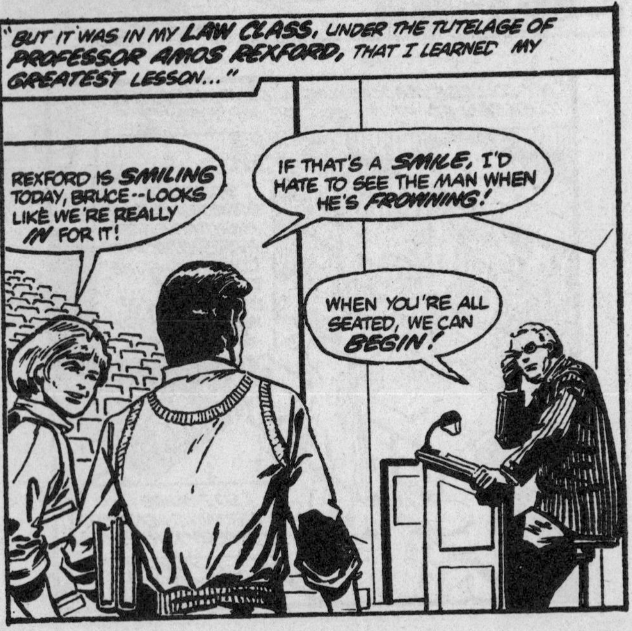
"BUT IT WAS IN MY LAW CLASS, UNDER THE TUTELAGE OF PROFESSOR AMOS REXFORD, THAT I LEARNED MY GREATEST LESSON..."
REXFORD IS SMILING TODAY, BRUCE--LOOKS LIKE WE'RE REALLY IN FOR IT!
IF THAT'S A SMILE, I'D HATE TO SEE THE MAN WHEN HE'S FROWNING!
WHEN YOU'RE ALL SEATED, WE CAN BEGIN!

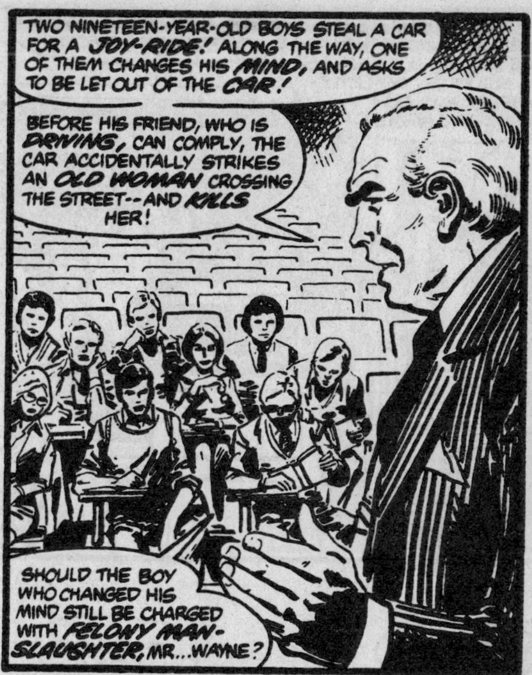
TWO NINETEEN-YEAR-OLD BOYS STEAL A CAR FOR A JOY-RIDE! ALONG THE WAY, ONE OF THEM CHANGES HIS MIND, AND ASKS TO BE LET OUT OF THE CAR!
BEFORE HIS FRIEND, WHO IS DRIVING, CAN COMPLY, THE CAR ACCIDENTALLY STRIKES AN OLD WOMAN CROSSING THE STREET--AND KILLS HER!
SHOULD THE BOY WHO CHANGED HIS MIND STILL BE CHARGED WITH FELONY MAN-SLAUGHTER, MR...WAYNE?

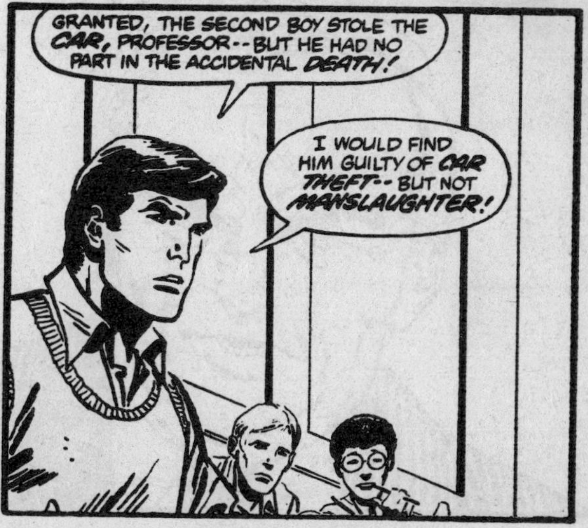
GRANTED, THE SECOND BOY STOLE THE CAR, PROFESSOR--BUT HE HAD NO PART IN THE ACCIDENTAL DEATH!
I WOULD FIND HIM GUILTY OF CAR THEFT--BUT NOT MANSLAUGHTER!

AND YOU WOULD BE WRONG! UNDER THE LAW, THE SECOND BOY WAS JUST AS GUILTY OF COMPLICITY AS IF HE HAD BEEN BEHIND THE WHEEL!
BUT IS THAT JUSTICE, PROFESSOR REXFORD?

NO, MISTER WAYNE...
...THAT'S THE LAW!

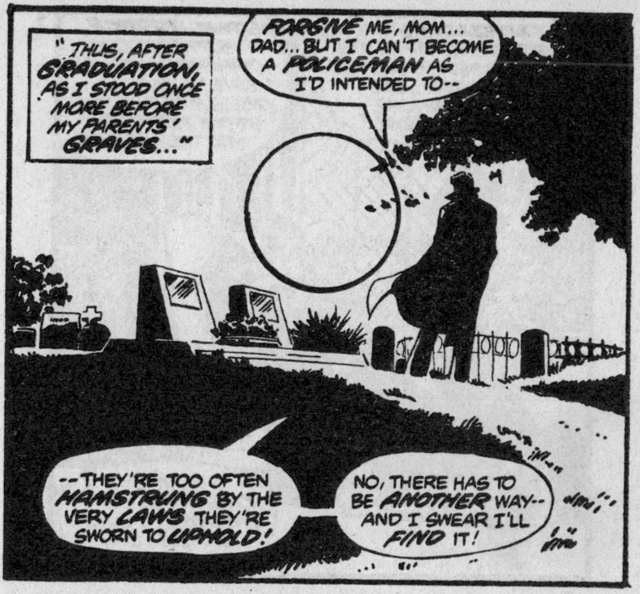
"THUS, AFTER GRADUATION, AS I STOOD ONCE MORE BEFORE MY PARENTS' GRAVES..."
FORGIVE ME, MOM... DAD... BUT I CAN'T BECOME A POLICEMAN AS I'D INTENDED TO--
--THEY'RE TOO OFTEN HAMSTRUNG BY THE VERY LAWS THEY'RE SWORN TO UPHOLD!
NO, THERE HAS TO BE ANOTHER WAY-- AND I SWEAR I'LL FIND IT!

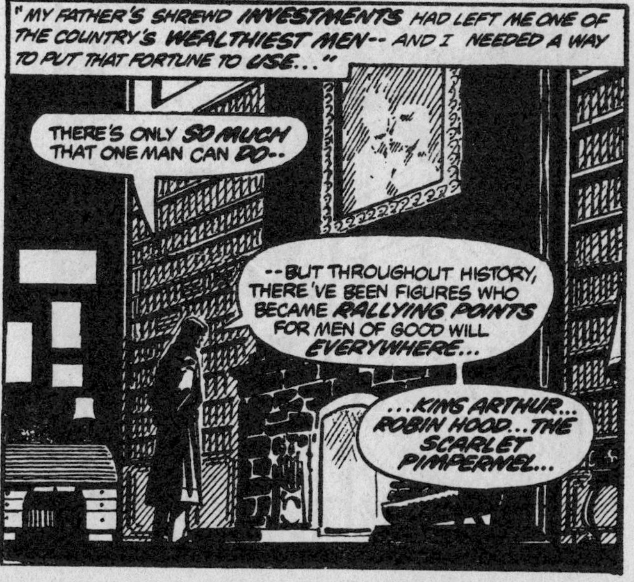
"MY FATHER'S SHREWD INVESTMENTS HAD LEFT ME ONE OF THE COUNTRY'S WEALTHIEST MEN-- AND I NEEDED A WAY TO PUT THAT FORTUNE TO USE..."
THERE'S ONLY SO MUCH THAT ONE MAN CAN DO--
--BUT THROUGHOUT HISTORY, THERE'VE BEEN FIGURES WHO BECAME RALLYING POINTS FOR MEN OF GOOD WILL EVERYWHERE...
...KING ARTHUR... ROBIN HOOD... THE SCARLET PIMPERNEL...

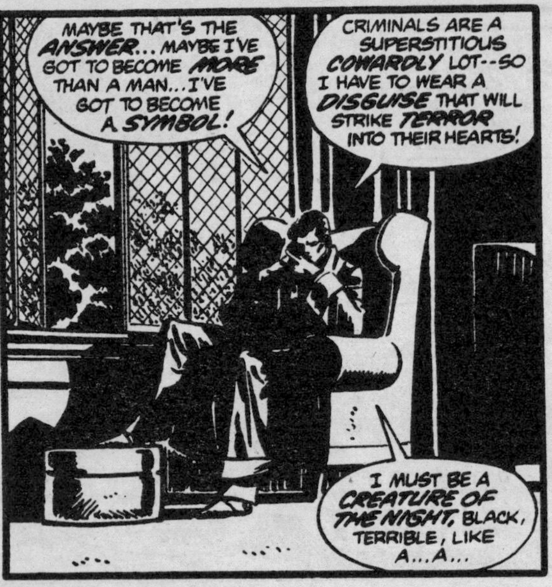
MAYBE THAT'S THE ANSWER... MAYBE I'VE GOT TO BECOME MORE THAN A MAN... I'VE GOT TO BECOME A SYMBOL!
CRIMINALS ARE A SUPERSTITIOUS COWARDLY LOT--SO I HAVE TO WEAR A DISGUISE THAT WILL STRIKE TERROR INTO THEIR HEARTS!
I MUST BE A CREATURE OF THE NIGHT, BLACK, TERRIBLE, LIKE A...A...

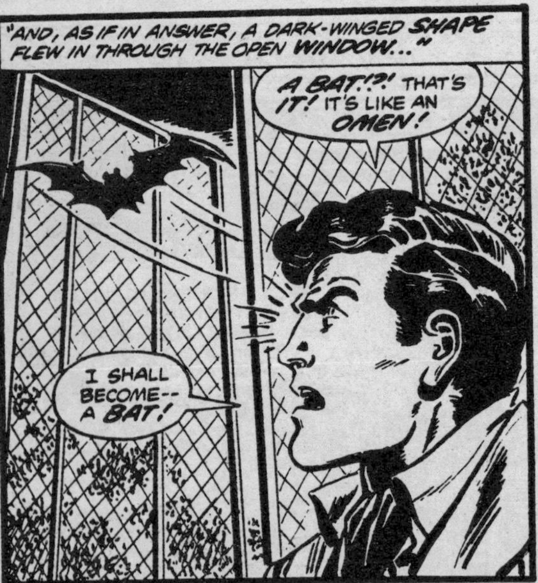
"AND, AS IF IN ANSWER, A DARK-WINGED SHAPE FLEW IN THROUGH THE OPEN WINDOW..."
A BAT!?! THAT'S IT! IT'S LIKE AN OMEN!
I SHALL BECOME-- A BAT!

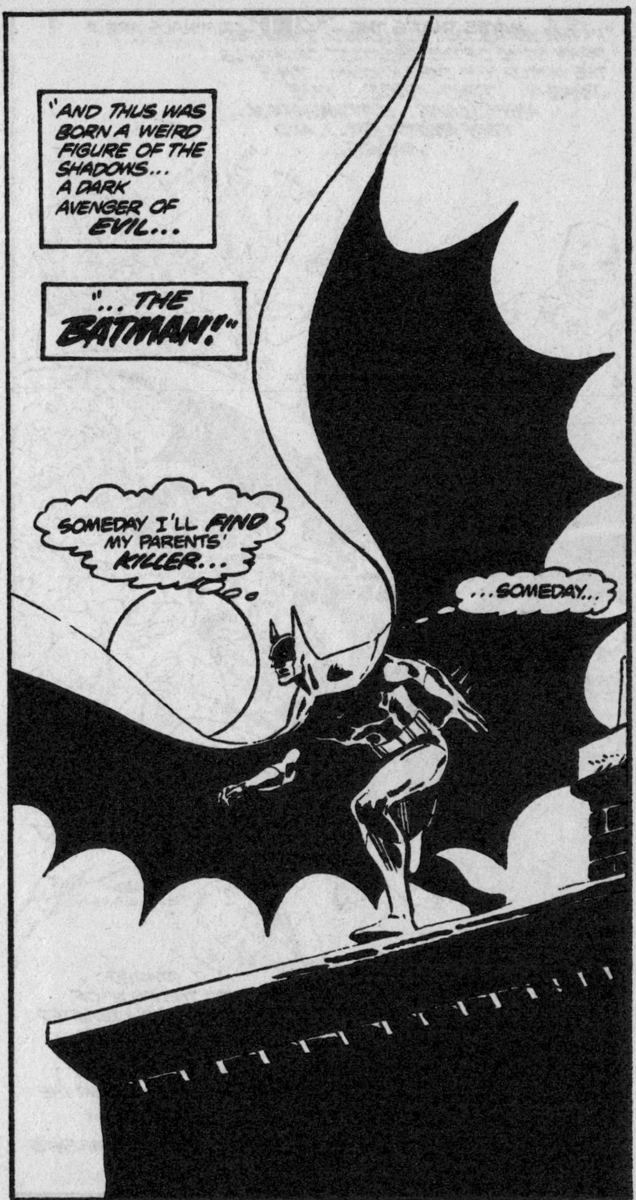
"AND THUS WAS BORN A WEIRD FIGURE OF THE SHADOWS... A DARK AVENGER OF EVIL...
"... THE BATMAN!"
SOMEDAY I'LL FIND MY PARENTS' KILLER...
...SOMEDAY...

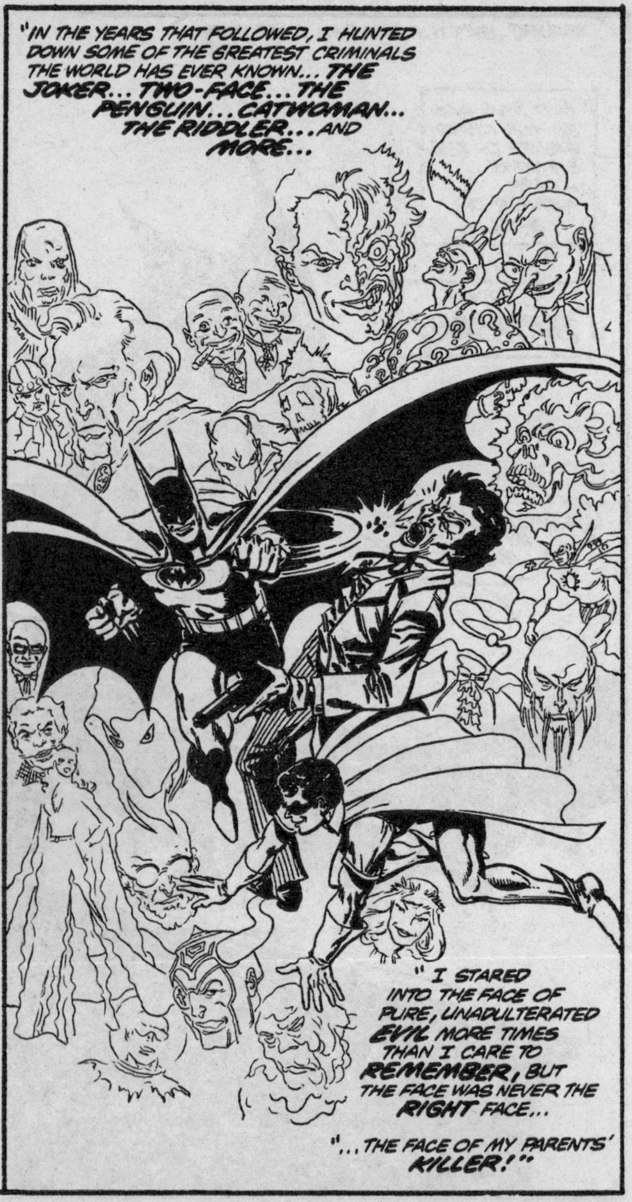
"IN THE YEARS THAT FOLLOWED, I HUNTED DOWN SOME OF THE GREATEST CRIMINALS THE WORLD HAS EVER KNOWN... THE JOKER... TWO-FACE... THE PENGUIN... CATWOMAN... THE RIDDLER... AND MORE...
"I STARED INTO THE FACE OF PURE, UNADULTERATED EVIL MORE TIMES THAN I CARE TO REMEMBER, BUT THE FACE WAS NEVER THE RIGHT FACE...
"...THE FACE OF MY PARENTS' KILLER!"

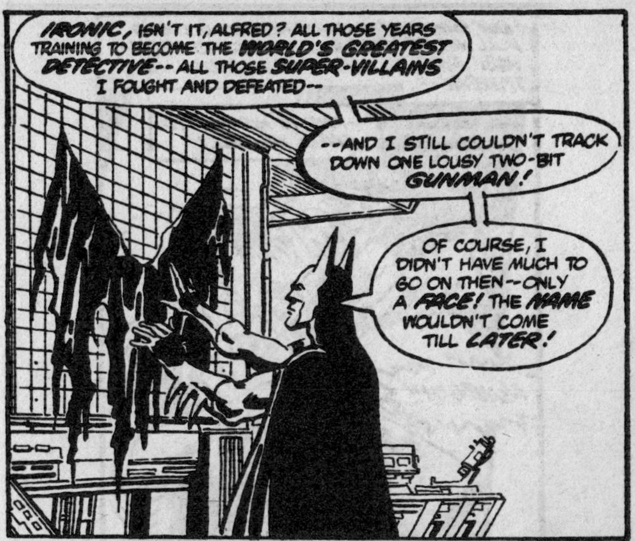
IRONIC, ISN'T IT, ALFRED? ALL THOSE YEARS TRAINING TO BECOME THE WORLD'S GREATEST DETECTIVE-- ALL THOSE SUPER-VILLAINS I FOUGHT AND DEFEATED--
--AND I STILL COULDN'T TRACK DOWN ONE LOUSY TWO-BIT GUNMAN!
OF COURSE, I DIDN'T HAVE MUCH TO GO ON THEN--ONLY A FACE! THE NAME WOULDN'T COME TILL LATER!

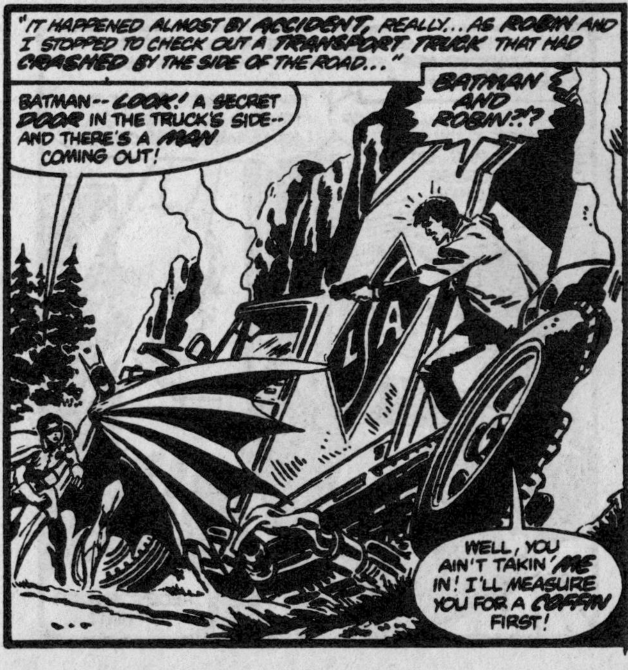
"IT HAPPENED ALMOST BY ACCIDENT, REALLY... AS ROBIN AND I STOPPED TO CHECK OUT A TRANSPORT TRUCK THAT HAD CRASHED BY THE SIDE OF THE ROAD..."
BATMAN--LOOK! A SECRET DOOR IN THE TRUCK'S SIDE-- AND THERE'S A MAN COMING OUT!
BATMAN AND ROBIN?!?
WELL, YOU AIN'T TAKIN' ME IN! I'LL MEASURE YOU FOR A COFFIN FIRST!

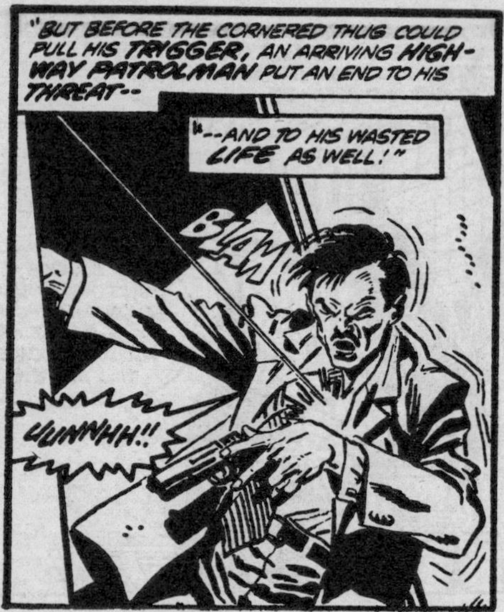
"BUT BEFORE THE CORNERED THUG COULD PULL HIS TRIGGER, AN ARRIVING HIGHWAY PATROLMAN PUT AN END TO HIS THREAT--
"--AND TO HIS WASTED LIFE AS WELL!"
BLAM
UUNNHH!!

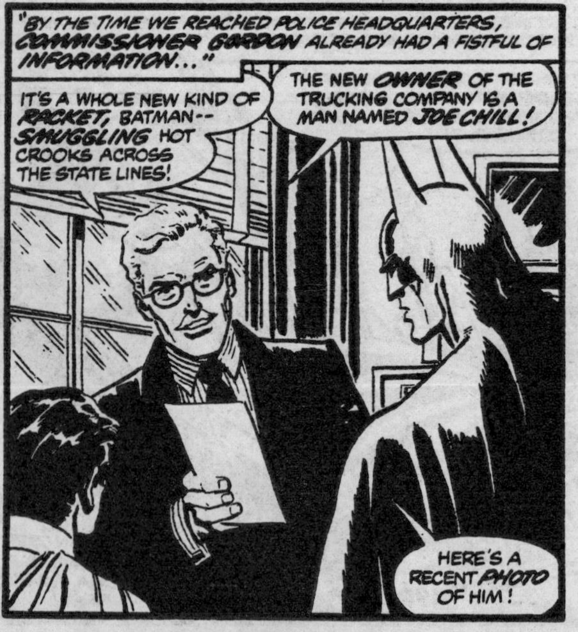
"BY THE TIME WE REACHED POLICE HEADQUARTERS, COMMISSIONER GORDON ALREADY HAD A FISTFUL OF INFORMATION..."
IT'S A WHOLE NEW KIND OF RACKET, BATMAN-- SMUGGLING HOT CROOKS ACROSS THE STATE LINES!
THE NEW OWNER OF THE TRUCKING COMPANY IS A MAN NAMED JOE CHILL!
HERE'S A RECENT PHOTO OF HIM!

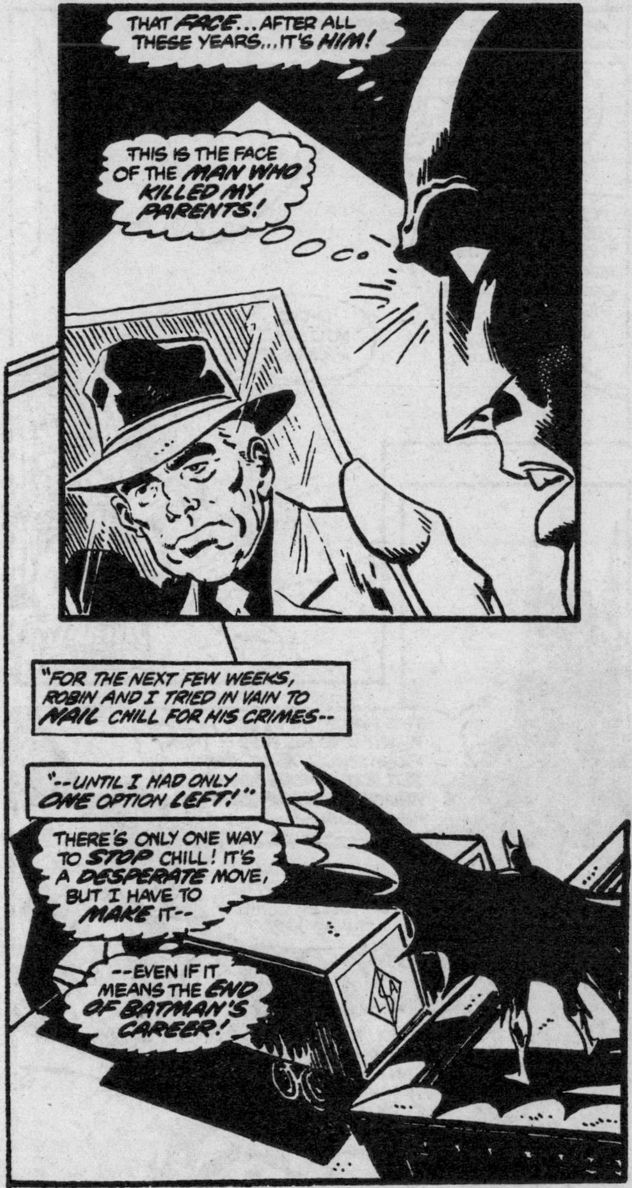
THAT FACE... AFTER ALL THESE YEARS... IT'S HIM!
THIS IS THE FACE OF THE MAN WHO KILLED MY PARENTS!
"FOR THE NEXT FEW WEEKS, ROBIN AND I TRIED IN VAIN TO NAIL CHILL FOR HIS CRIMES--
"--UNTIL I HAD ONLY ONE OPTION LEFT!"
THERE'S ONLY ONE WAY TO STOP CHILL! IT'S A DESPERATE MOVE, BUT I HAVE TO MAKE IT--
--EVEN IF IT MEANS THE END OF BATMAN'S CAREER!

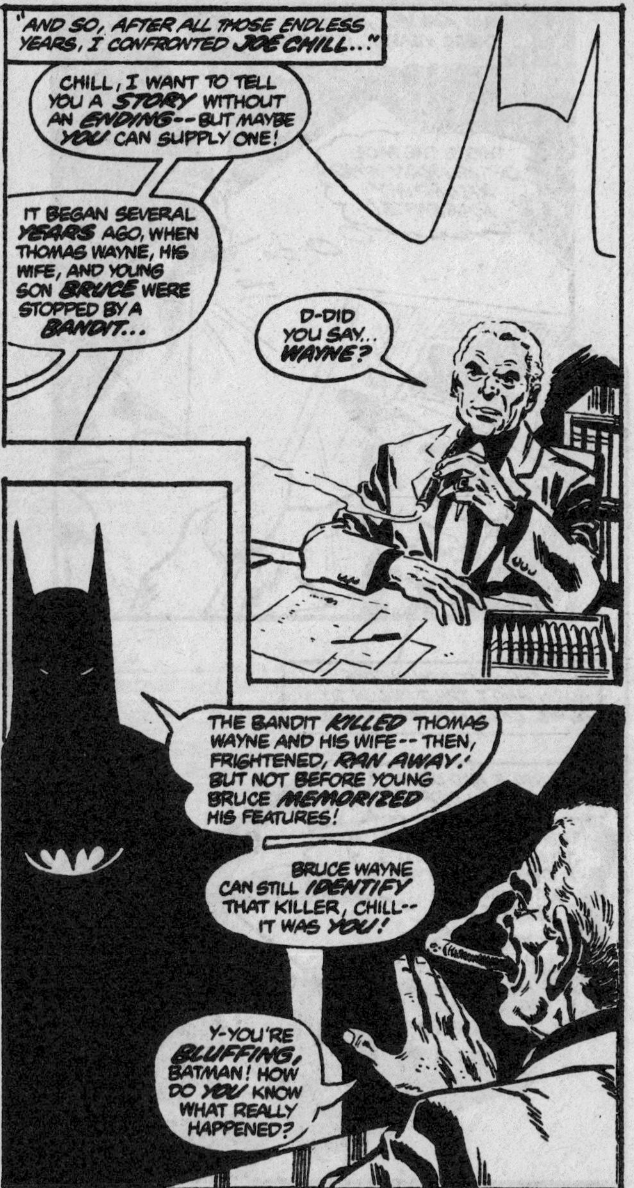
"AND SO, AFTER ALL THOSE ENDLESS YEARS, I CONFRONTED JOE CHILL..."
CHILL, I WANT TO TELL YOU A STORY WITHOUT AN ENDING-- BUT MAYBE YOU CAN SUPPLY ONE!
IT BEGAN SEVERAL YEARS AGO, WHEN THOMAS WAYNE, HIS WIFE, AND YOUNG SON BRUCE WERE STOPPED BY A BANDIT...
D-DID YOU SAY... WAYNE?
THE BANDIT KILLED THOMAS WAYNE AND HIS WIFE-- THEN, FRIGHTENED, RAN AWAY! BUT NOT BEFORE YOUNG BRUCE MEMORIZED HIS FEATURES!
BRUCE WAYNE CAN STILL IDENTIFY THAT KILLER, CHILL-- IT WAS YOU!
Y-YOU'RE BLUFFING, BATMAN! HOW DO YOU KNOW WHAT REALLY HAPPENED?

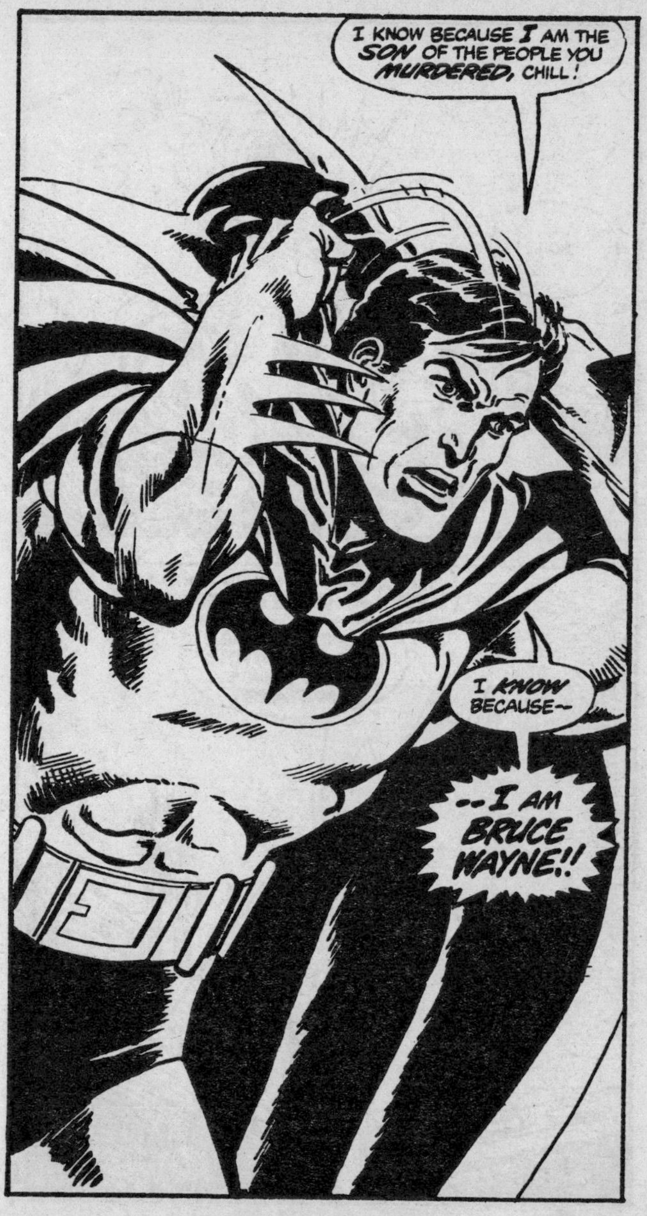
I KNOW BECAUSE I AM THE SON OF THE PEOPLE YOU MURDERED, CHILL!
I KNOW BECAUSE--
--I AM BRUCE WAYNE!!

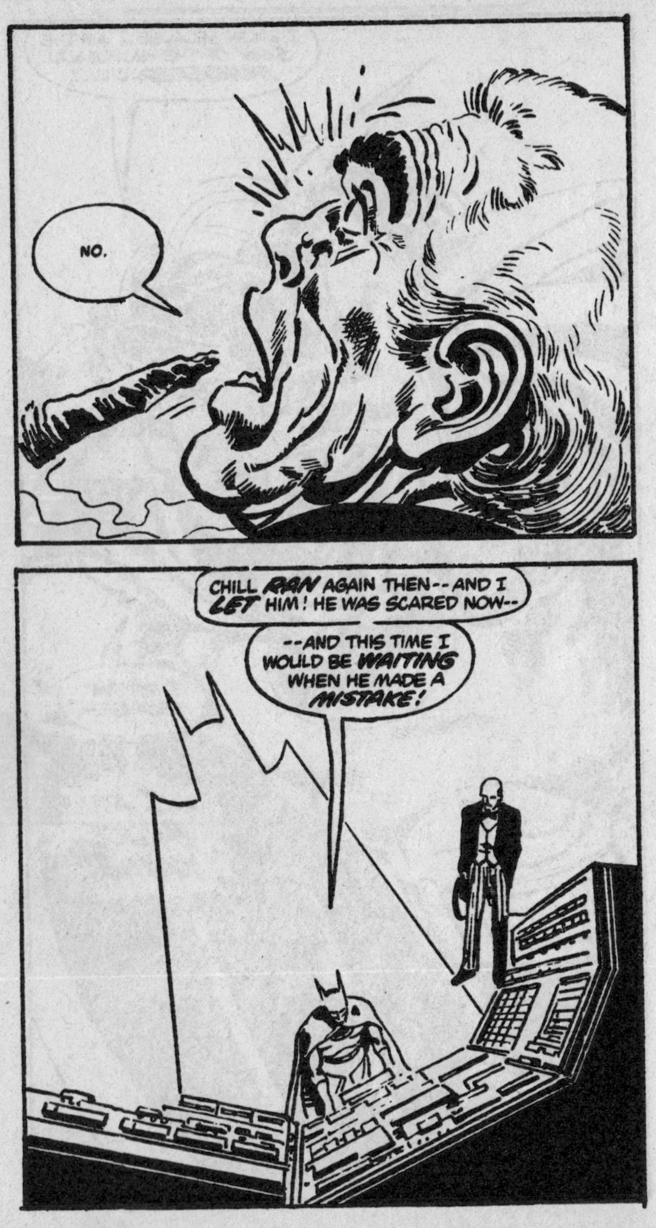
NO.
CHILL RAN AGAIN THEN--AND I LET HIM! HE WAS SCARED NOW--
--AND THIS TIME I WOULD BE WAITING WHEN HE MADE A MISTAKE!

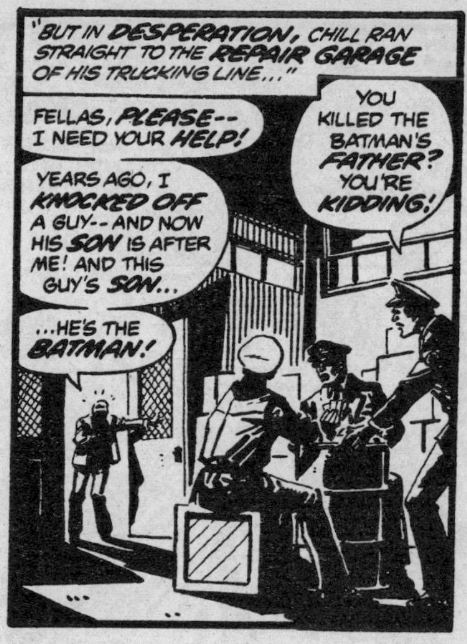
"BUT IN DESPERATION, CHILL RAN STRAIGHT TO THE REPAIR GARAGE OF HIS TRUCKING LINE..."
FELLAS, PLEASE-- I NEED YOUR HELP!
YEARS AGO, I KNOCKED OFF A GUY-- AND NOW HIS SON IS AFTER ME! AND THIS GUY'S SON...
...HE'S THE BATMAN!
YOU KILLED THE BATMAN'S FATHER? YOU'RE KIDDING!

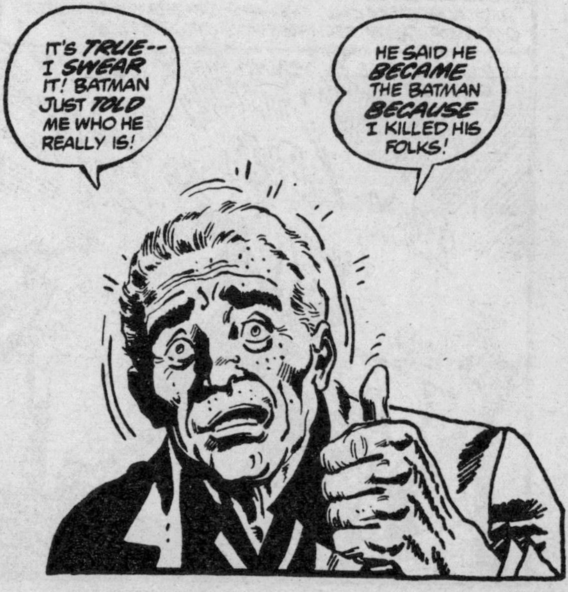
IT'S TRUE-- I SWEAR IT! BATMAN JUST TOLD ME WHO HE REALLY IS!
HE SAID HE BECAME THE BATMAN BECAUSE I KILLED HIS FOLKS!

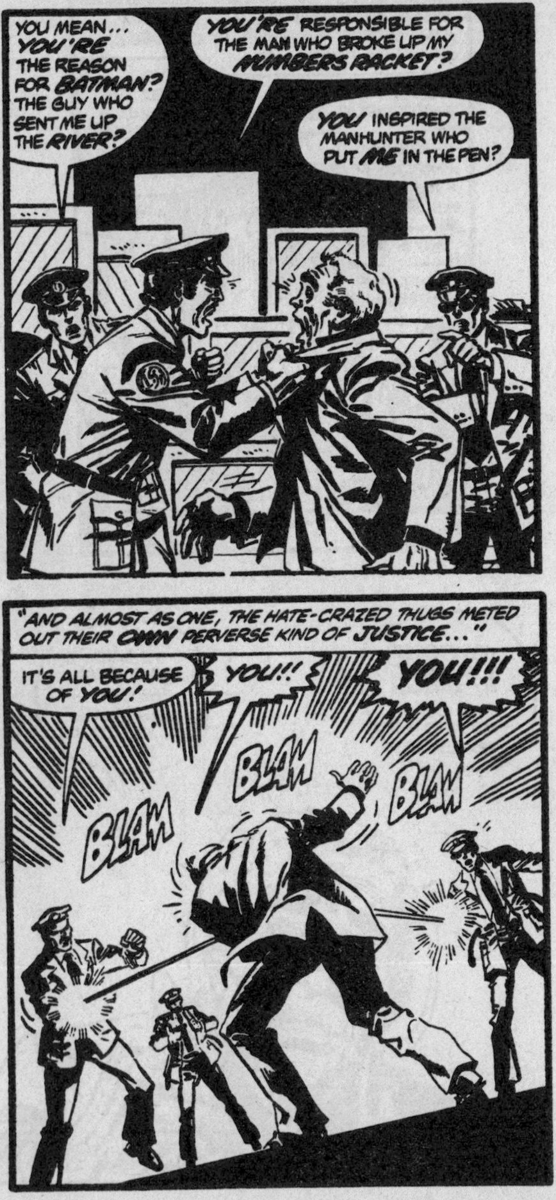
YOU MEAN... YOU'RE THE REASON FOR BATMAN? THE GUY WHO SENT ME UP THE RIVER?
YOU'RE RESPONSIBLE FOR THE MAN WHO BROKE UP MY NUMBERS RACKET?
YOU INSPIRED THE MANHUNTER WHO PUT ME IN THE PEN?
"AND ALMOST AS ONE, THE HATE-CRAZED THUGS METED OUT THEIR OWN PERVERSE KIND OF JUSTICE..."
IT'S ALL BECAUSE OF YOU!
YOU!!
YOU!!!
BLAM
BLAM
BLAM
BLAM

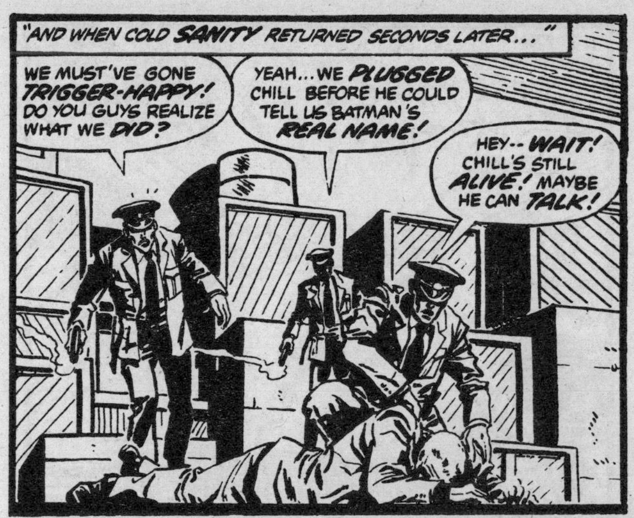
"AND WHEN COLD SANITY RETURNED SECONDS LATER..."
WE MUST'VE GONE TRIGGER-HAPPY! DO YOU GUYS REALIZE WHAT WE DID?
YEAH...WE PLUGGED CHILL BEFORE HE COULD TELL US BATMAN'S REAL NAME!
HEY-- WAIT! CHILL'S STILL ALIVE! MAYBE HE CAN TALK!

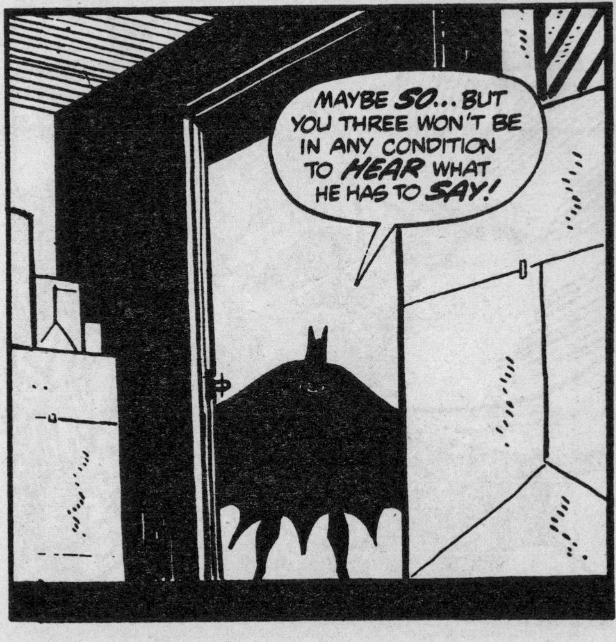
MAYBE SO...BUT YOU THREE WON'T BE IN ANY CONDITION TO HEAR WHAT HE HAS TO SAY!

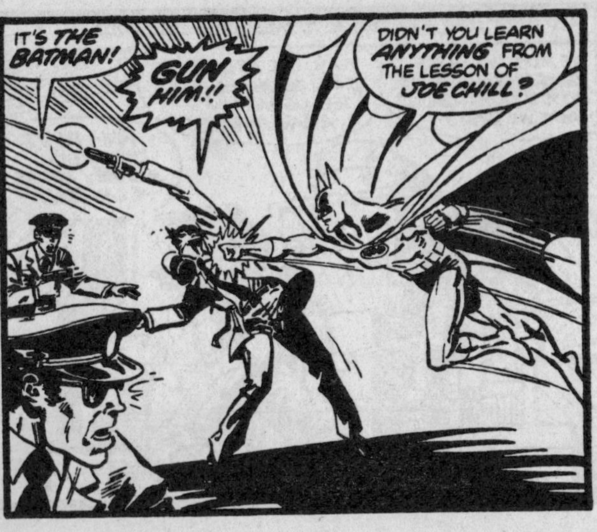
IT'S THE BATMAN!
GUN HIM!!
DIDN'T YOU LEARN ANYTHING FROM THE LESSON OF JOE CHILL?

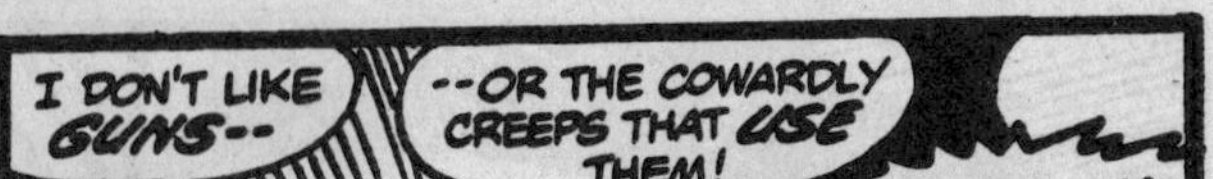
I DON'T LIKE GUNS--
--OR THE COWARDLY CREEPS THAT USE THEM!
UUNNFF!!

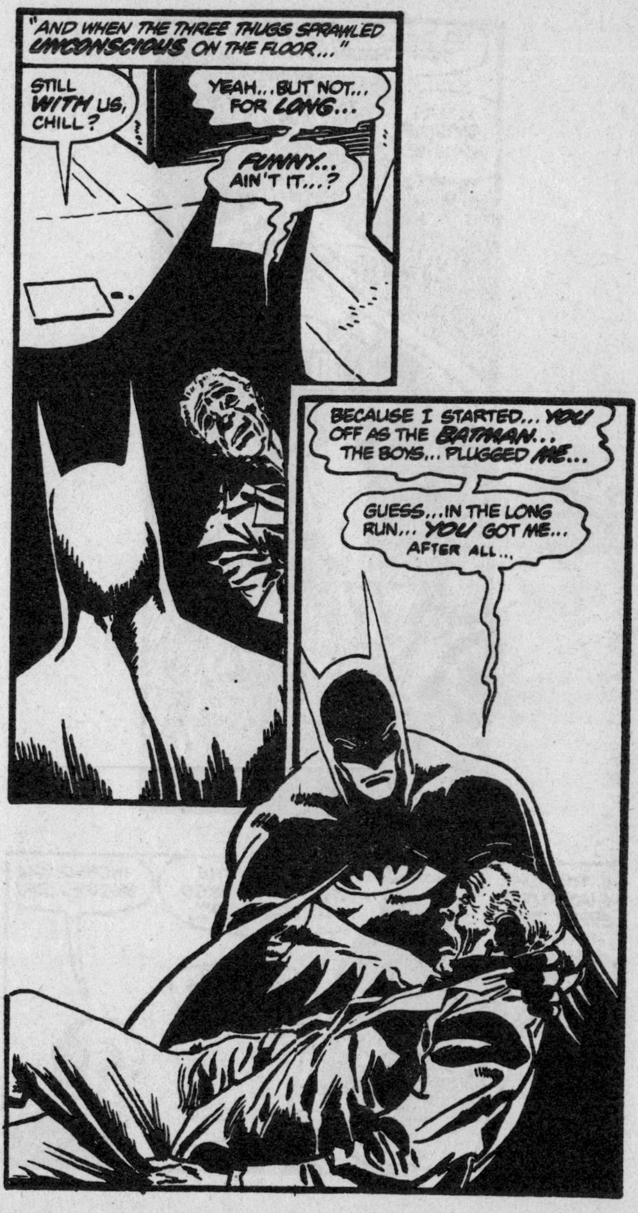
"AND WHEN THE THREE THUGS SPRAWLED UNCONSCIOUS ON THE FLOOR..."
STILL WITH US, CHILL?
YEAH...BUT NOT... FOR LONG...
FUNNY... AIN'T IT...?
BECAUSE I STARTED... YOU OFF AS THE BATMAN... THE BOYS... PLUGGED ME...
GUESS...IN THE LONG RUN... YOU GOT ME... AFTER ALL...

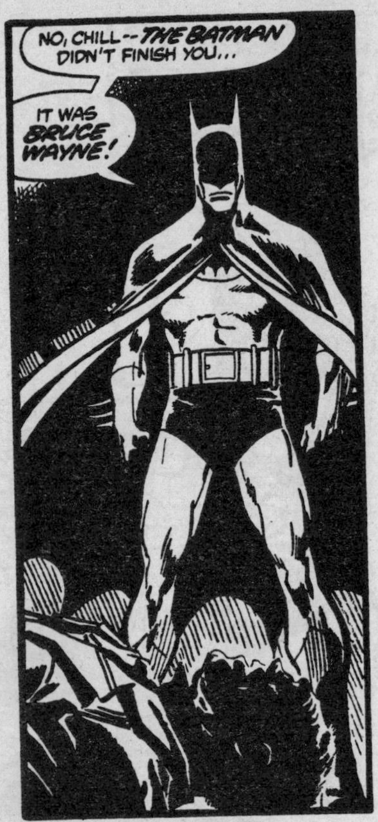
NO, CHILL-- THE BATMAN DIDN'T FINISH YOU...
IT WAS BRUCE WAYNE!

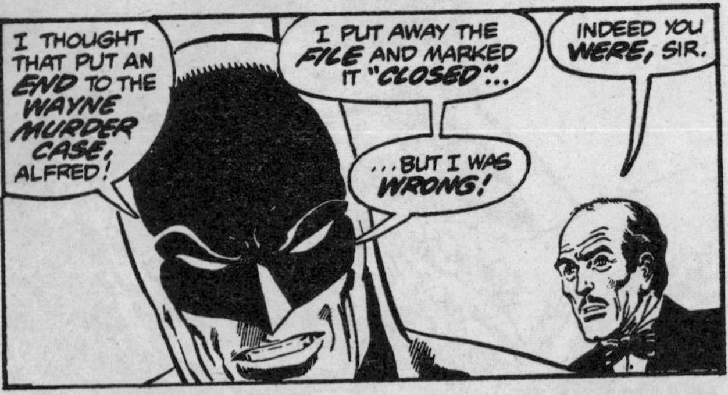
I THOUGHT THAT PUT AN END TO THE WAYNE MURDER CASE, ALFRED!
I PUT AWAY THE FILE AND MARKED IT "CLOSED"...
...BUT I WAS WRONG!
INDEED YOU WERE, SIR.

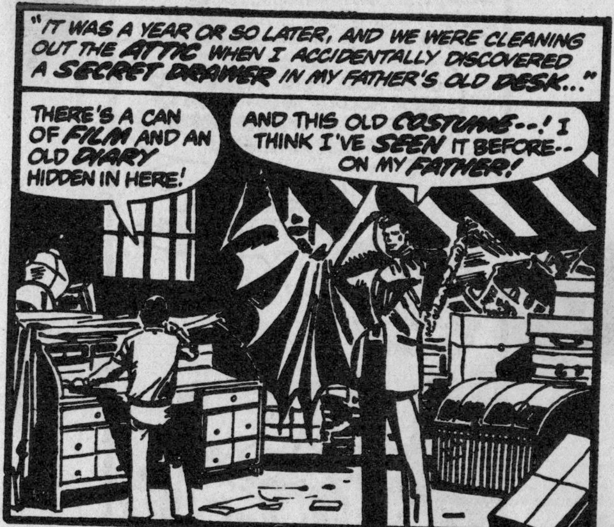
"IT WAS A YEAR OR SO LATER, AND WE WERE CLEANING OUT THE ATTIC WHEN I ACCIDENTALLY DISCOVERED A SECRET DRAWER IN MY FATHER'S OLD DESK..."
THERE'S A CAN OF FILM AND AN OLD DIARY HIDDEN IN HERE!
AND THIS OLD COSTUME--! I THINK I'VE SEEN IT BEFORE--ON MY FATHER!

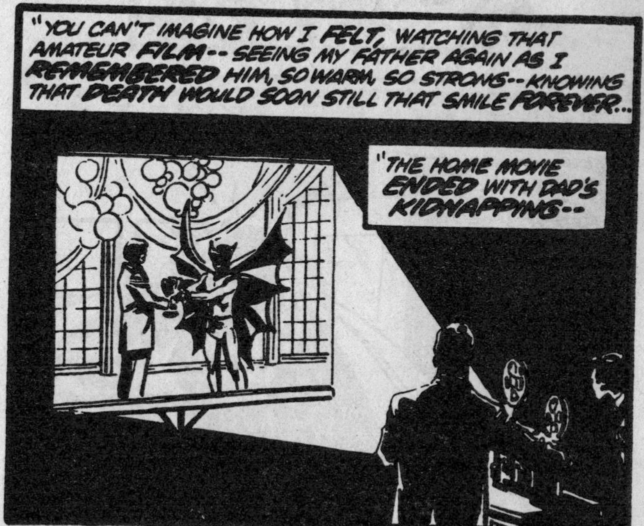
"YOU CAN'T IMAGINE HOW I FELT, WATCHING THAT AMATEUR FILM--SEEING MY FATHER AGAIN AS I REMEMBERED HIM, SO WARM, SO STRONG--KNOWING THAT DEATH WOULD SOON STILL THAT SMILE FOREVER...
"THE HOME MOVIE ENDED WITH DAD'S KIDNAPPING--

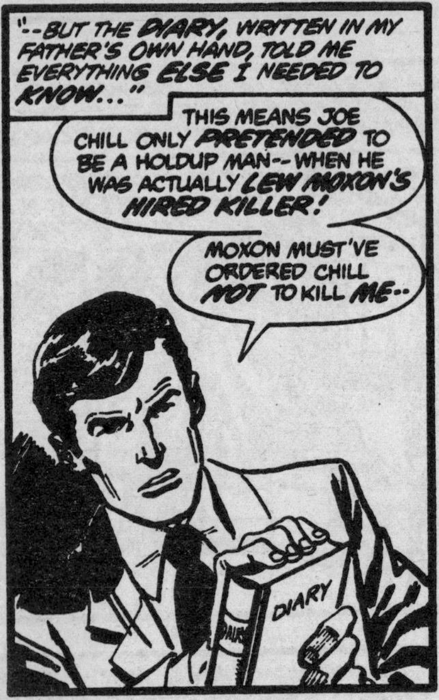
"--BUT THE DIARY, WRITTEN IN MY FATHER'S OWN HAND, TOLD ME EVERYTHING ELSE I NEEDED TO KNOW..."
THIS MEANS JOE CHILL ONLY PRETENDED TO BE A HOLDUP MAN--WHEN HE WAS ACTUALLY LEW MOXON'S HIRED KILLER!
MOXON MUST'VE ORDERED CHILL NOT TO KILL ME--
DIARY

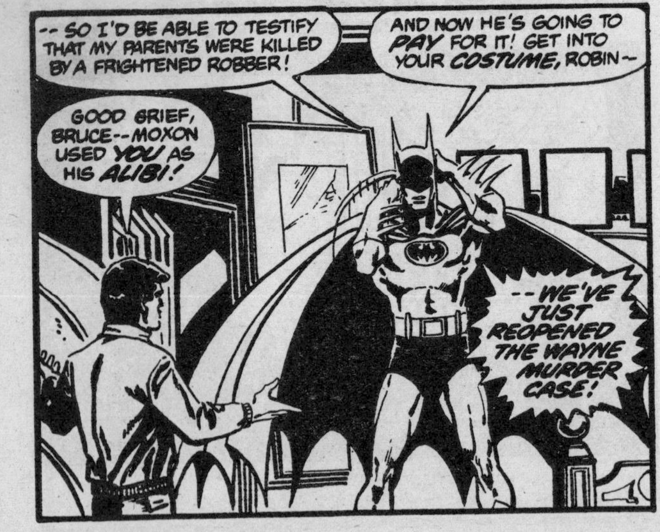
--SO I'D BE ABLE TO TESTIFY THAT MY PARENTS WERE KILLED BY A FRIGHTENED ROBBER!
AND NOW HE'S GOING TO PAY FOR IT! GET INTO YOUR COSTUME, ROBIN--
GOOD GRIEF, BRUCE--MOXON USED YOU AS HIS ALIBI!
--WE'VE JUST REOPENED THE WAYNE MURDER CASE!

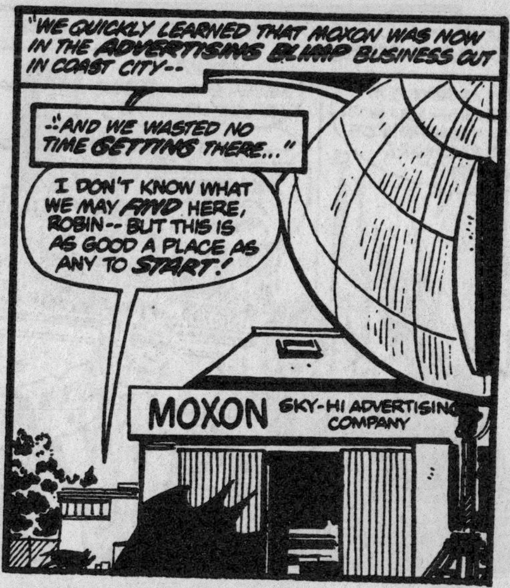
"WE QUICKLY LEARNED THAT MOXON WAS NOW IN THE ADVERTISING BLIMP BUSINESS OUT IN COAST CITY--
--"AND WE WASTED NO TIME GETTING THERE..."
I DON'T KNOW WHAT WE MAY FIND HERE, ROBIN-- BUT THIS IS AS GOOD A PLACE AS ANY TO START!
MOXON SKY-HI ADVERTISING COMPANY

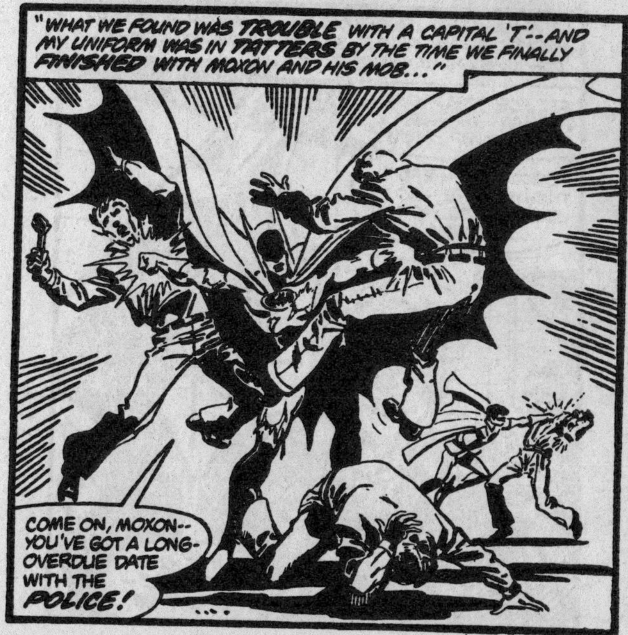
"WHAT WE FOUND WAS TROUBLE WITH A CAPITAL 'T'--AND MY UNIFORM WAS IN TATTERS BY THE TIME WE FINALLY FINISHED WITH MOXON AND HIS MOB..."
COME ON, MOXON-- YOU'VE GOT A LONG-OVERDUE DATE WITH THE POLICE!
...

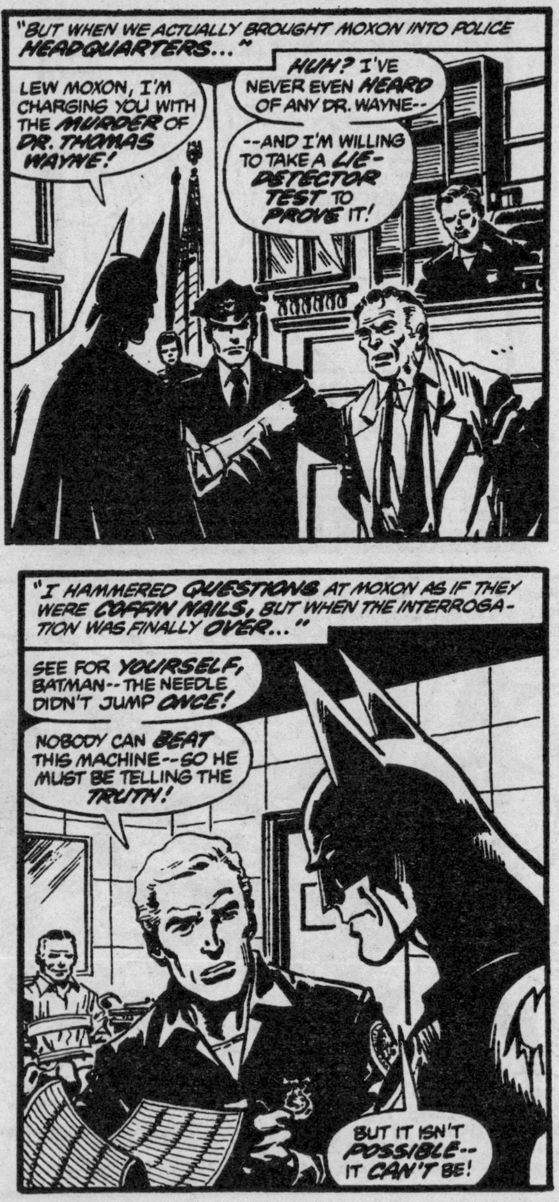
"BUT WHEN WE ACTUALLY BROUGHT MOXON INTO POLICE HEADQUARTERS..."
LEW MOXON, I'M CHARGING YOU WITH THE MURDER OF DR. THOMAS WAYNE!
HUH? I'VE NEVER EVEN HEARD OF ANY DR. WAYNE--
--AND I'M WILLING TO TAKE A LIE-DETECTOR TEST TO PROVE IT!
"I HAMMERED QUESTIONS AT MOXON AS IF THEY WERE COFFIN NAILS, BUT WHEN THE INTERROGATION WAS FINALLY OVER..."
SEE FOR YOURSELF, BATMAN--THE NEEDLE DIDN'T JUMP ONCE!
NOBODY CAN BEAT THIS MACHINE--SO HE MUST BE TELLING THE TRUTH!
BUT IT ISN'T POSSIBLE--IT CAN'T BE!

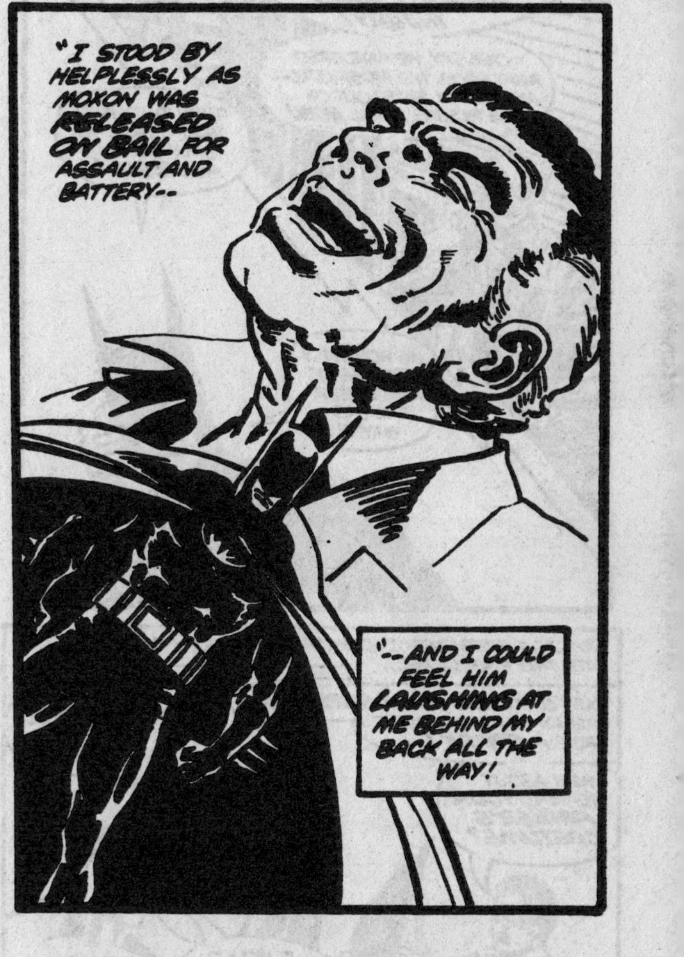
"I STOOD BY HELPLESSLY AS MOXON WAS RELEASED ON BAIL FOR ASSAULT AND BATTERY--
"--AND I COULD FEEL HIM LAUGHING AT ME BEHIND MY BACK ALL THE WAY!

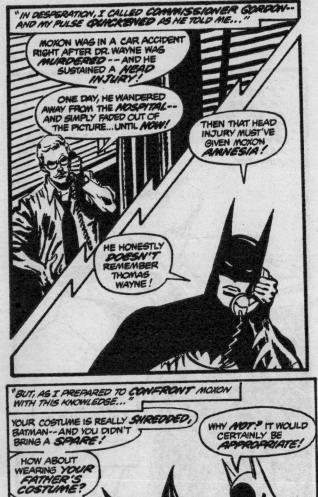

"IN DESPERATION, I CALLED *COMMISSIONER GORDON*-- AND MY PULSE *QUICKENED* AS HE TOLD ME..."

MOXON WAS IN A CAR ACCIDENT RIGHT AFTER DR. WAYNE WAS *MURDERED* -- AND HE SUSTAINED A *HEAD INJURY!*

ONE DAY, HE WANDERED AWAY FROM THE *HOSPITAL*-- AND SIMPLY FADED OUT OF THE PICTURE...UNTIL *NOW!*

THEN THAT HEAD INJURY MUST'VE GIVEN MOXON *AMNESIA!*

HE HONESTLY *DOESN'T* REMEMBER THOMAS WAYNE!

"BUT, AS I PREPARED TO *CONFRONT* MOXON WITH THIS KNOWLEDGE..."

YOUR COSTUME IS REALLY *SHREDDED,* BATMAN--AND YOU DIDN'T BRING A *SPARE!*

WHY *NOT?* IT WOULD CERTAINLY BE *APPROPRIATE!*

HOW ABOUT WEARING *YOUR FATHER'S* COSTUME?

IT WOULD BE ALMOST AS IF *DAD* WERE ARRESTING MOXON!

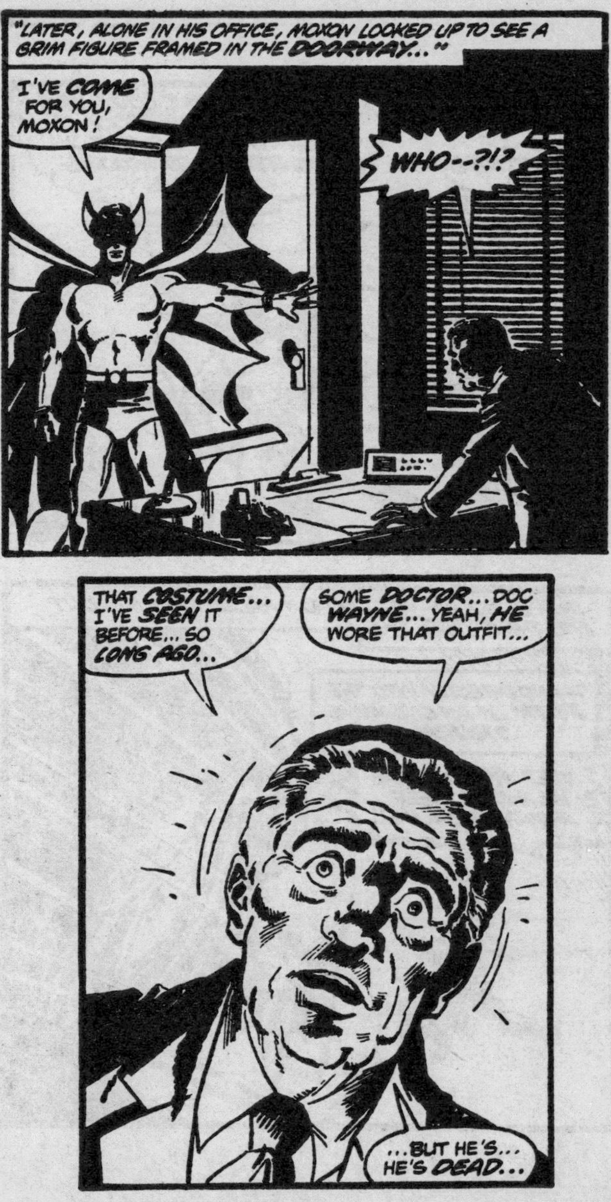
"LATER, ALONE IN HIS OFFICE, MOXON LOOKED UP TO SEE A GRIM FIGURE FRAMED IN THE DOORWAY..."
I'VE COME FOR YOU, MOXON!
WHO--?!?
THAT COSTUME... I'VE SEEN IT BEFORE... SO LONG AGO...
SOME DOCTOR... DOC WAYNE... YEAH, HE WORE THAT OUTFIT...
...BUT HE'S... HE'S DEAD...

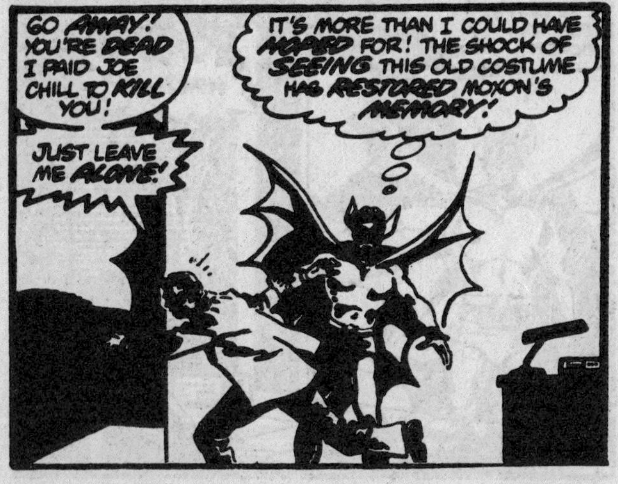
GO AWAY! YOU'RE DEAD I PAID JOE CHILL TO KILL YOU!
IT'S MORE THAN I COULD HAVE HOPED FOR! THE SHOCK OF SEEING THIS OLD COSTUME HAS RESTORED MOXON'S MEMORY!
JUST LEAVE ME ALONE!

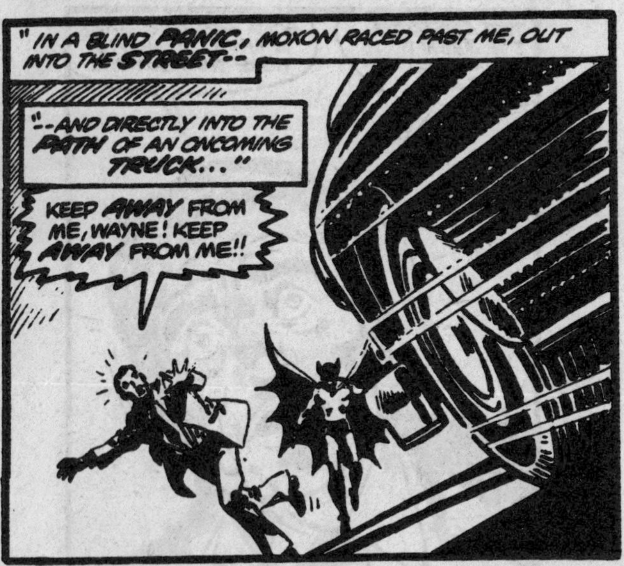
"IN A BLIND PANIC, MOXON RACED PAST ME, OUT INTO THE STREET--
"--AND DIRECTLY INTO THE PATH OF AN ONCOMING TRUCK..."
KEEP AWAY FROM ME, WAYNE! KEEP AWAY FROM ME!!

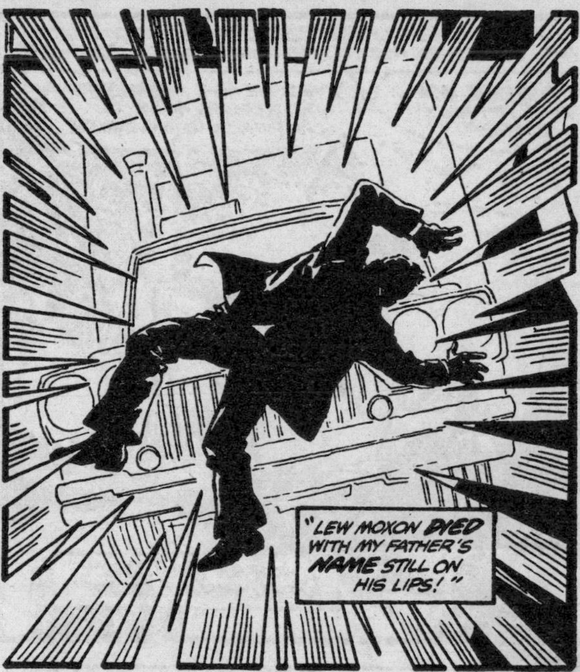
"LEW MOXON DIED WITH MY FATHER'S NAME STILL ON HIS LIPS!"

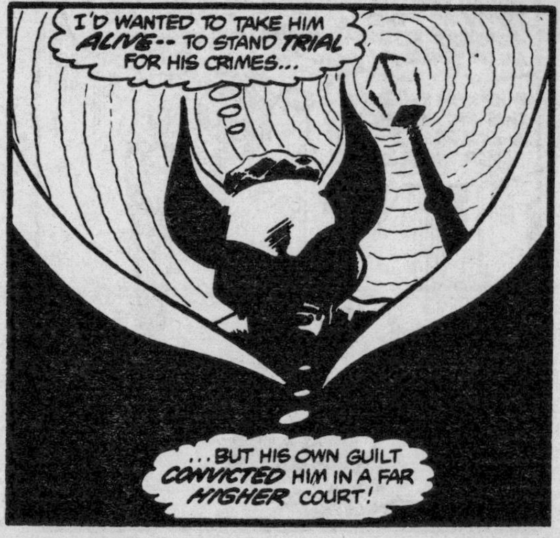
I'D WANTED TO TAKE HIM ALIVE-- TO STAND TRIAL FOR HIS CRIMES...
...BUT HIS OWN GUILT CONVICTED HIM IN A FAR HIGHER COURT!

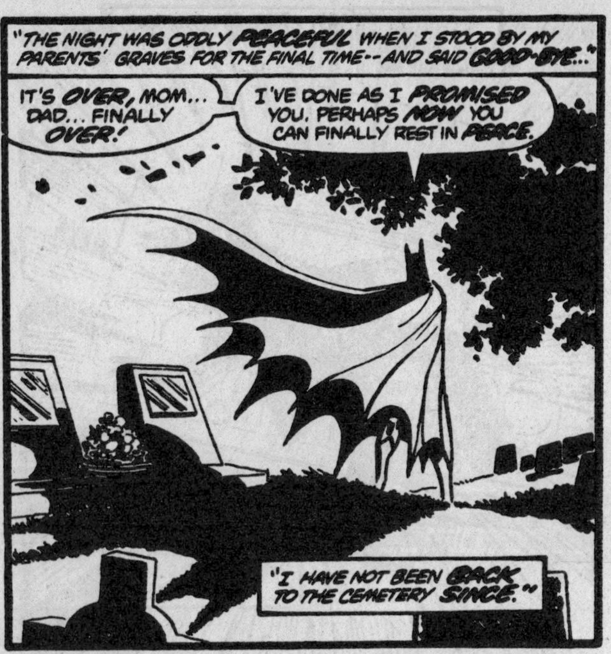
"THE NIGHT WAS ODDLY PEACEFUL WHEN I STOOD BY MY PARENTS' GRAVES FOR THE FINAL TIME--AND SAID GOOD-BYE..."
IT'S OVER, MOM... DAD... FINALLY OVER!
I'VE DONE AS I PROMISED YOU. PERHAPS NOW YOU CAN FINALLY REST IN PEACE.
"I HAVE NOT BEEN BACK TO THE CEMETERY SINCE."

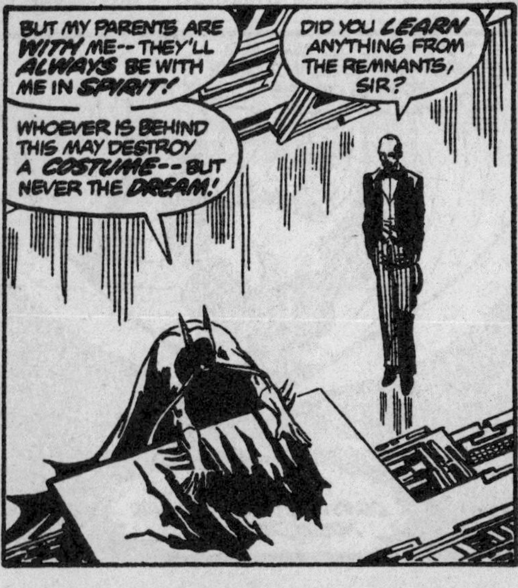
BUT MY PARENTS ARE WITH ME--THEY'LL ALWAYS BE WITH ME IN SPIRIT!
DID YOU LEARN ANYTHING FROM THE REMNANTS, SIR?
WHOEVER IS BEHIND THIS MAY DESTROY A COSTUME--BUT NEVER THE DREAM!

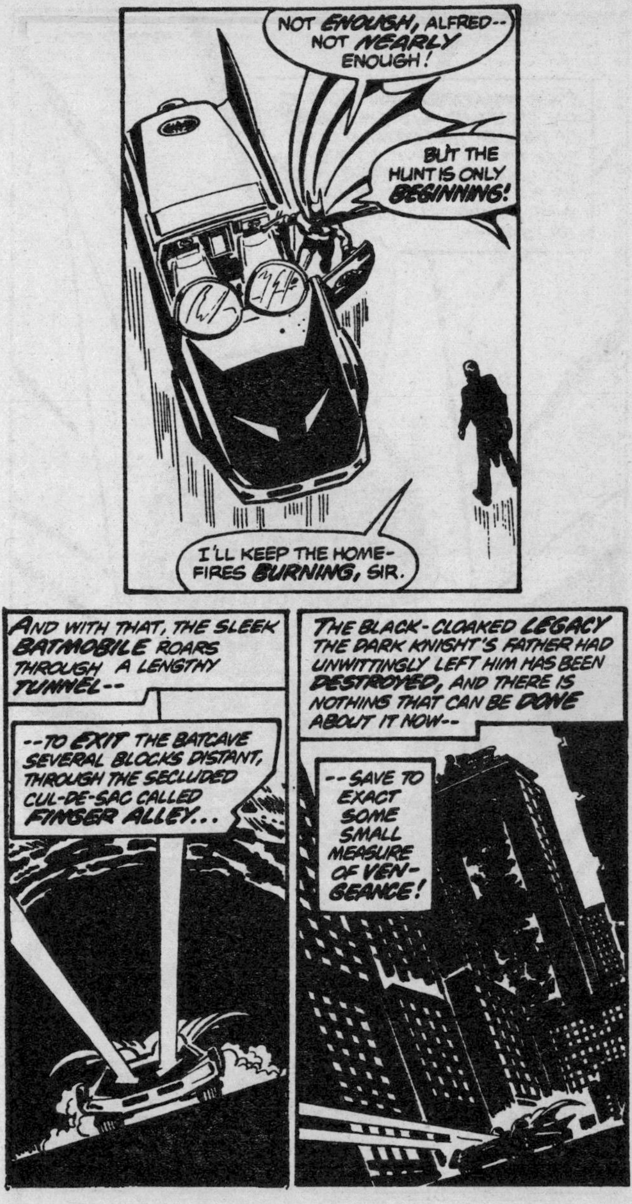
NOT ENOUGH, ALFRED-- NOT NEARLY ENOUGH!
BUT THE HUNT IS ONLY BEGINNING!
I'LL KEEP THE HOME-FIRES BURNING, SIR.
AND WITH THAT, THE SLEEK BATMOBILE ROARS THROUGH A LENGTHY TUNNEL--
--TO EXIT THE BATCAVE SEVERAL BLOCKS DISTANT, THROUGH THE SECLUDED CUL-DE-SAC CALLED FINGER ALLEY...
THE BLACK-CLOAKED LEGACY THE DARK KNIGHT'S FATHER HAD UNWITTINGLY LEFT HIM HAS BEEN DESTROYED, AND THERE IS NOTHING THAT CAN BE DONE ABOUT IT NOW--
--SAVE TO EXACT SOME SMALL MEASURE OF VEN-GEANCE!

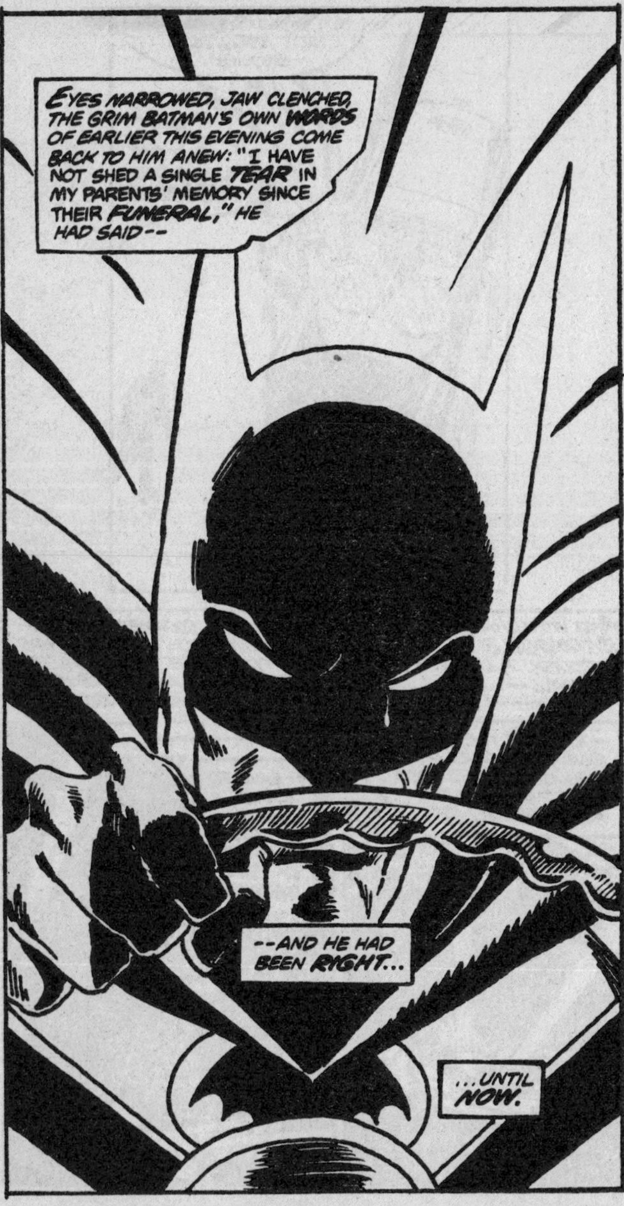
EYES NARROWED, JAW CLENCHED, THE GRIM BATMAN'S OWN WORDS OF EARLIER THIS EVENING COME BACK TO HIM ANEW: "I HAVE NOT SHED A SINGLE TEAR IN MY PARENTS' MEMORY SINCE THEIR FUNERAL," HE HAD SAID--
--AND HE HAD BEEN RIGHT...
...UNTIL NOW.

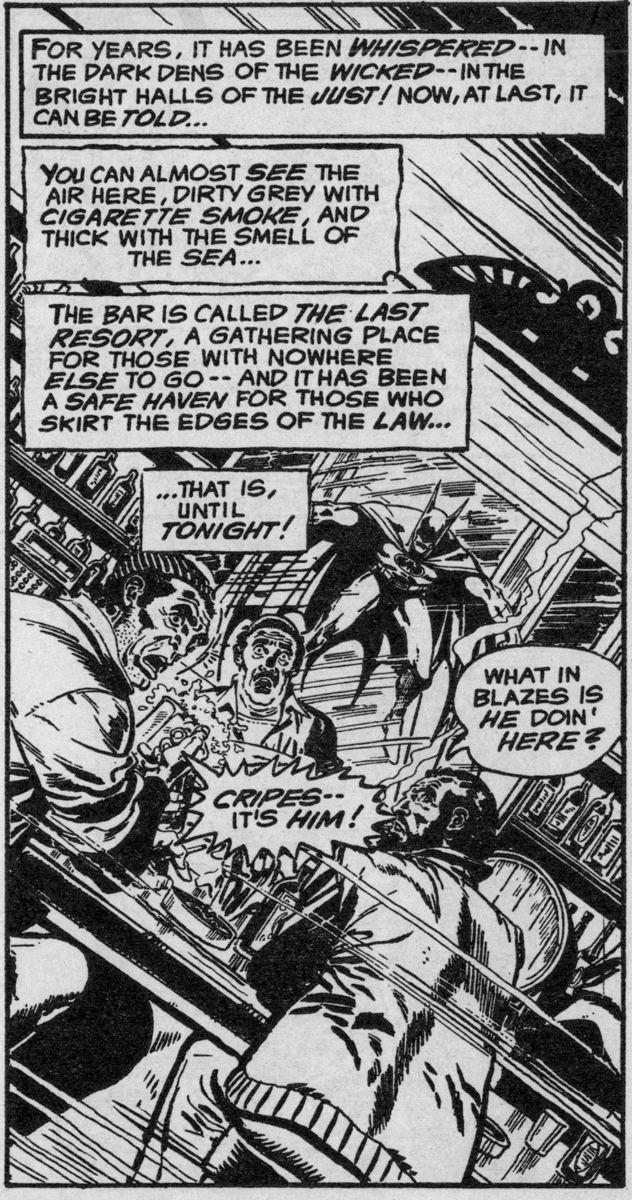
FOR YEARS, IT HAS BEEN WHISPERED-- IN THE DARK DENS OF THE WICKED-- IN THE BRIGHT HALLS OF THE JUST! NOW, AT LAST, IT CAN BE TOLD...
YOU CAN ALMOST SEE THE AIR HERE, DIRTY GREY WITH CIGARETTE SMOKE, AND THICK WITH THE SMELL OF THE SEA...
THE BAR IS CALLED THE LAST RESORT, A GATHERING PLACE FOR THOSE WITH NOWHERE ELSE TO GO-- AND IT HAS BEEN A SAFE HAVEN FOR THOSE WHO SKIRT THE EDGES OF THE LAW...
...THAT IS, UNTIL TONIGHT!
WHAT IN BLAZES IS HE DOIN' HERE?
CRIPES-- IT'S HIM!

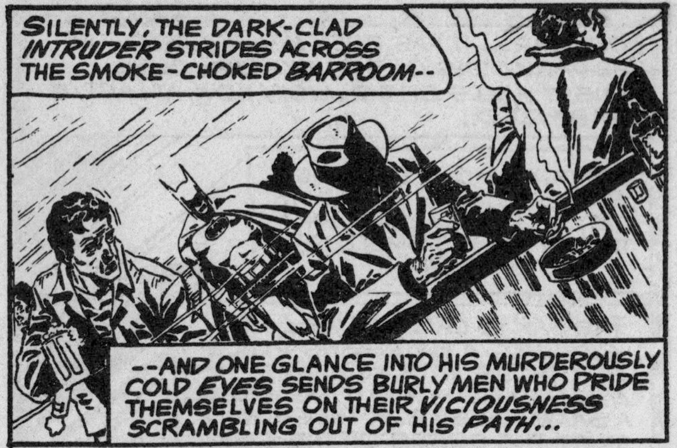
SILENTLY, THE DARK-CLAD INTRUDER STRIDES ACROSS THE SMOKE-CHOKED BARROOM--
--AND ONE GLANCE INTO HIS MURDEROUSLY COLD EYES SENDS BURLY MEN WHO PRIDE THEMSELVES ON THEIR VICIOUSNESS SCRAMBLING OUT OF HIS PATH...

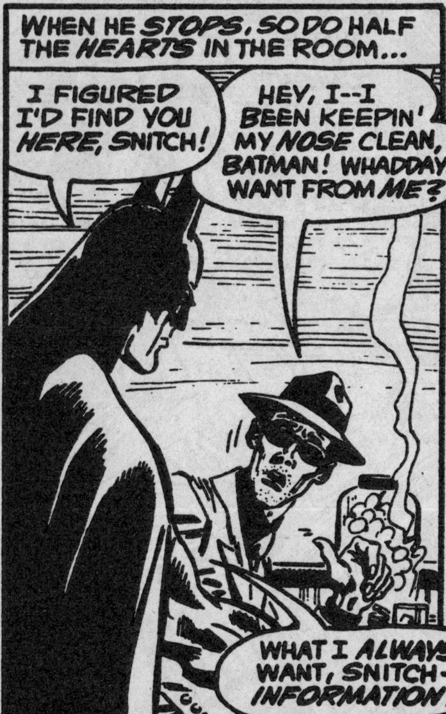
WHEN HE STOPS, SO DO HALF THE HEARTS IN THE ROOM...
I FIGURED I'D FIND YOU HERE, SNITCH!
HEY, I--I BEEN KEEPIN' MY NOSE CLEAN, BATMAN! WHADDAYA WANT FROM ME?
WHAT I ALWAYS WANT, SNITCH-- INFORMATION!

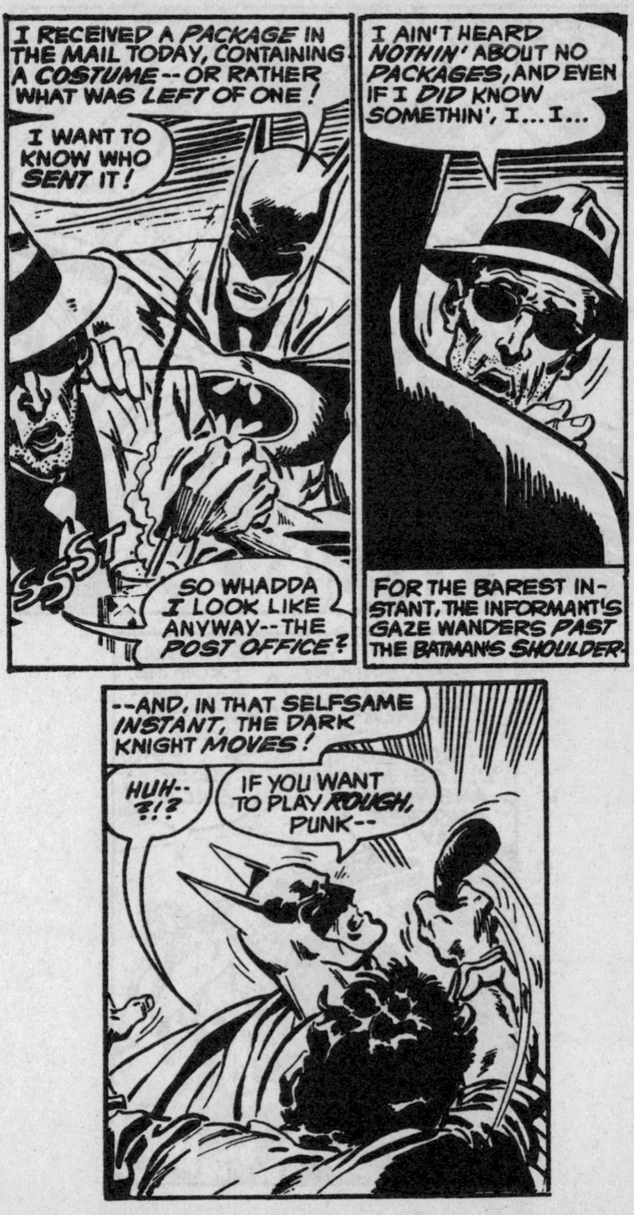
I RECEIVED A PACKAGE IN THE MAIL TODAY, CONTAINING A COSTUME -- OR RATHER WHAT WAS LEFT OF ONE!
I WANT TO KNOW WHO SENT IT!
SSSST
SO WHADDA I LOOK LIKE ANYWAY-- THE POST OFFICE?
I AIN'T HEARD NOTHIN' ABOUT NO PACKAGES, AND EVEN IF I DID KNOW SOMETHIN', I... I...
FOR THE BAREST IN-STANT, THE INFORMANT'S GAZE WANDERS PAST THE BATMAN'S SHOULDER-
--AND, IN THAT SELFSAME INSTANT, THE DARK KNIGHT MOVES!
HUH-- ?!?
IF YOU WANT TO PLAY ROUGH, PUNK--

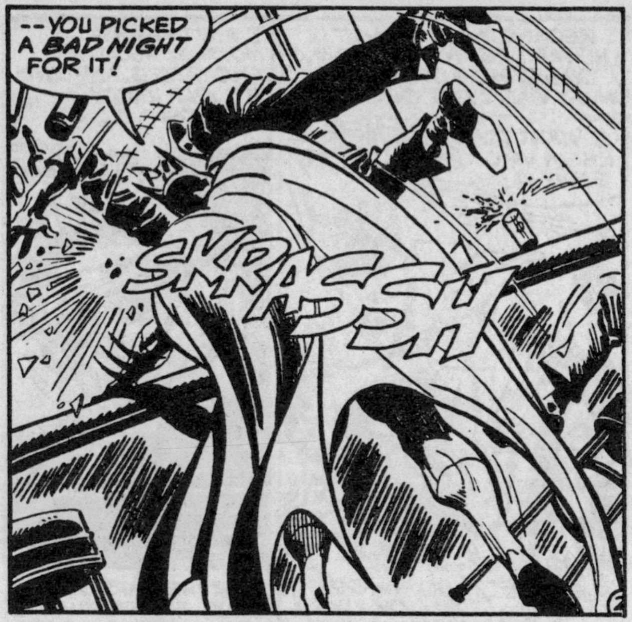
--YOU PICKED A BAD NIGHT FOR IT!
SKRASSH
SMASH

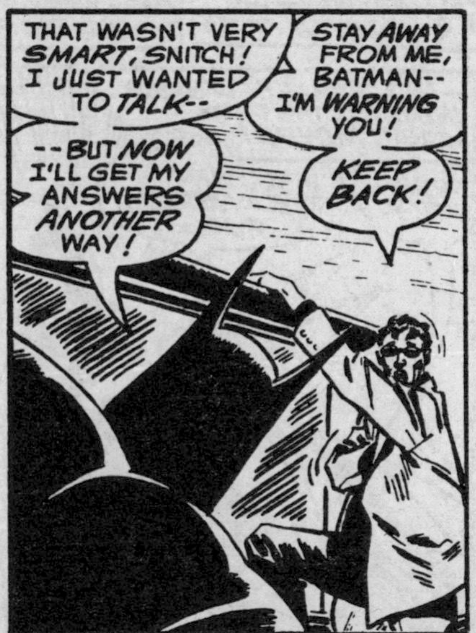
THAT WASN'T VERY SMART, SNITCH! I JUST WANTED TO TALK--
STAY AWAY FROM ME, BATMAN-- I'M WARNING YOU!
--BUT NOW I'LL GET MY ANSWERS ANOTHER WAY!
KEEP BACK!

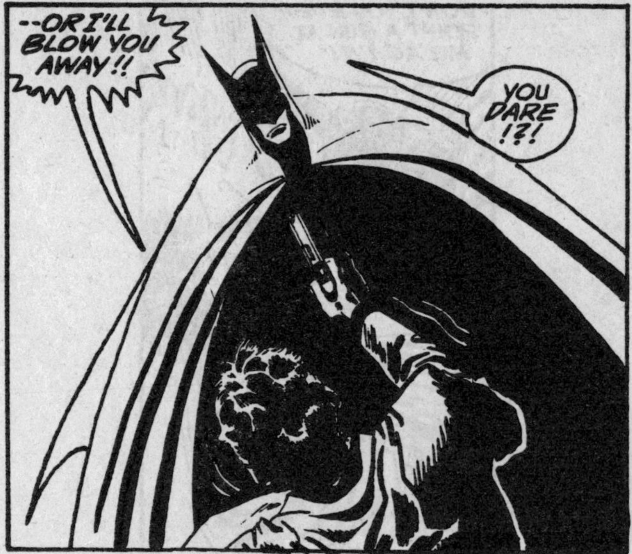
--OR I'LL BLOW YOU AWAY!!
YOU DARE !?!

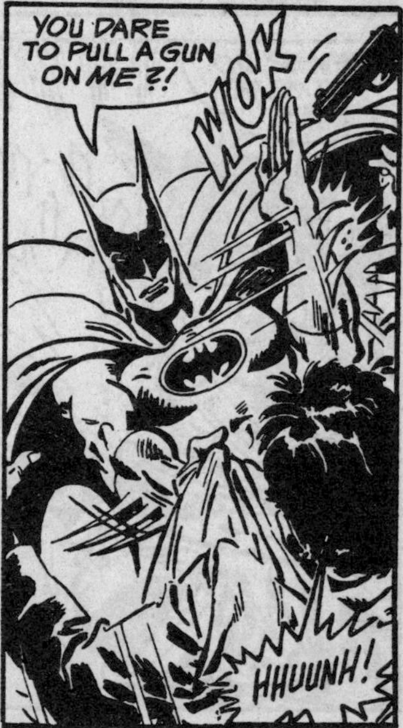
YOU DARE TO PULL A GUN ON ME ?!
WOK
HHUUNH!

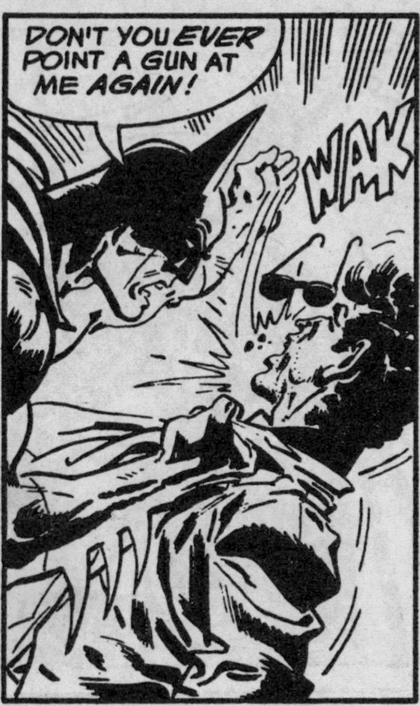
DON'T YOU EVER POINT A GUN AT ME AGAIN!
WAK

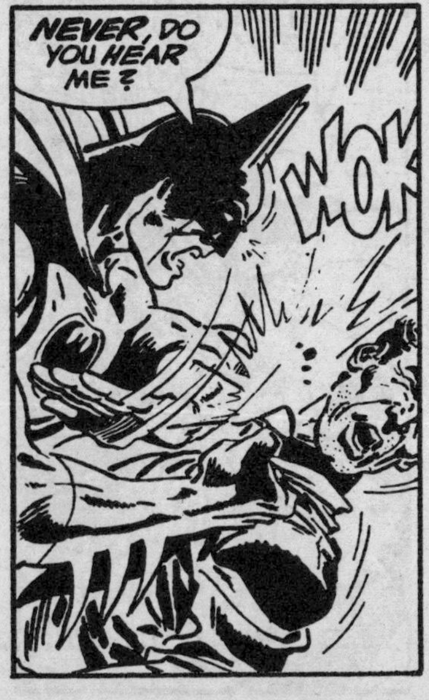
NEVER, DO YOU HEAR ME?
WOK

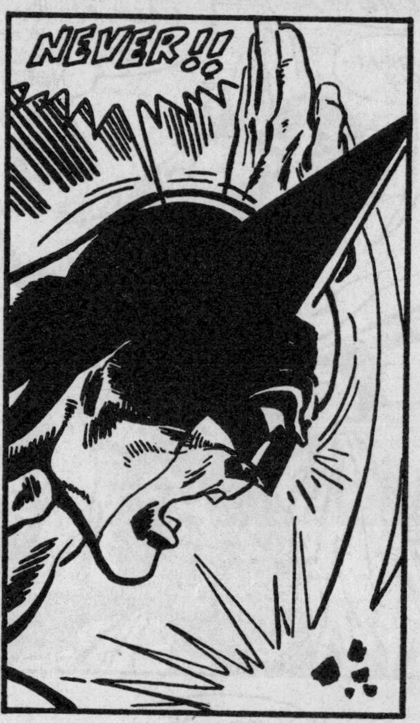
NEVER!!

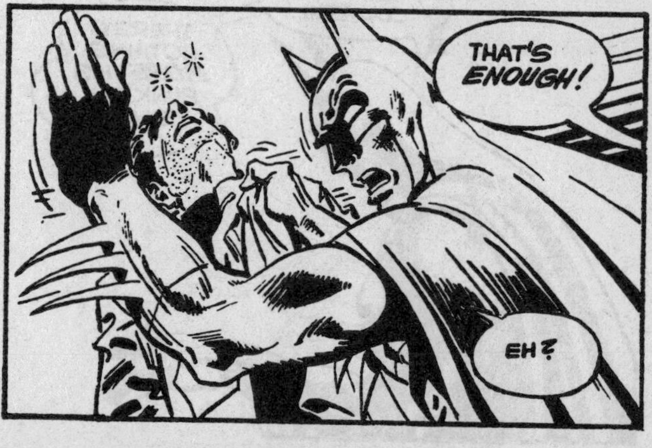
THAT'S ENOUGH!
EH?

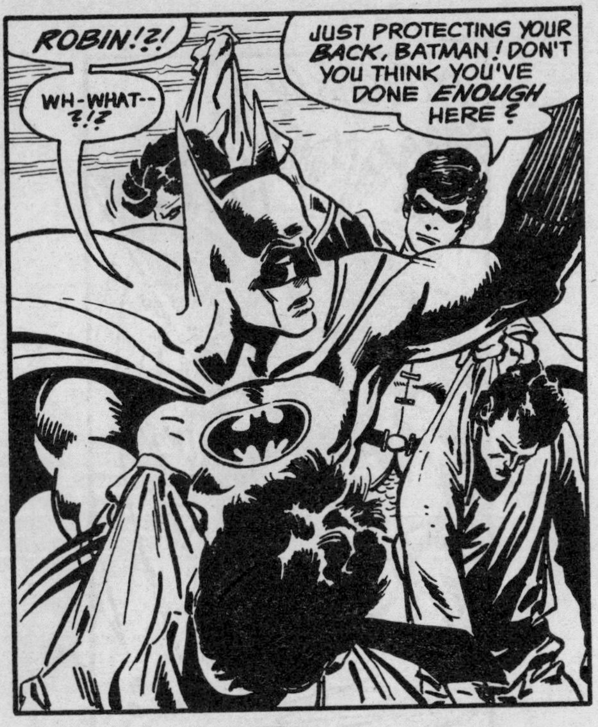
ROBIN!?!
WH-WHAT-- ?!?
JUST PROTECTING YOUR BACK, BATMAN! DON'T YOU THINK YOU'VE DONE ENOUGH HERE?

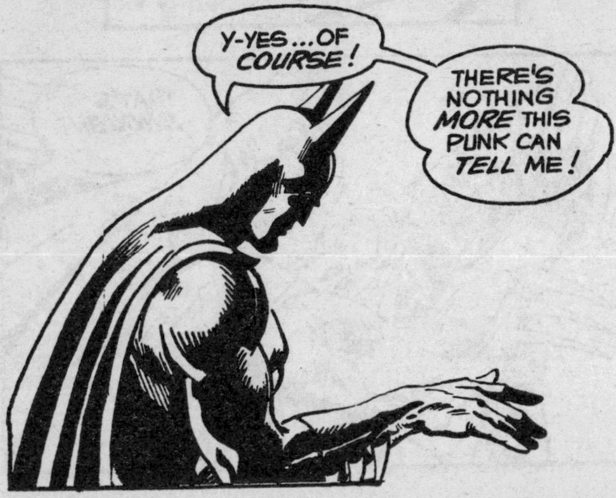
Y-YES...OF COURSE!
THERE'S NOTHING MORE THIS PUNK CAN TELL ME!

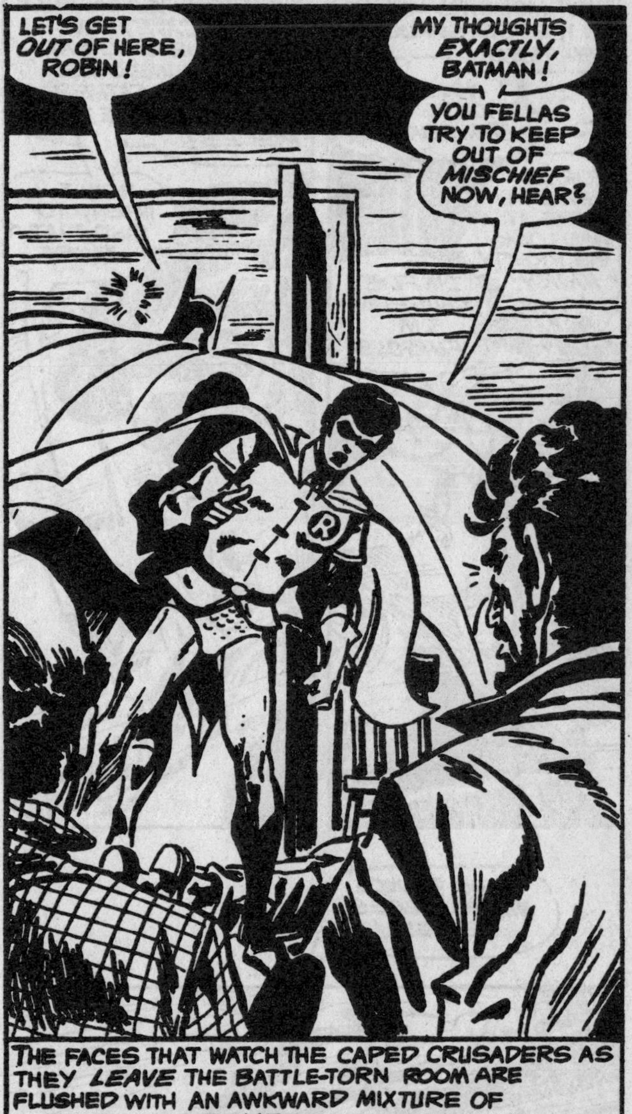
LET'S GET OUT OF HERE, ROBIN!
MY THOUGHTS EXACTLY, BATMAN!
YOU FELLAS TRY TO KEEP OUT OF MISCHIEF NOW, HEAR?

THE FACES THAT WATCH THE CAPED CRUSADERS AS THEY *LEAVE* THE BATTLE-TORN ROOM ARE FLUSHED WITH AN AWKWARD MIXTURE OF *HATRED*-- AND *RELIEF*...

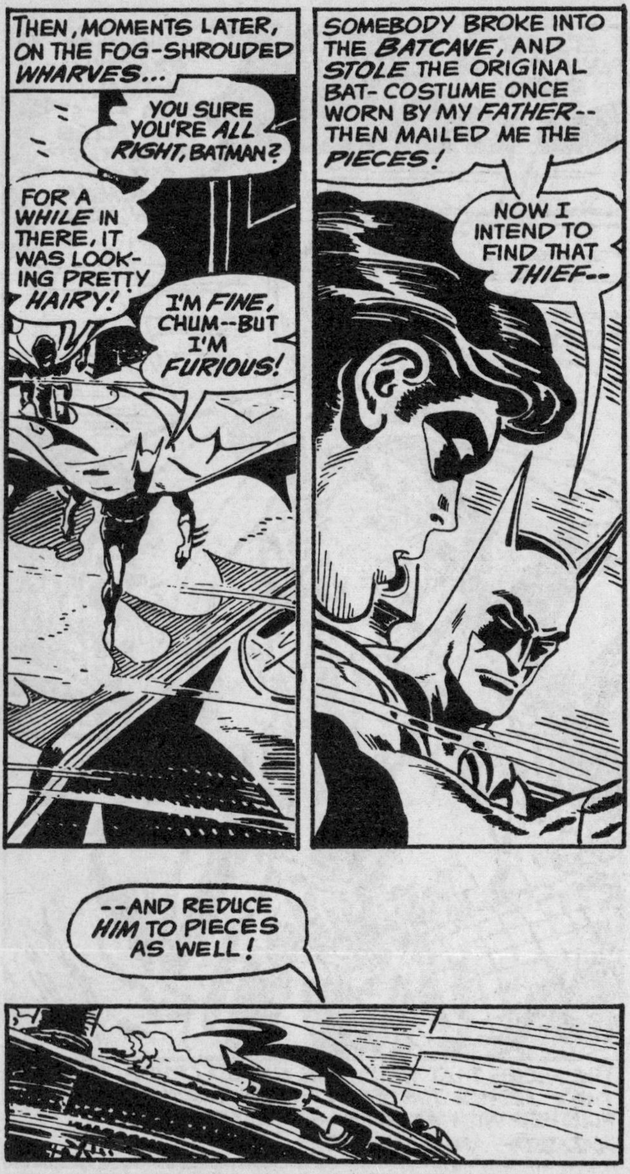
THEN, MOMENTS LATER, ON THE FOG-SHROUDED WHARVES...
YOU SURE YOU'RE ALL RIGHT, BATMAN?
FOR A WHILE IN THERE, IT WAS LOOKING PRETTY HAIRY!
I'M FINE, CHUM--BUT I'M FURIOUS!
SOMEBODY BROKE INTO THE BATCAVE, AND STOLE THE ORIGINAL BAT-COSTUME ONCE WORN BY MY FATHER--THEN MAILED ME THE PIECES!
NOW I INTEND TO FIND THAT THIEF--
--AND REDUCE HIM TO PIECES AS WELL!

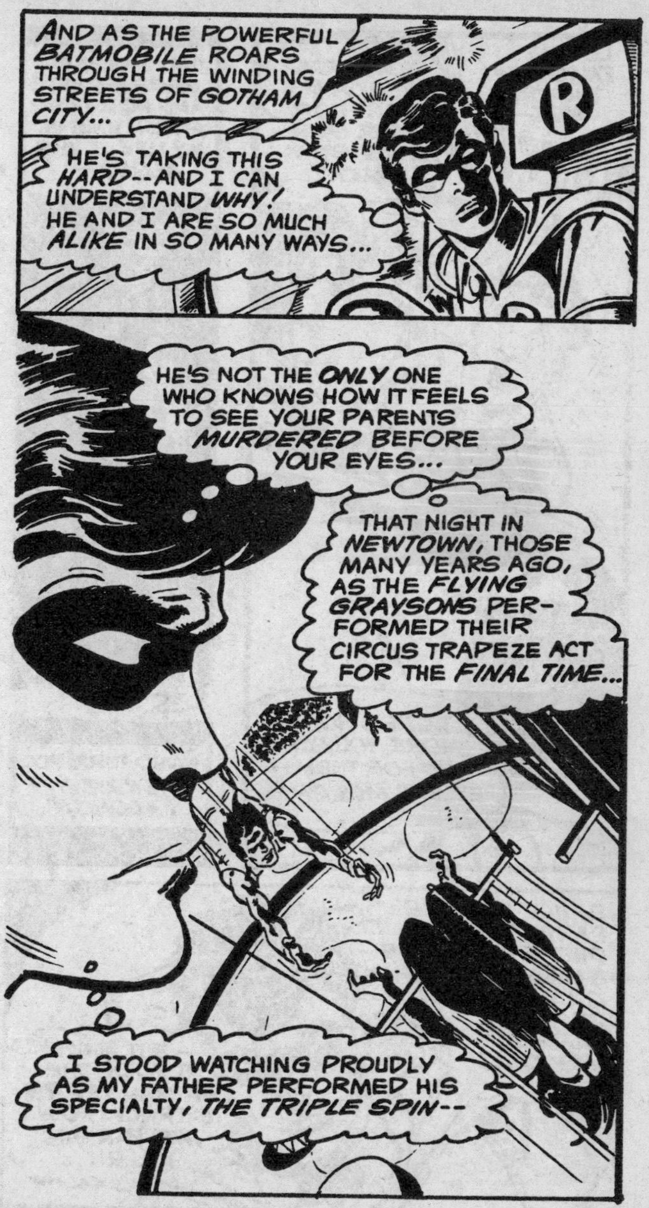
AND AS THE POWERFUL BATMOBILE ROARS THROUGH THE WINDING STREETS OF GOTHAM CITY...
HE'S TAKING THIS HARD--AND I CAN UNDERSTAND WHY! HE AND I ARE SO MUCH ALIKE IN SO MANY WAYS...
HE'S NOT THE ONLY ONE WHO KNOWS HOW IT FEELS TO SEE YOUR PARENTS MURDERED BEFORE YOUR EYES...
THAT NIGHT IN NEWTOWN, THOSE MANY YEARS AGO, AS THE FLYING GRAYSONS PER-FORMED THEIR CIRCUS TRAPEZE ACT FOR THE FINAL TIME...
I STOOD WATCHING PROUDLY AS MY FATHER PERFORMED HIS SPECIALTY, THE TRIPLE SPIN--

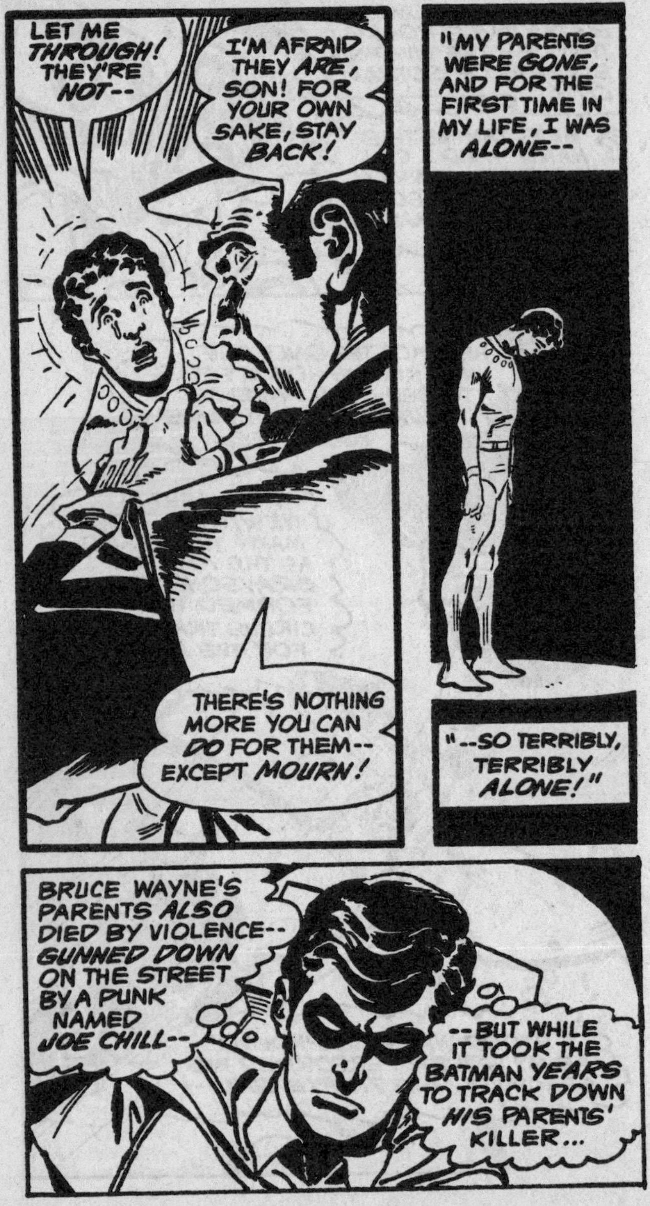

LET ME THROUGH! THEY'RE NOT--
I'M AFRAID THEY ARE, SON! FOR YOUR OWN SAKE, STAY BACK!
THERE'S NOTHING MORE YOU CAN DO FOR THEM-- EXCEPT MOURN!
"MY PARENTS WERE GONE, AND FOR THE FIRST TIME IN MY LIFE, I WAS ALONE--
"--SO TERRIBLY, TERRIBLY ALONE!"
BRUCE WAYNE'S PARENTS ALSO DIED BY VIOLENCE-- GUNNED DOWN ON THE STREET BY A PUNK NAMED JOE CHILL--
--BUT WHILE IT TOOK THE BATMAN YEARS TO TRACK DOWN HIS PARENTS' KILLER...

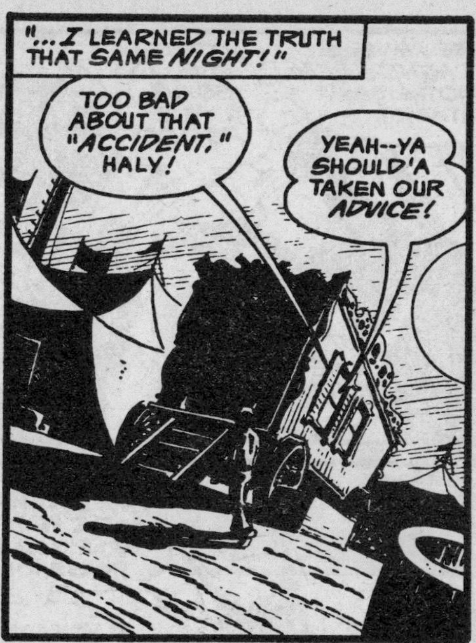
"...I LEARNED THE TRUTH THAT SAME NIGHT!"
TOO BAD ABOUT THAT "ACCIDENT," HALY!
YEAH--YA SHOULD'A TAKEN OUR ADVICE!

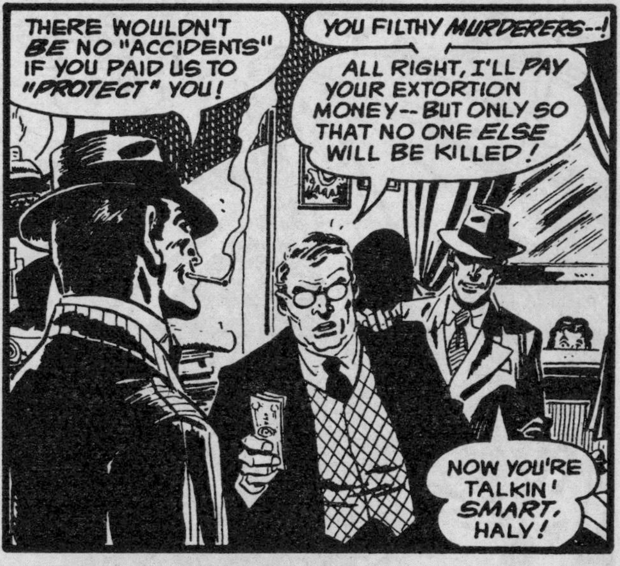
THERE WOULDN'T BE NO "ACCIDENTS" IF YOU PAID US TO "PROTECT" YOU!
YOU FILTHY MURDERERS--!
ALL RIGHT, I'LL PAY YOUR EXTORTION MONEY-- BUT ONLY SO THAT NO ONE ELSE WILL BE KILLED!
NOW YOU'RE TALKIN' SMART, HALY!

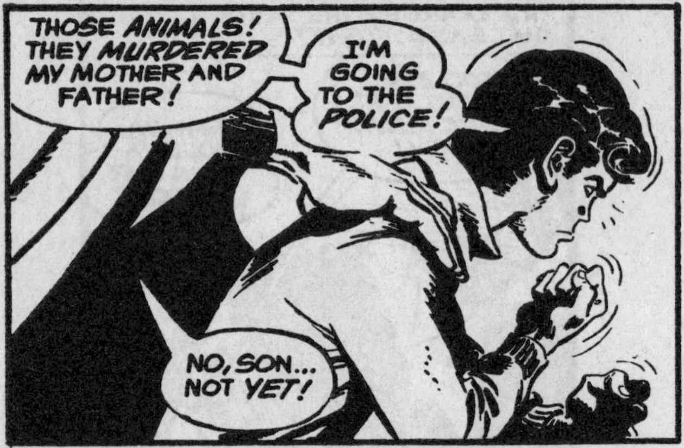
THOSE ANIMALS! THEY MURDERED MY MOTHER AND FATHER!
I'M GOING TO THE POLICE!
NO, SON... NOT YET!

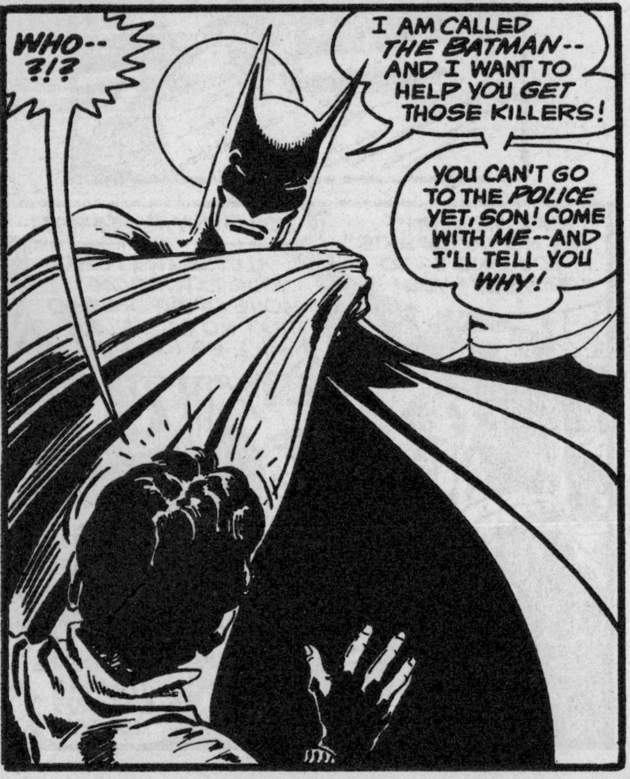
WHO-- ?!?
I AM CALLED THE BATMAN-- AND I WANT TO HELP YOU GET THOSE KILLERS!
YOU CAN'T GO TO THE POLICE YET, SON! COME WITH ME--AND I'LL TELL YOU WHY!

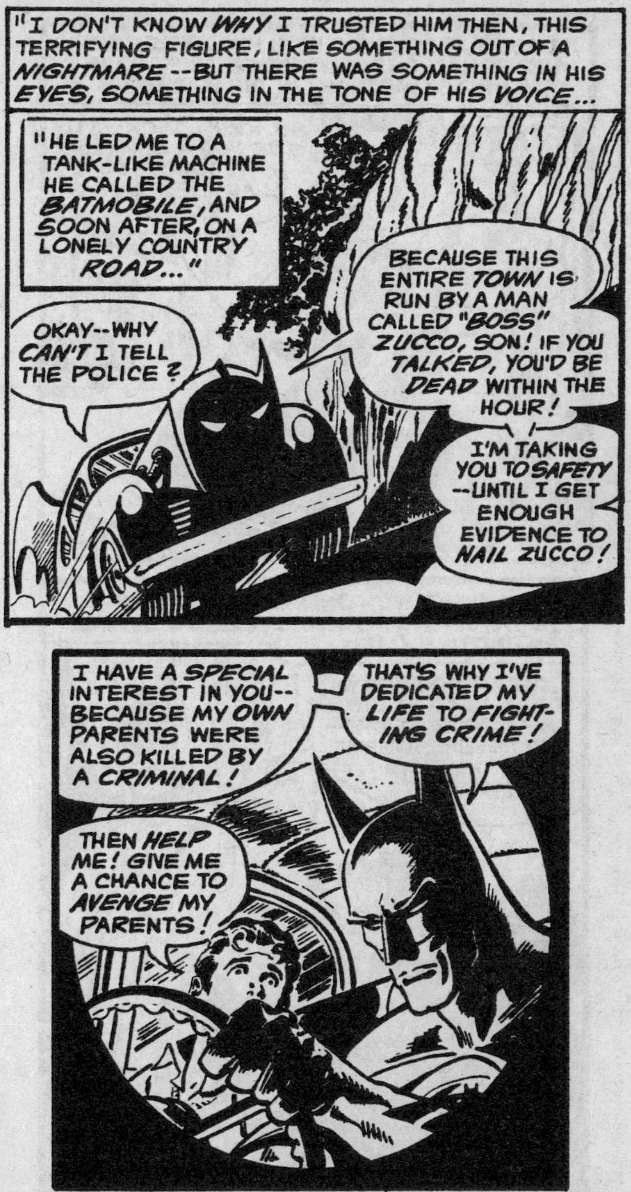
"I DON'T KNOW WHY I TRUSTED HIM THEN, THIS TERRIFYING FIGURE, LIKE SOMETHING OUT OF A NIGHTMARE --BUT THERE WAS SOMETHING IN HIS EYES, SOMETHING IN THE TONE OF HIS VOICE...
"HE LED ME TO A TANK-LIKE MACHINE HE CALLED THE BATMOBILE, AND SOON AFTER, ON A LONELY COUNTRY ROAD..."
OKAY--WHY CAN'T I TELL THE POLICE?
BECAUSE THIS ENTIRE TOWN IS RUN BY A MAN CALLED "BOSS" ZUCCO, SON! IF YOU TALKED, YOU'D BE DEAD WITHIN THE HOUR!
I'M TAKING YOU TO SAFETY --UNTIL I GET ENOUGH EVIDENCE TO NAIL ZUCCO!
I HAVE A SPECIAL INTEREST IN YOU-- BECAUSE MY OWN PARENTS WERE ALSO KILLED BY A CRIMINAL!
THAT'S WHY I'VE DEDICATED MY LIFE TO FIGHTING CRIME!
THEN HELP ME! GIVE ME A CHANCE TO AVENGE MY PARENTS!

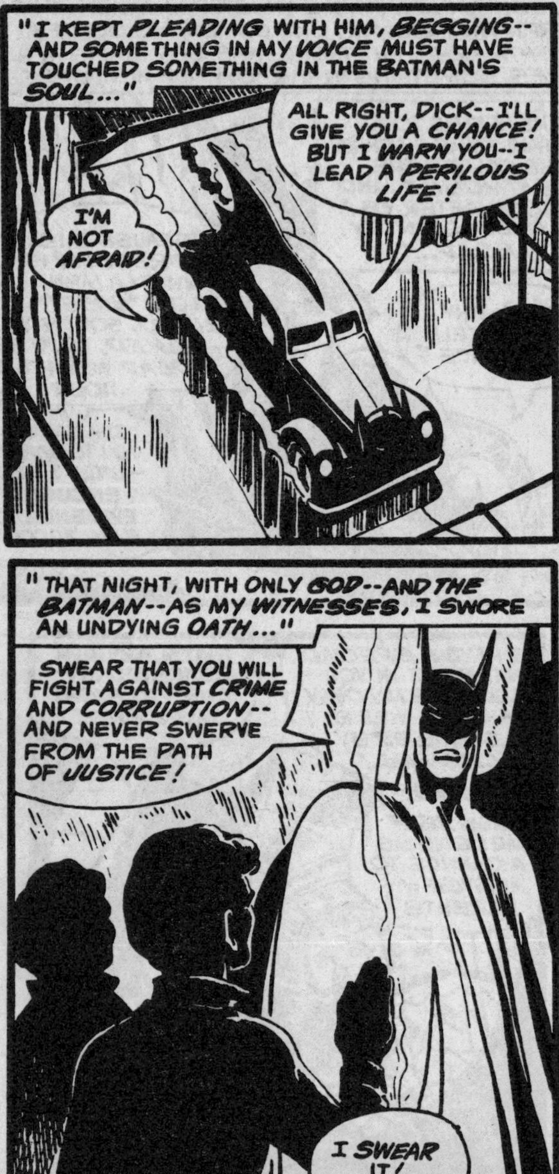
"I KEPT PLEADING WITH HIM, BEGGING--AND SOMETHING IN MY VOICE MUST HAVE TOUCHED SOMETHING IN THE BATMAN'S SOUL..."
ALL RIGHT, DICK--I'LL GIVE YOU A CHANCE! BUT I WARN YOU--I LEAD A PERILOUS LIFE!
I'M NOT AFRAID!
"THAT NIGHT, WITH ONLY GOD--AND THE BATMAN--AS MY WITNESSES, I SWORE AN UNDYING OATH..."
SWEAR THAT YOU WILL FIGHT AGAINST CRIME AND CORRUPTION--AND NEVER SWERVE FROM THE PATH OF JUSTICE!
I SWEAR IT!

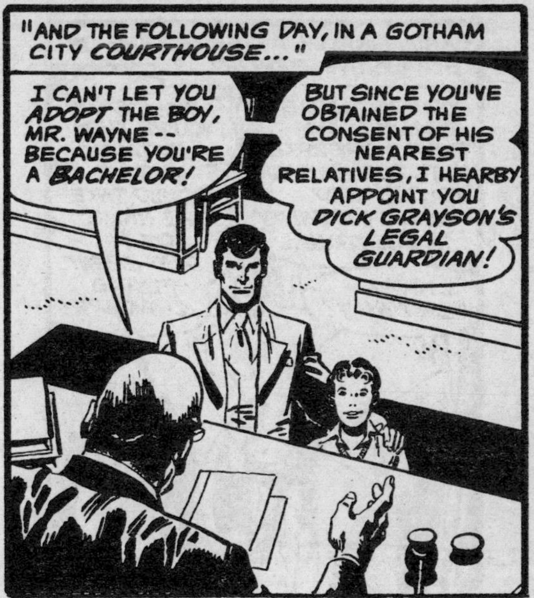
"AND THE FOLLOWING DAY, IN A GOTHAM CITY COURTHOUSE..."
I CAN'T LET YOU ADOPT THE BOY, MR. WAYNE -- BECAUSE YOU'RE A BACHELOR!
BUT SINCE YOU'VE OBTAINED THE CONSENT OF HIS NEAREST RELATIVES, I HEARBY APPOINT YOU DICK GRAYSON'S LEGAL GUARDIAN!

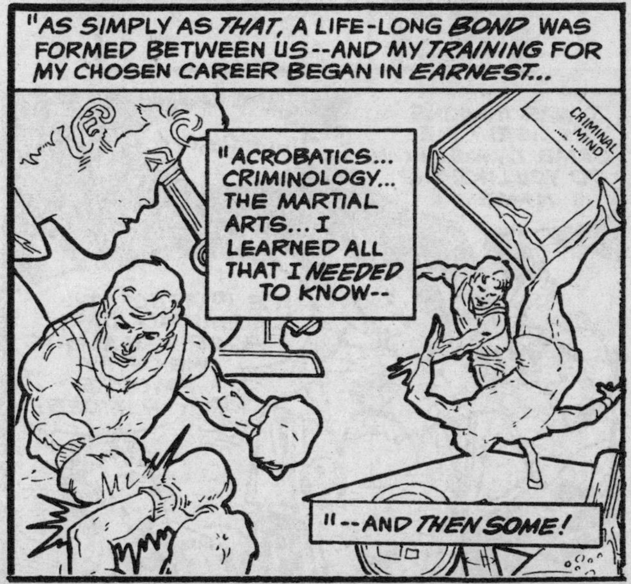
"AS SIMPLY AS THAT, A LIFE-LONG BOND WAS FORMED BETWEEN US--AND MY TRAINING FOR MY CHOSEN CAREER BEGAN IN EARNEST...
CRIMINAL MIND
"ACROBATICS... CRIMINOLOGY... THE MARTIAL ARTS... I LEARNED ALL THAT I NEEDED TO KNOW--
"--AND THEN SOME!

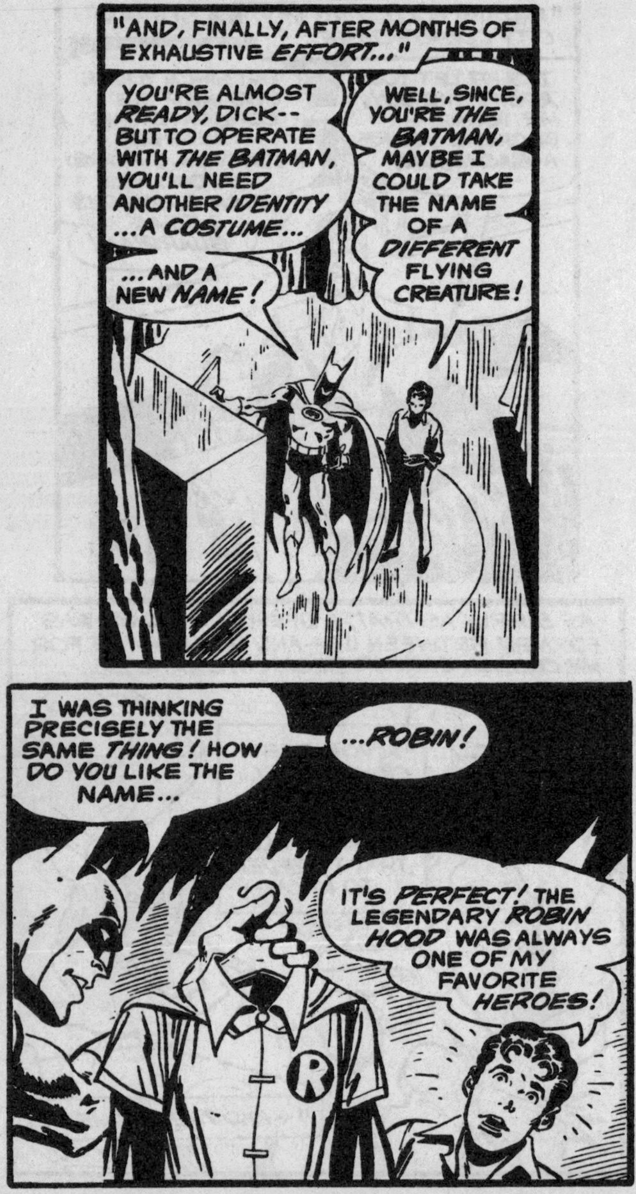
"AND, FINALLY, AFTER MONTHS OF EXHAUSTIVE EFFORT..."
YOU'RE ALMOST READY, DICK-- BUT TO OPERATE WITH THE BATMAN, YOU'LL NEED ANOTHER IDENTITY ...A COSTUME...
...AND A NEW NAME!
WELL, SINCE, YOU'RE THE BATMAN, MAYBE I COULD TAKE THE NAME OF A DIFFERENT FLYING CREATURE!
I WAS THINKING PRECISELY THE SAME THING! HOW DO YOU LIKE THE NAME...
...ROBIN!
IT'S PERFECT! THE LEGENDARY ROBIN HOOD WAS ALWAYS ONE OF MY FAVORITE HEROES!
R

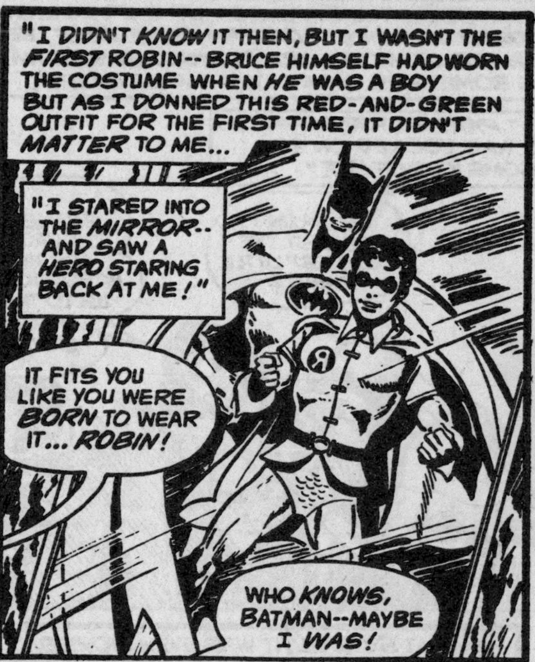
"I DIDN'T KNOW IT THEN, BUT I WASN'T THE FIRST ROBIN-- BRUCE HIMSELF HAD WORN THE COSTUME WHEN HE WAS A BOY BUT AS I DONNED THIS RED-AND-GREEN OUTFIT FOR THE FIRST TIME, IT DIDN'T MATTER TO ME...
"I STARED INTO THE MIRROR-- AND SAW A HERO STARING BACK AT ME!"
IT FITS YOU LIKE YOU WERE BORN TO WEAR IT... ROBIN!
WHO KNOWS, BATMAN--MAYBE I WAS!

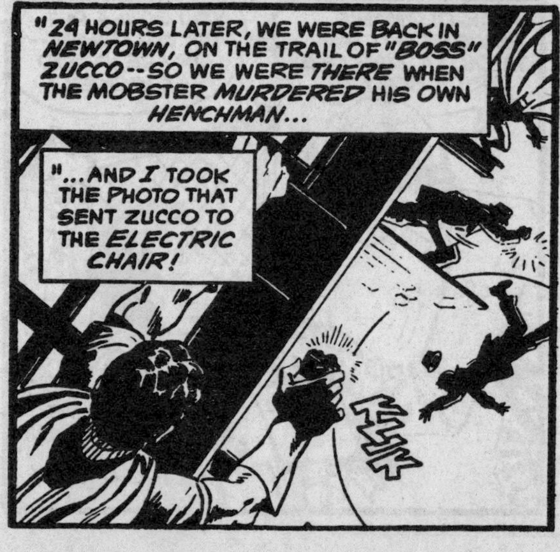
"24 HOURS LATER, WE WERE BACK IN NEWTOWN, ON THE TRAIL OF "BOSS" ZUCCO--SO WE WERE THERE WHEN THE MOBSTER MURDERED HIS OWN HENCHMAN...
"...AND I TOOK THE PHOTO THAT SENT ZUCCO TO THE ELECTRIC CHAIR!

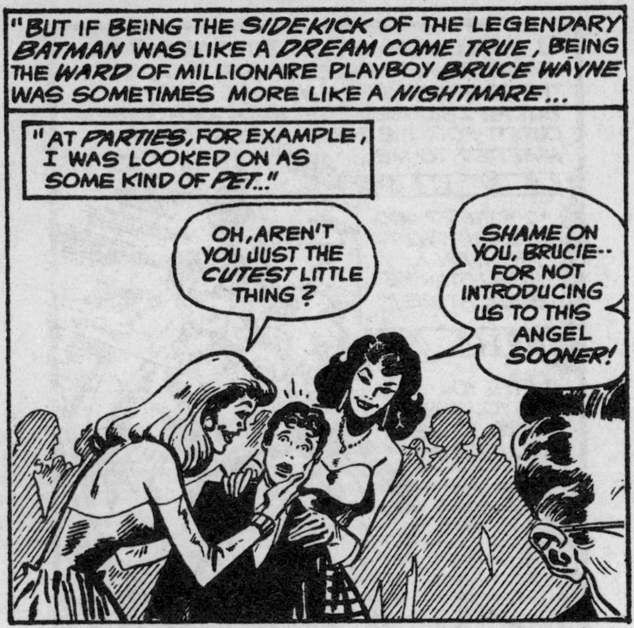
"BUT IF BEING THE SIDEKICK OF THE LEGENDARY BATMAN WAS LIKE A DREAM COME TRUE, BEING THE WARD OF MILLIONAIRE PLAYBOY BRUCE WAYNE WAS SOMETIMES MORE LIKE A NIGHTMARE...
"AT PARTIES, FOR EXAMPLE, I WAS LOOKED ON AS SOME KIND OF PET..."
OH, AREN'T YOU JUST THE CUTEST LITTLE THING?
SHAME ON YOU, BRUCIE-- FOR NOT INTRODUCING US TO THIS ANGEL SOONER!

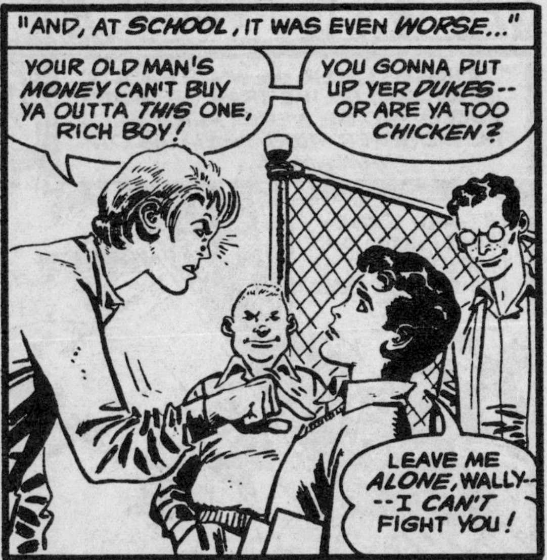
"AND, AT SCHOOL, IT WAS EVEN WORSE..."
YOUR OLD MAN'S MONEY CAN'T BUY YA OUTTA THIS ONE, RICH BOY!
YOU GONNA PUT UP YER DUKES-- OR ARE YA TOO CHICKEN?
LEAVE ME ALONE, WALLY-- --I CAN'T FIGHT YOU!

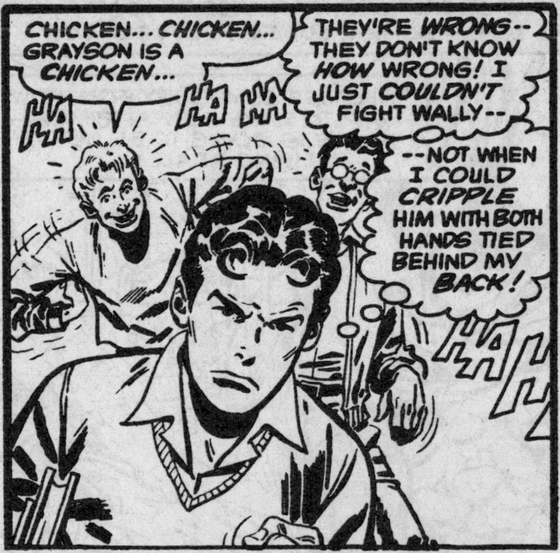
CHICKEN... CHICKEN... GRAYSON IS A CHICKEN...
HA HA HA
THEY'RE WRONG-- THEY DON'T KNOW HOW WRONG! I JUST COULDN'T FIGHT WALLY--
--NOT WHEN I COULD CRIPPLE HIM WITH BOTH HANDS TIED BEHIND MY BACK!
HA

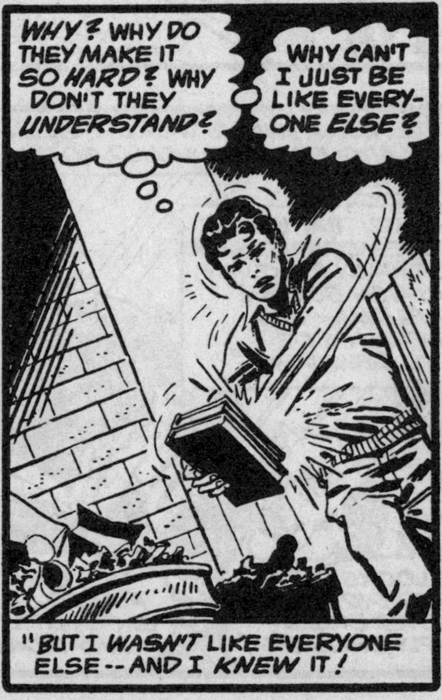
WHY? WHY DO THEY MAKE IT SO HARD? WHY DON'T THEY UNDERSTAND?
WHY CAN'T I JUST BE LIKE EVERY-ONE ELSE?
"BUT I WASN'T LIKE EVERYONE ELSE--AND I KNEW IT!

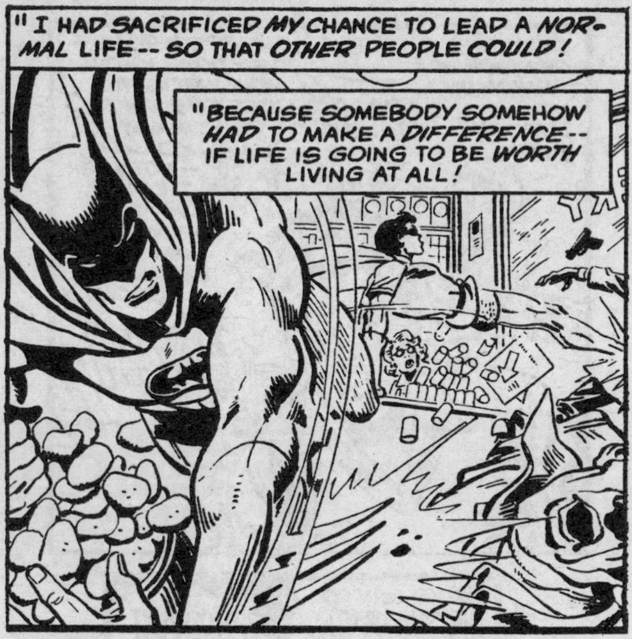
"I HAD SACRIFICED MY CHANCE TO LEAD A NORMAL LIFE -- SO THAT OTHER PEOPLE COULD!
"BECAUSE SOMEBODY SOMEHOW HAD TO MAKE A DIFFERENCE -- IF LIFE IS GOING TO BE WORTH LIVING AT ALL!

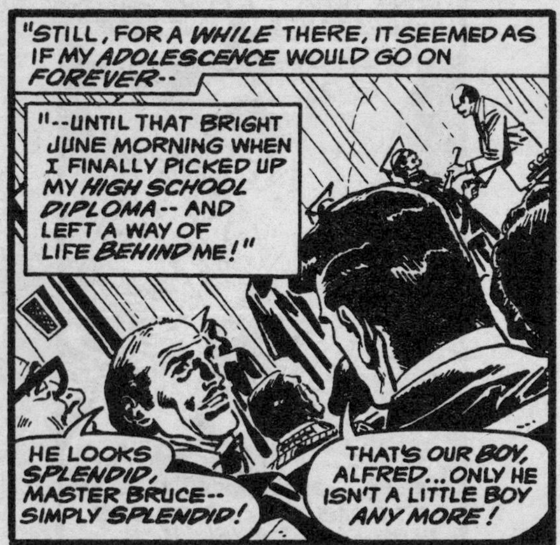
"STILL, FOR A WHILE THERE, IT SEEMED AS IF MY ADOLESCENCE WOULD GO ON FOREVER--
"--UNTIL THAT BRIGHT JUNE MORNING WHEN I FINALLY PICKED UP MY HIGH SCHOOL DIPLOMA -- AND LEFT A WAY OF LIFE BEHIND ME!"
HE LOOKS SPLENDID, MASTER BRUCE-- SIMPLY SPLENDID!
THAT'S OUR BOY, ALFRED...ONLY HE ISN'T A LITTLE BOY ANY MORE!

"THAT FALL, I LEFT WAYNE MANOR FOR *HUDSON UNIVERSITY*-- AND THAT SPRAWLING OLD MANSION SUDDENLY CEASED TO BE A *HOME*..."

THIS PLACE IS TOO *BIG* FOR JUST THE *TWO* OF US, ALFRED-- IT'S TIME FOR A *CHANGE!*

"WITHIN THE WEEK, BRUCE HAD *CLOSED* WAYNE MANOR --AND MOVED LOCK, STOCK, AND ALFRED INTO THE *PENTHOUSE* CROWNING THE OFFICES OF THE *WAYNE FOUNDATION*..."

ONCE AGAIN, THE *BATMAN* BECAME A VITAL *PART* OF THE CITY THAT HE *LOVED!*

THE *DARKNIGHT AVENGER* HAD FINALLY COME *HOME!*

FOR A MOMENT THE TEEN WONDER *PAUSES* IN HIS REVERIE, AS THE SLEEK BATMOBILE SLIPS *UN-SEEN* INTO THE SECLUDED CUL-DE-SAC CALLED *FINGER ALLEY*--

--THEN ALONG A HIDDEN *TUNNEL*--

--WHICH LEADS TO THE SPRAWLING *BATCAVE* HIDDEN BENEATH THE TOWERING *WAYNE FOUNDATION BUILDING*...

WELCOME *HOME,* SIRS!

WOULD YOU CARE FOR SOMETHING TO *DRINK?*

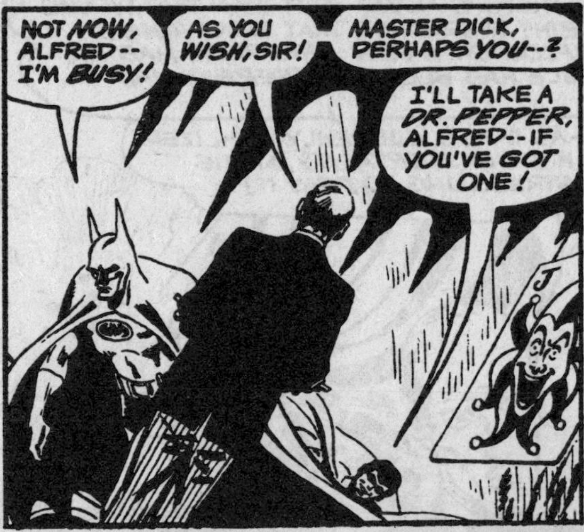
NOT NOW, ALFRED-- I'M BUSY!
AS YOU WISH, SIR!
MASTER DICK, PERHAPS YOU--?
I'LL TAKE A DR. PEPPER, ALFRED--IF YOU'VE GOT ONE!

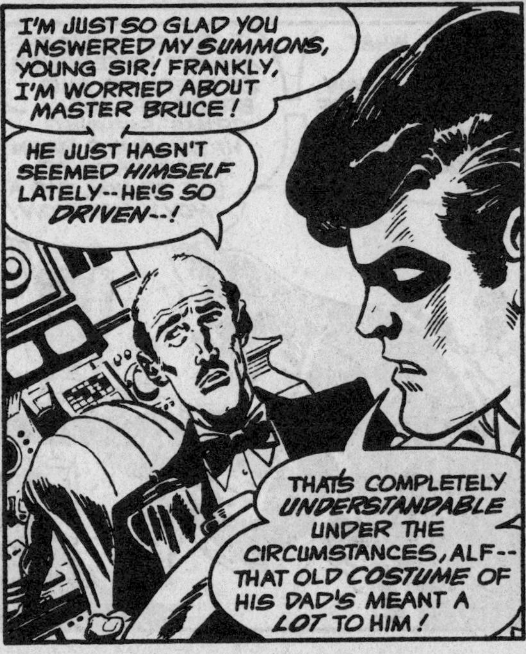
I'M JUST SO GLAD YOU ANSWERED MY SUMMONS, YOUNG SIR! FRANKLY, I'M WORRIED ABOUT MASTER BRUCE!
HE JUST HASN'T SEEMED HIMSELF LATELY--HE'S SO DRIVEN--!
THAT'S COMPLETELY UNDERSTANDABLE UNDER THE CIRCUMSTANCES, ALF--THAT OLD COSTUME OF HIS DAD'S MEANT A LOT TO HIM!

BUT THERE'S *MORE* TO IT THAN THAT, YOUNG ROBIN! EVER SINCE THAT *WAREHOUSE EXPLOSION* A FEW DAYS PAST, MASTER BRUCE HAS BEEN A *DIFFERENT MAN*--

--AS IF HE'S *SUDDENLY* REALIZED HIS OWN *MORTALITY*, AND IS STRUGGLING TO *DENY* IT!

I KNOW WHAT YOU *MEAN*, ALFRED--I SAW AN *EXAMPLE* OF IT A LITTLE BIT *EARLIER* TONIGHT!

I GUESS THAT'S THE *MAJOR* DIFFERENCE BETWEEN ME AND BRUCE--TO ME, CRIME-FIGHTING HAS ALWAYS BEEN AN *ADVENTURE*-- BUT TO *HIM*, IT'S A *HOLY MISSION!*

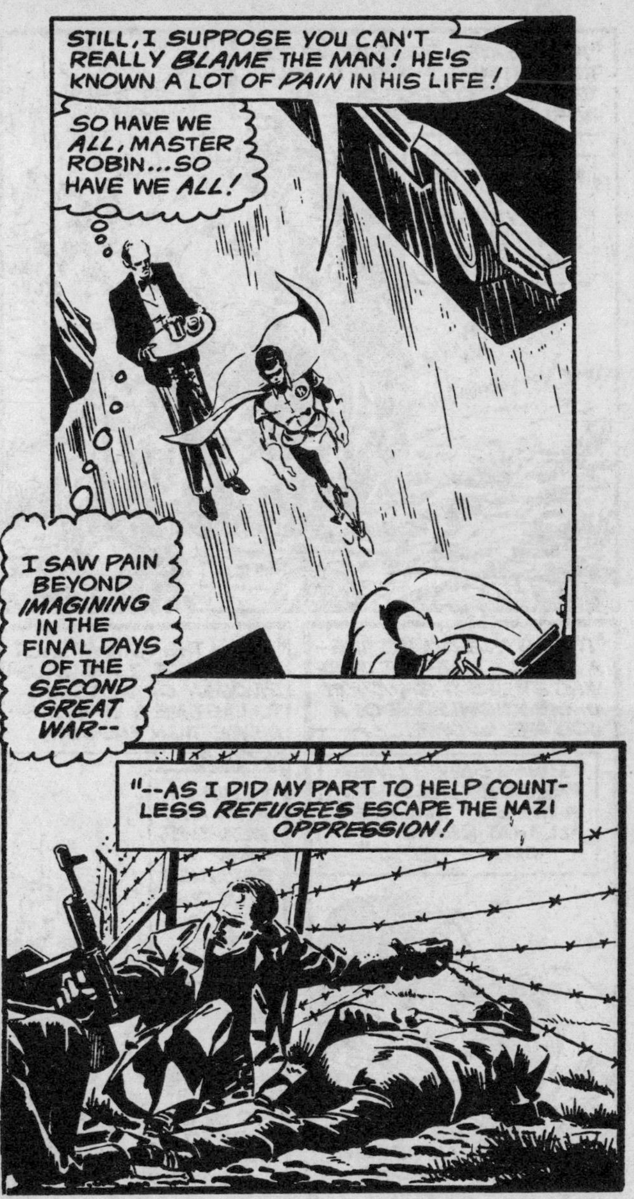
STILL, I SUPPOSE YOU CAN'T REALLY BLAME THE MAN! HE'S KNOWN A LOT OF PAIN IN HIS LIFE!
SO HAVE WE ALL, MASTER ROBIN... SO HAVE WE ALL!
I SAW PAIN BEYOND IMAGINING IN THE FINAL DAYS OF THE SECOND GREAT WAR--
"--AS I DID MY PART TO HELP COUNTLESS REFUGEES ESCAPE THE NAZI OPPRESSION!

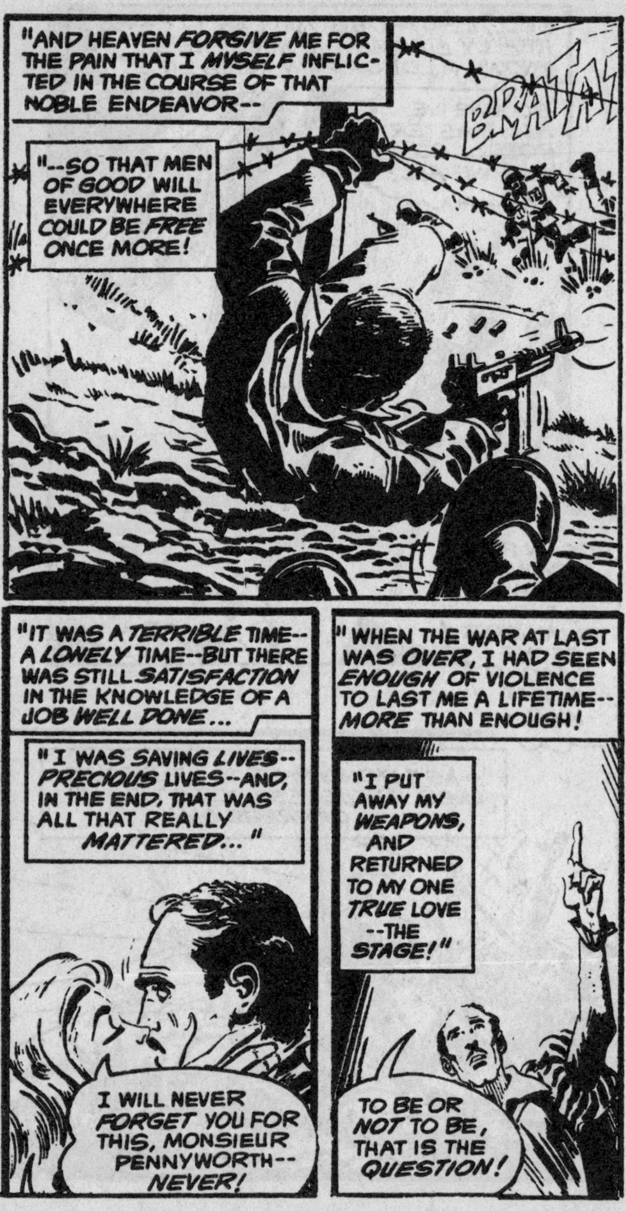
"AND HEAVEN FORGIVE ME FOR THE PAIN THAT I MYSELF INFLICTED IN THE COURSE OF THAT NOBLE ENDEAVOR--
"--SO THAT MEN OF GOOD WILL EVERYWHERE COULD BE FREE ONCE MORE!
BRATAT
"IT WAS A TERRIBLE TIME--A LONELY TIME--BUT THERE WAS STILL SATISFACTION IN THE KNOWLEDGE OF A JOB WELL DONE...
"I WAS SAVING LIVES--PRECIOUS LIVES--AND, IN THE END, THAT WAS ALL THAT REALLY MATTERED..."
I WILL NEVER FORGET YOU FOR THIS, MONSIEUR PENNYWORTH--NEVER!
"WHEN THE WAR AT LAST WAS OVER, I HAD SEEN ENOUGH OF VIOLENCE TO LAST ME A LIFETIME--MORE THAN ENOUGH!
"I PUT AWAY MY WEAPONS, AND RETURNED TO MY ONE TRUE LOVE --THE STAGE!"
TO BE OR NOT TO BE, THAT IS THE QUESTION!

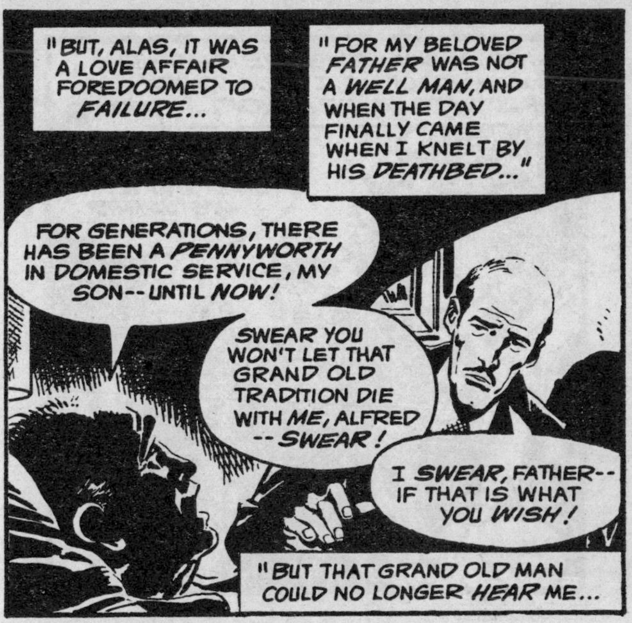
"BUT, ALAS, IT WAS A LOVE AFFAIR FOREDOOMED TO FAILURE...
"FOR MY BELOVED FATHER WAS NOT A WELL MAN, AND WHEN THE DAY FINALLY CAME WHEN I KNELT BY HIS DEATHBED..."
FOR GENERATIONS, THERE HAS BEEN A PENNYWORTH IN DOMESTIC SERVICE, MY SON--UNTIL NOW!
SWEAR YOU WON'T LET THAT GRAND OLD TRADITION DIE WITH ME, ALFRED --SWEAR!
I SWEAR, FATHER--IF THAT IS WHAT YOU WISH!
"BUT THAT GRAND OLD MAN COULD NO LONGER HEAR ME...
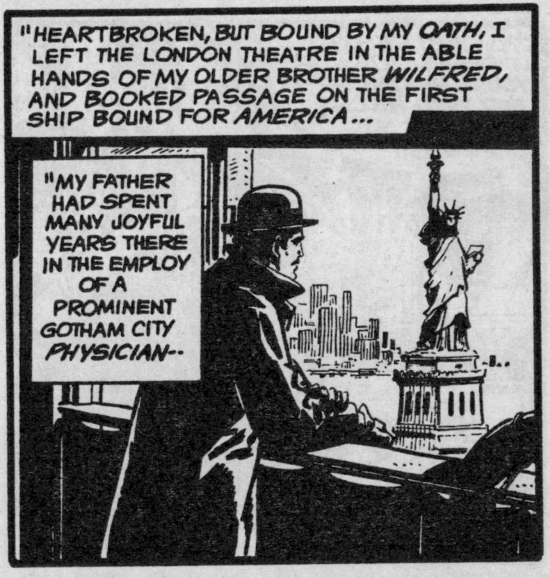
"HEARTBROKEN, BUT BOUND BY MY OATH, I LEFT THE LONDON THEATRE IN THE ABLE HANDS OF MY OLDER BROTHER WILFRED, AND BOOKED PASSAGE ON THE FIRST SHIP BOUND FOR AMERICA...
"MY FATHER HAD SPENT MANY JOYFUL YEARS THERE IN THE EMPLOY OF A PROMINENT GOTHAM CITY PHYSICIAN--

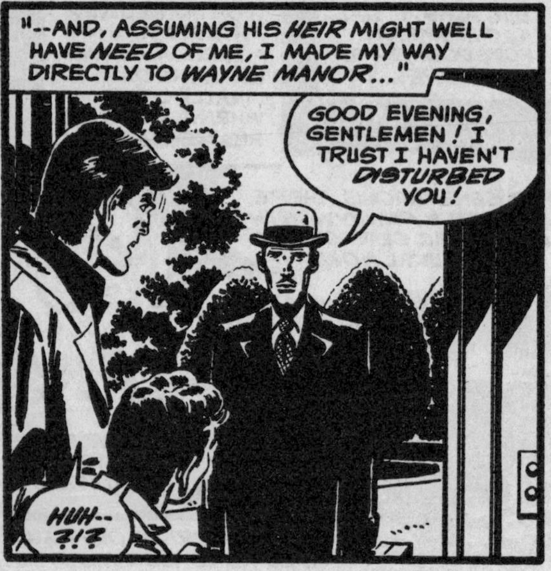
"--AND, ASSUMING HIS HEIR MIGHT WELL HAVE NEED OF ME, I MADE MY WAY DIRECTLY TO WAYNE MANOR..."
GOOD EVENING, GENTLEMEN! I TRUST I HAVEN'T DISTURBED YOU!
HUH-- ?!?

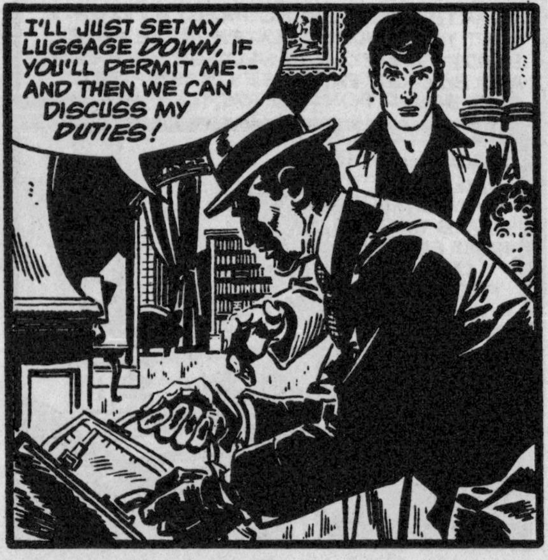
I'LL JUST SET MY LUGGAGE DOWN, IF YOU'LL PERMIT ME-- AND THEN WE CAN DISCUSS MY DUTIES!

NOW WAIT JUST ONE MINUTE! EXACTLY WHAT CAN I DO FOR YOU, MISTER--?
YOU MAY CALL ME ALFRED, WITHOUT THE "MISTER"--AND IT IS I WHO WILL DO FOR YOU, SIR! I TRUST YOU'LL FIND MY REFERENCES IN GOOD ORDER!
YOU SEE--I'M YOUR NEW BUTLER!
BUTLER? BUT I HAVEN'T HAD ONE IN YEARS! I DIDN'T SEND FOR ONE--AND I'M AFRAID I DON'T REALLY WANT ONE!
WE'VE FOUND WE CAN GET ALONG BETTER WITHOUT SERVANTS OF ANY KIND!
IT MAY BE A BIT AWKWARD AT FIRST, SIR--BUT I DARE SAY YOU'LL GET USED TO ME!

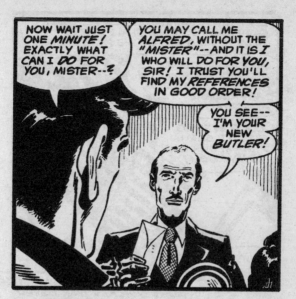

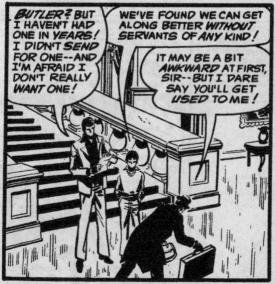

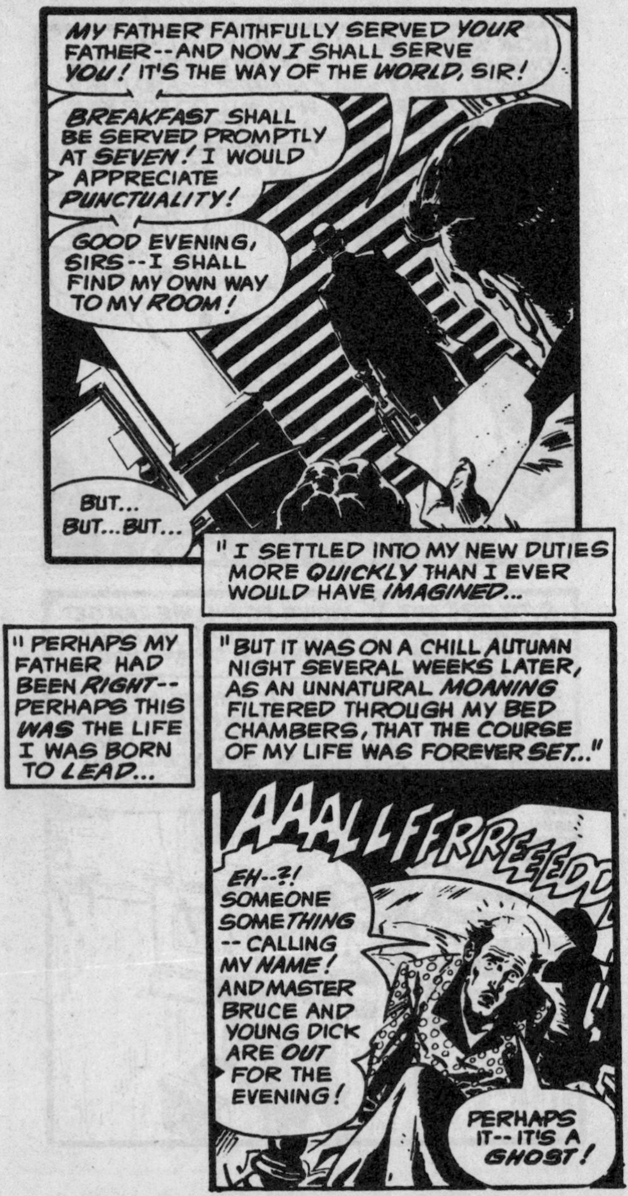
MY FATHER FAITHFULLY SERVED YOUR FATHER--AND NOW I SHALL SERVE YOU! IT'S THE WAY OF THE WORLD, SIR!
BREAKFAST SHALL BE SERVED PROMPTLY AT SEVEN! I WOULD APPRECIATE PUNCTUALITY!
GOOD EVENING, SIRS--I SHALL FIND MY OWN WAY TO MY ROOM!
BUT... BUT...BUT...
"I SETTLED INTO MY NEW DUTIES MORE QUICKLY THAN I EVER WOULD HAVE IMAGINED...
"PERHAPS MY FATHER HAD BEEN RIGHT--PERHAPS THIS WAS THE LIFE I WAS BORN TO LEAD...
"BUT IT WAS ON A CHILL AUTUMN NIGHT SEVERAL WEEKS LATER, AS AN UNNATURAL MOANING FILTERED THROUGH MY BED CHAMBERS, THAT THE COURSE OF MY LIFE WAS FOREVER SET..."
AAALLFFRREEEDD
EH--?! SOMEONE SOMETHING--CALLING MY NAME! AND MASTER BRUCE AND YOUNG DICK ARE OUT FOR THE EVENING!
PERHAPS IT--IT'S A GHOST!

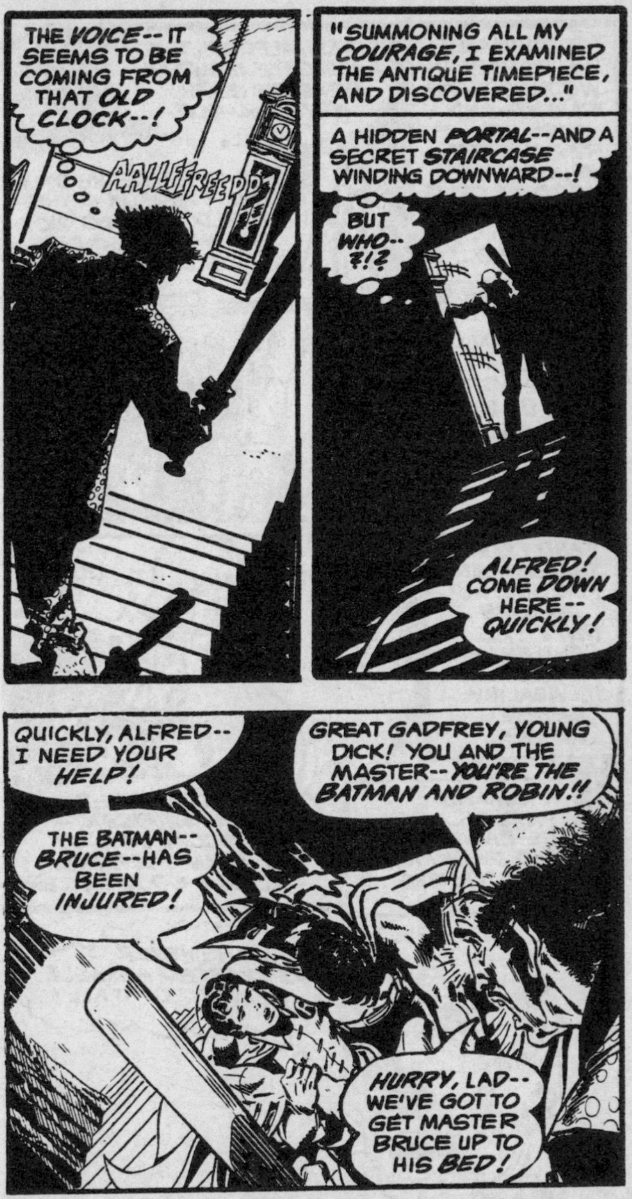
THE VOICE-- IT SEEMS TO BE COMING FROM THAT OLD CLOCK--!
AALLFFREEDD
"SUMMONING ALL MY COURAGE, I EXAMINED THE ANTIQUE TIMEPIECE, AND DISCOVERED..."
A HIDDEN PORTAL--AND A SECRET STAIRCASE WINDING DOWNWARD--!
BUT WHO-- ?!?
ALFRED! COME DOWN HERE-- QUICKLY!
QUICKLY, ALFRED-- I NEED YOUR HELP!
THE BATMAN-- BRUCE--HAS BEEN INJURED!
GREAT GADFREY, YOUNG DICK! YOU AND THE MASTER--YOU'RE THE BATMAN AND ROBIN!!
HURRY, LAD-- WE'VE GOT TO GET MASTER BRUCE UP TO HIS BED!

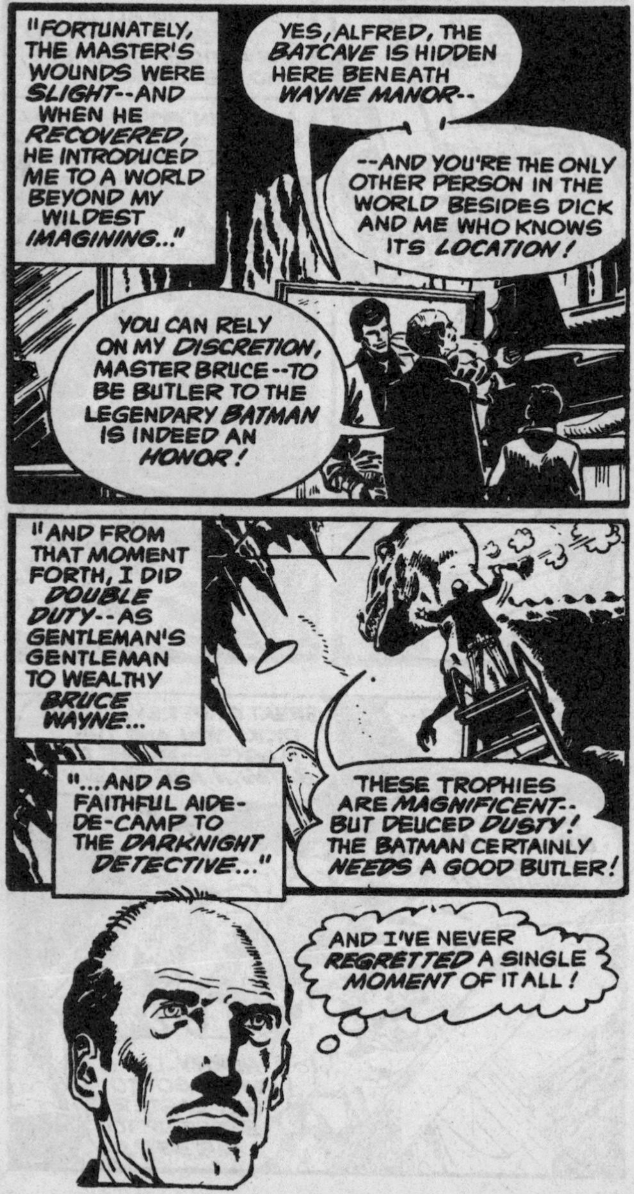
"FORTUNATELY, THE MASTER'S WOUNDS WERE SLIGHT--AND WHEN HE RECOVERED, HE INTRODUCED ME TO A WORLD BEYOND MY WILDEST IMAGINING..."
YES, ALFRED, THE BATCAVE IS HIDDEN HERE BENEATH WAYNE MANOR--
--AND YOU'RE THE ONLY OTHER PERSON IN THE WORLD BESIDES DICK AND ME WHO KNOWS ITS LOCATION!
YOU CAN RELY ON MY DISCRETION, MASTER BRUCE--TO BE BUTLER TO THE LEGENDARY BATMAN IS INDEED AN HONOR!
"AND FROM THAT MOMENT FORTH, I DID DOUBLE DUTY--AS GENTLEMAN'S GENTLEMAN TO WEALTHY BRUCE WAYNE...
"...AND AS FAITHFUL AIDE-DE-CAMP TO THE DARKNIGHT DETECTIVE..."
THESE TROPHIES ARE MAGNIFICENT--BUT DEUCED DUSTY! THE BATMAN CERTAINLY NEEDS A GOOD BUTLER!
AND I'VE NEVER REGRETTED A SINGLE MOMENT OF IT ALL!

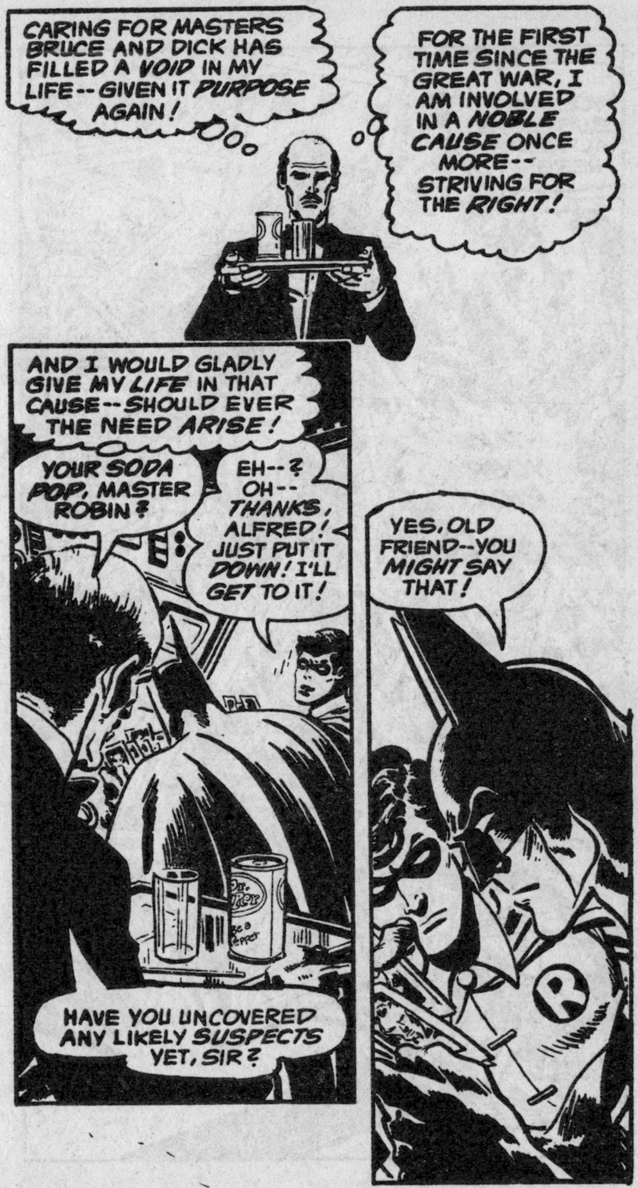
CARING FOR MASTERS BRUCE AND DICK HAS FILLED A VOID IN MY LIFE -- GIVEN IT PURPOSE AGAIN!
FOR THE FIRST TIME SINCE THE GREAT WAR, I AM INVOLVED IN A NOBLE CAUSE ONCE MORE-- STRIVING FOR THE RIGHT!
AND I WOULD GLADLY GIVE MY LIFE IN THAT CAUSE -- SHOULD EVER THE NEED ARISE!
YOUR SODA POP, MASTER ROBIN?
EH--? OH-- THANKS, ALFRED! JUST PUT IT DOWN! I'LL GET TO IT!
HAVE YOU UNCOVERED ANY LIKELY SUSPECTS YET, SIR?
YES, OLD FRIEND--YOU MIGHT SAY THAT!

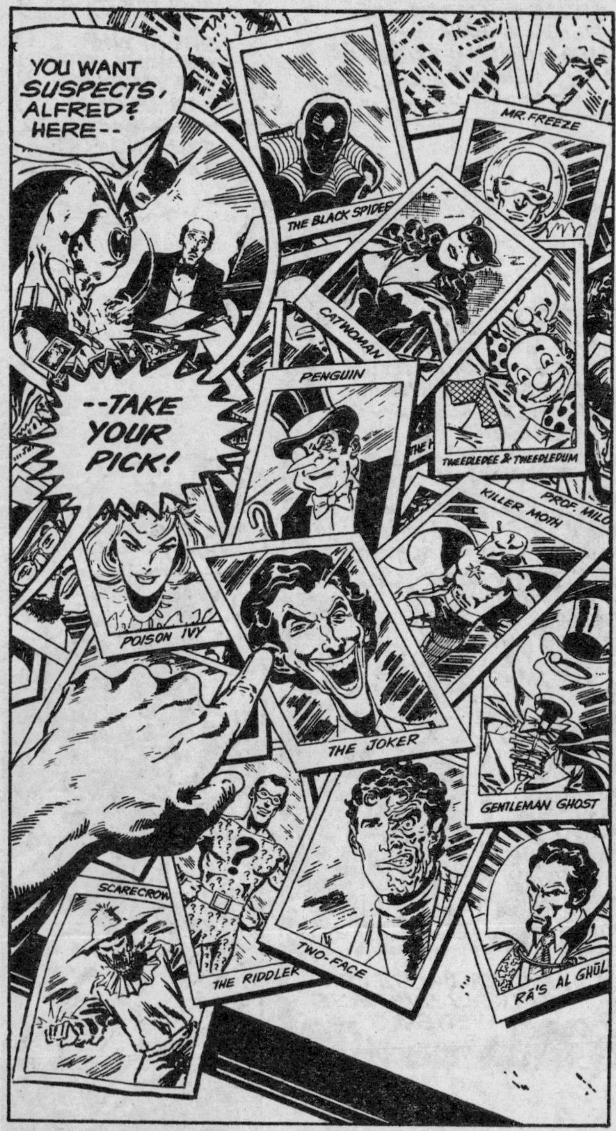
YOU WANT SUSPECTS, ALFRED? HERE--
--TAKE YOUR PICK!
THE BLACK SPIDER
MR. FREEZE
CATWOMAN
PENGUIN
TWEEDLEDEE & TWEEDLEDUM
KILLER MOTH
PROF. MILO
POISON IVY
THE JOKER
GENTLEMAN GHOST
SCARECROW
THE RIDDLER
TWO-FACE
RĀ'S AL GHŪL

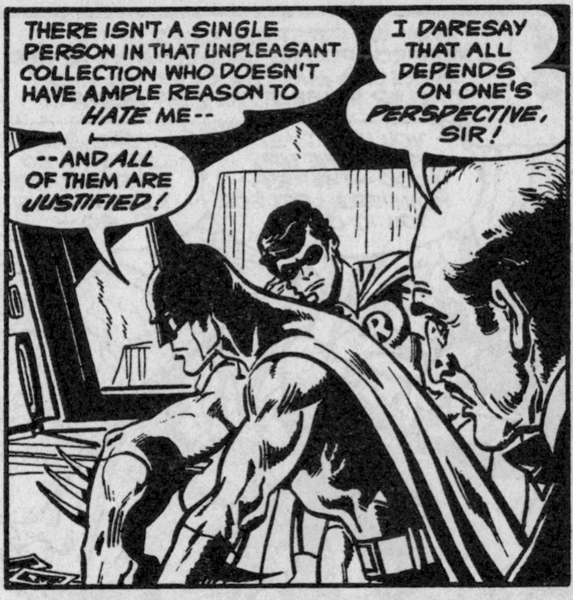
THERE ISN'T A SINGLE PERSON IN THAT UNPLEASANT COLLECTION WHO DOESN'T HAVE AMPLE REASON TO HATE ME--
--AND ALL OF THEM ARE JUSTIFIED!
I DARESAY THAT ALL DEPENDS ON ONE'S PERSPECTIVE, SIR!

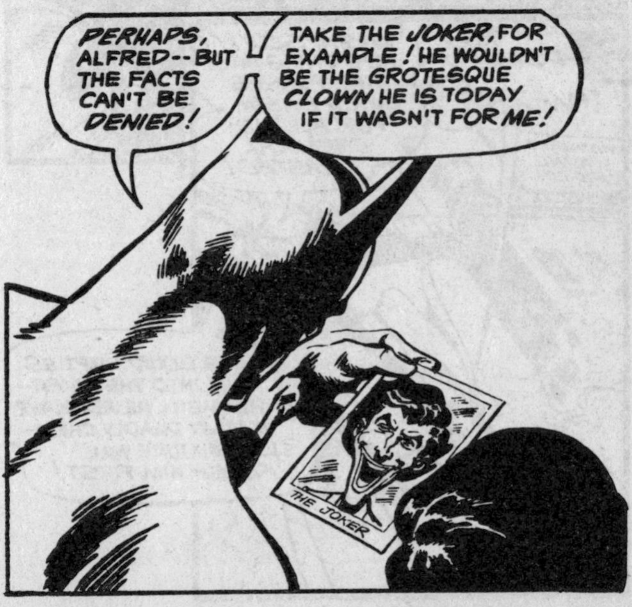
PERHAPS, ALFRED--BUT THE FACTS CAN'T BE DENIED!
TAKE THE JOKER, FOR EXAMPLE! HE WOULDN'T BE THE GROTESQUE CLOWN HE IS TODAY IF IT WASN'T FOR ME!
THE JOKER

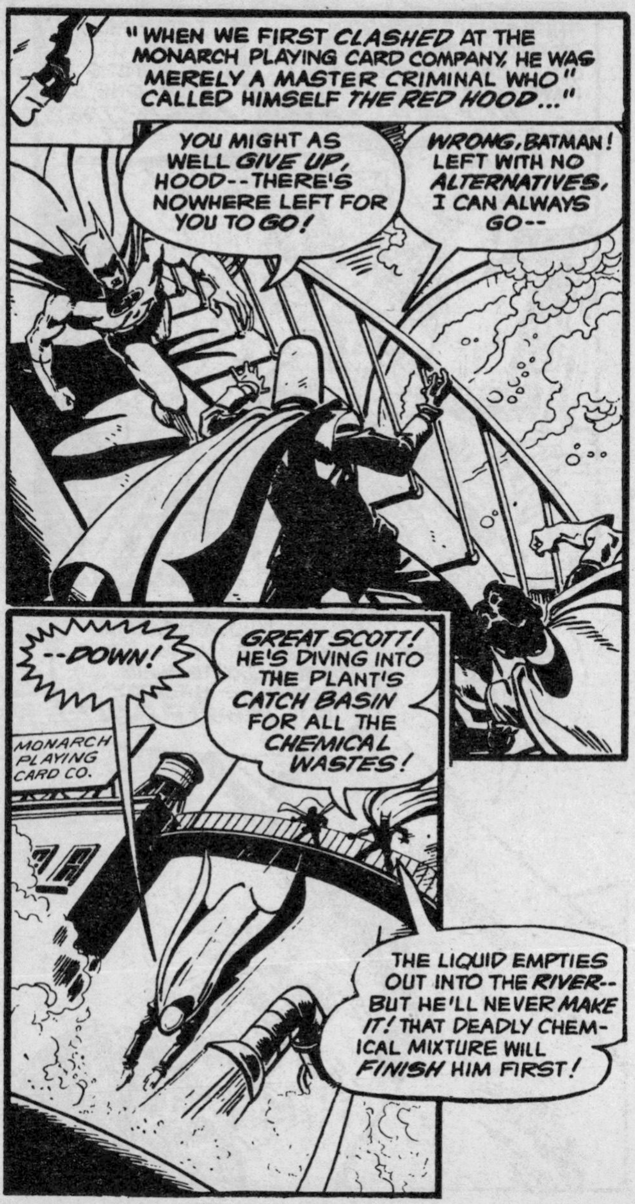
"WHEN WE FIRST CLASHED AT THE MONARCH PLAYING CARD COMPANY, HE WAS MERELY A MASTER CRIMINAL WHO CALLED HIMSELF THE RED HOOD..."
YOU MIGHT AS WELL GIVE UP, HOOD--THERE'S NOWHERE LEFT FOR YOU TO GO!
WRONG, BATMAN! LEFT WITH NO ALTERNATIVES, I CAN ALWAYS GO--
--DOWN!
GREAT SCOTT! HE'S DIVING INTO THE PLANT'S CATCH BASIN FOR ALL THE CHEMICAL WASTES!
MONARCH PLAYING CARD CO.
THE LIQUID EMPTIES OUT INTO THE RIVER--BUT HE'LL NEVER MAKE IT! THAT DEADLY CHEMICAL MIXTURE WILL FINISH HIM FIRST!

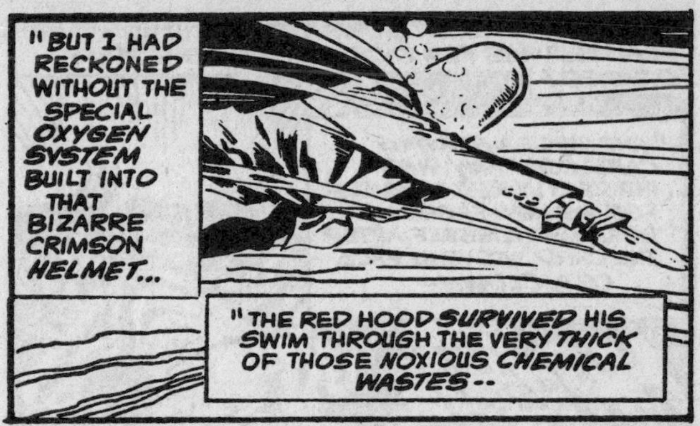
"BUT I HAD RECKONED WITHOUT THE SPECIAL OXYGEN SYSTEM BUILT INTO THAT BIZARRE CRIMSON HELMET...
"THE RED HOOD SURVIVED HIS SWIM THROUGH THE VERY THICK OF THOSE NOXIOUS CHEMICAL WASTES--

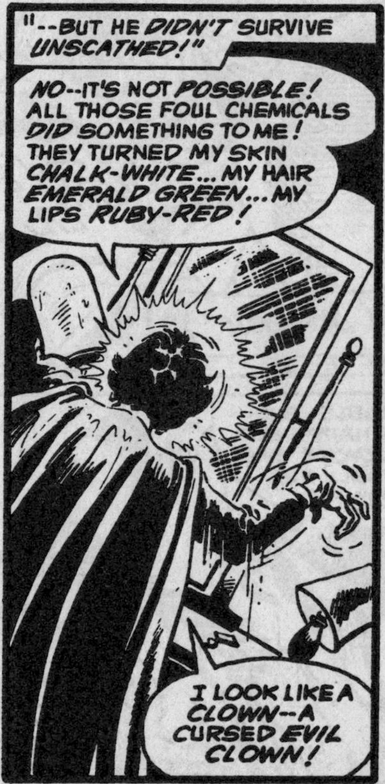
"--BUT HE DIDN'T SURVIVE UNSCATHED!"
NO--IT'S NOT POSSIBLE! ALL THOSE FOUL CHEMICALS DID SOMETHING TO ME! THEY TURNED MY SKIN CHALK-WHITE... MY HAIR EMERALD GREEN... MY LIPS RUBY-RED!
I LOOK LIKE A CLOWN--A CURSED EVIL CLOWN!

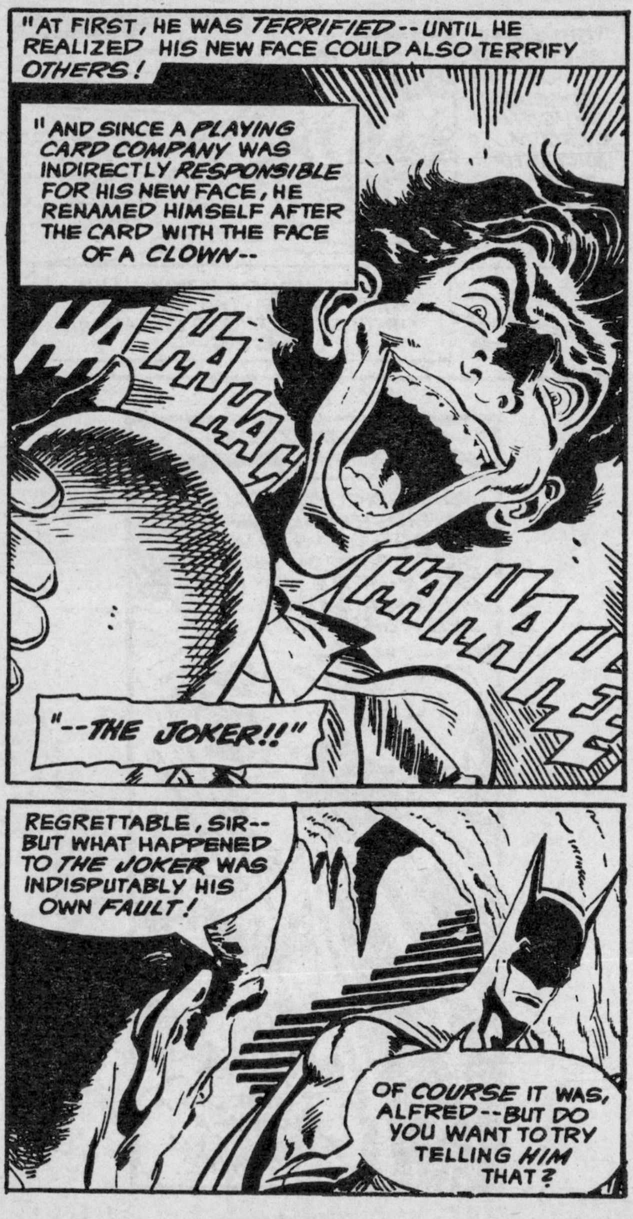
"AT FIRST, HE WAS TERRIFIED--UNTIL HE REALIZED HIS NEW FACE COULD ALSO TERRIFY OTHERS!
"AND SINCE A PLAYING CARD COMPANY WAS INDIRECTLY RESPONSIBLE FOR HIS NEW FACE, HE RENAMED HIMSELF AFTER THE CARD WITH THE FACE OF A CLOWN--
"--THE JOKER!!"
REGRETTABLE, SIR--BUT WHAT HAPPENED TO THE JOKER WAS INDISPUTABLY HIS OWN FAULT!
OF COURSE IT WAS, ALFRED--BUT DO YOU WANT TO TRY TELLING HIM THAT?

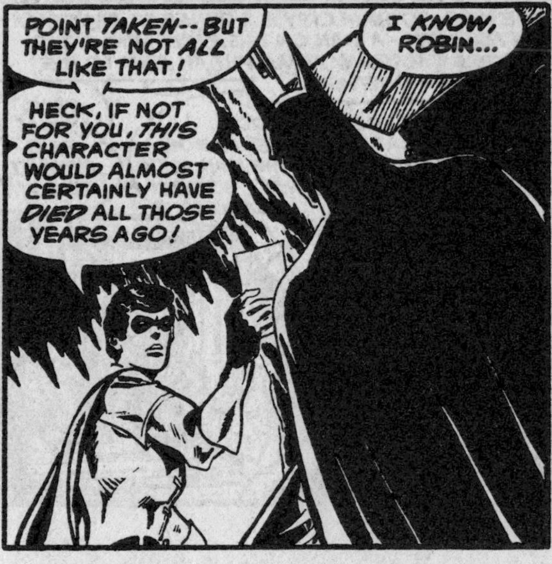
POINT TAKEN--BUT THEY'RE NOT ALL LIKE THAT!
HECK, IF NOT FOR YOU, THIS CHARACTER WOULD ALMOST CERTAINLY HAVE DIED ALL THOSE YEARS AGO!
I KNOW, ROBIN...

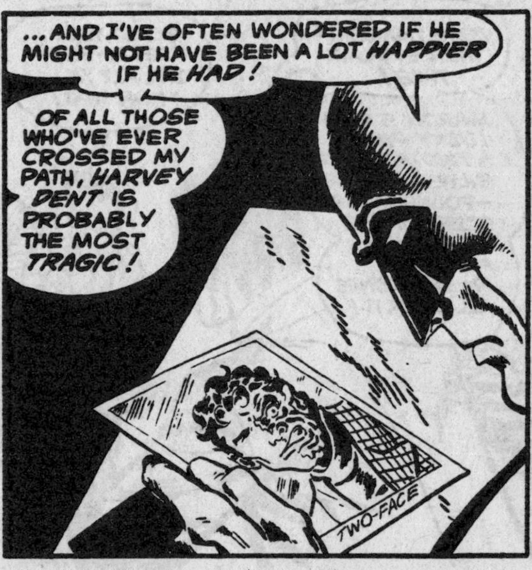
...AND I'VE OFTEN WONDERED IF HE MIGHT NOT HAVE BEEN A LOT HAPPIER IF HE HAD!
OF ALL THOSE WHO'VE EVER CROSSED MY PATH, HARVEY DENT IS PROBABLY THE MOST TRAGIC!
TWO-FACE

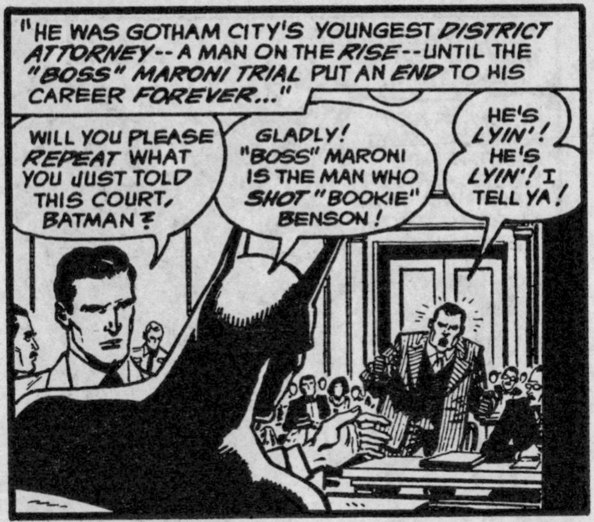
"HE WAS GOTHAM CITY'S YOUNGEST DISTRICT ATTORNEY-- A MAN ON THE RISE--UNTIL THE "BOSS" MARONI TRIAL PUT AN END TO HIS CAREER FOREVER..."
WILL YOU PLEASE REPEAT WHAT YOU JUST TOLD THIS COURT, BATMAN?
GLADLY! "BOSS" MARONI IS THE MAN WHO SHOT "BOOKIE" BENSON!
HE'S LYIN'! HE'S LYIN'! I TELL YA!

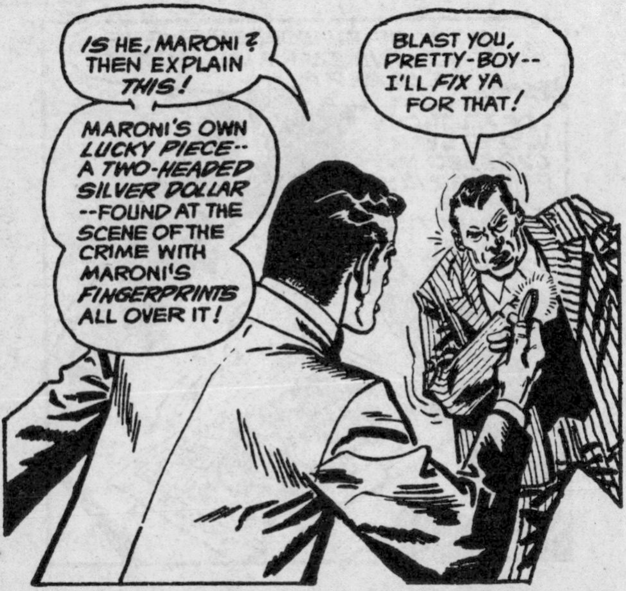
IS HE, MARONI? THEN EXPLAIN THIS!
MARONI'S OWN LUCKY PIECE-- A TWO-HEADED SILVER DOLLAR --FOUND AT THE SCENE OF THE CRIME WITH MARONI'S FINGERPRINTS ALL OVER IT!
BLAST YOU, PRETTY-BOY-- I'LL FIX YA FOR THAT!

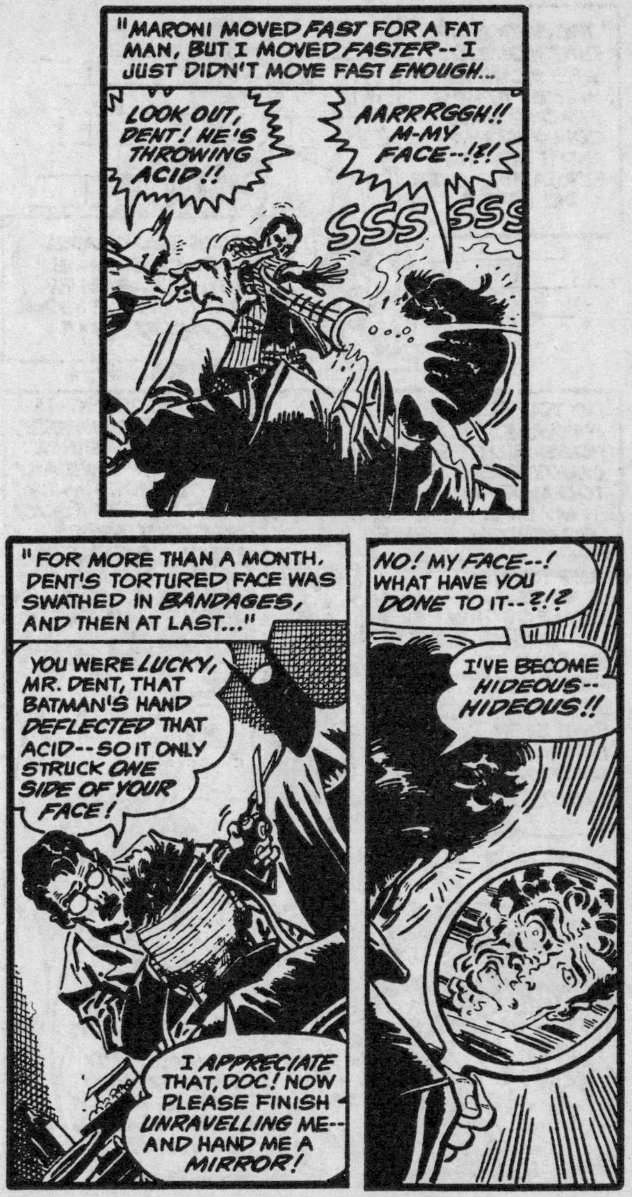
"MARONI MOVED FAST FOR A FAT MAN, BUT I MOVED FASTER-- I JUST DIDN'T MOVE FAST ENOUGH...
LOOK OUT, DENT! HE'S THROWING ACID!!
AARRRGGH!! M-MY FACE--!?!
SSS SSS
"FOR MORE THAN A MONTH, DENT'S TORTURED FACE WAS SWATHED IN BANDAGES, AND THEN AT LAST..."
YOU WERE LUCKY, MR. DENT, THAT BATMAN'S HAND DEFLECTED THAT ACID--SO IT ONLY STRUCK ONE SIDE OF YOUR FACE!
I APPRECIATE THAT, DOC! NOW PLEASE FINISH UNRAVELLING ME-- AND HAND ME A MIRROR!
NO! MY FACE--! WHAT HAVE YOU DONE TO IT--?!?
I'VE BECOME HIDEOUS-- HIDEOUS!!

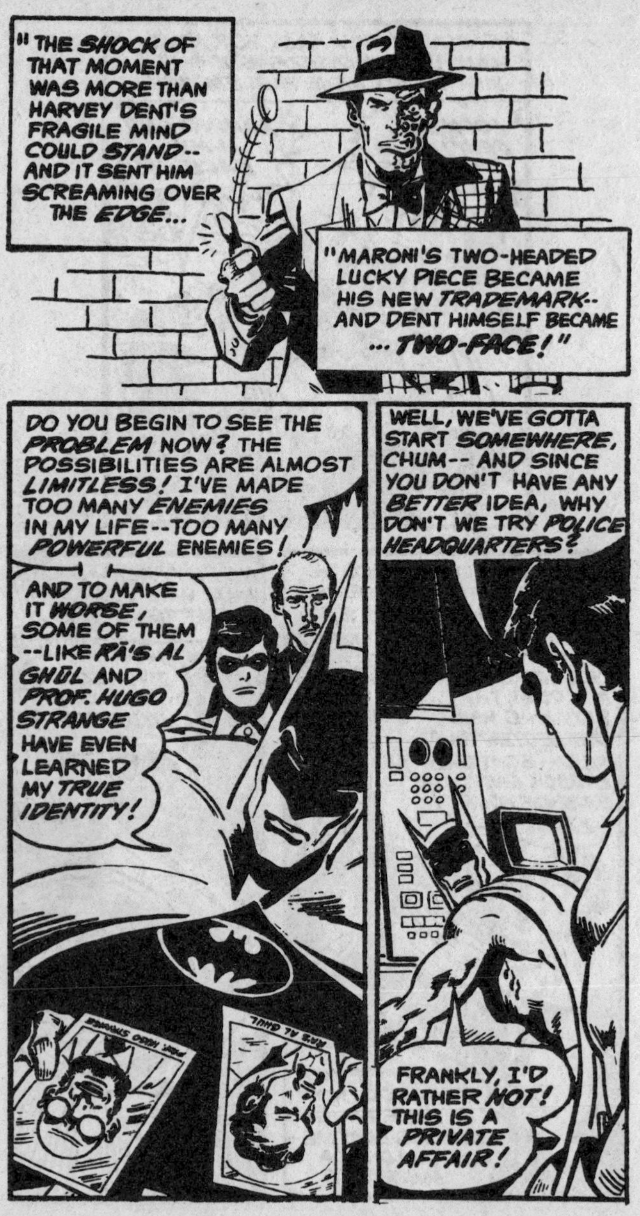
"THE SHOCK OF THAT MOMENT WAS MORE THAN HARVEY DENT'S FRAGILE MIND COULD STAND-- AND IT SENT HIM SCREAMING OVER THE EDGE...
"MARONI'S TWO-HEADED LUCKY PIECE BECAME HIS NEW TRADEMARK-- AND DENT HIMSELF BECAME ...TWO-FACE!"
DO YOU BEGIN TO SEE THE PROBLEM NOW? THE POSSIBILITIES ARE ALMOST LIMITLESS! I'VE MADE TOO MANY ENEMIES IN MY LIFE--TOO MANY POWERFUL ENEMIES!
AND TO MAKE IT WORSE, SOME OF THEM --LIKE RĀ'S AL GHŪL AND PROF. HUGO STRANGE HAVE EVEN LEARNED MY TRUE IDENTITY!
PROF. HUGO STRANGE
RA'S AL GHUL
WELL, WE'VE GOTTA START SOMEWHERE, CHUM-- AND SINCE YOU DON'T HAVE ANY BETTER IDEA, WHY DON'T WE TRY POLICE HEADQUARTERS?
FRANKLY, I'D RATHER NOT! THIS IS A PRIVATE AFFAIR!

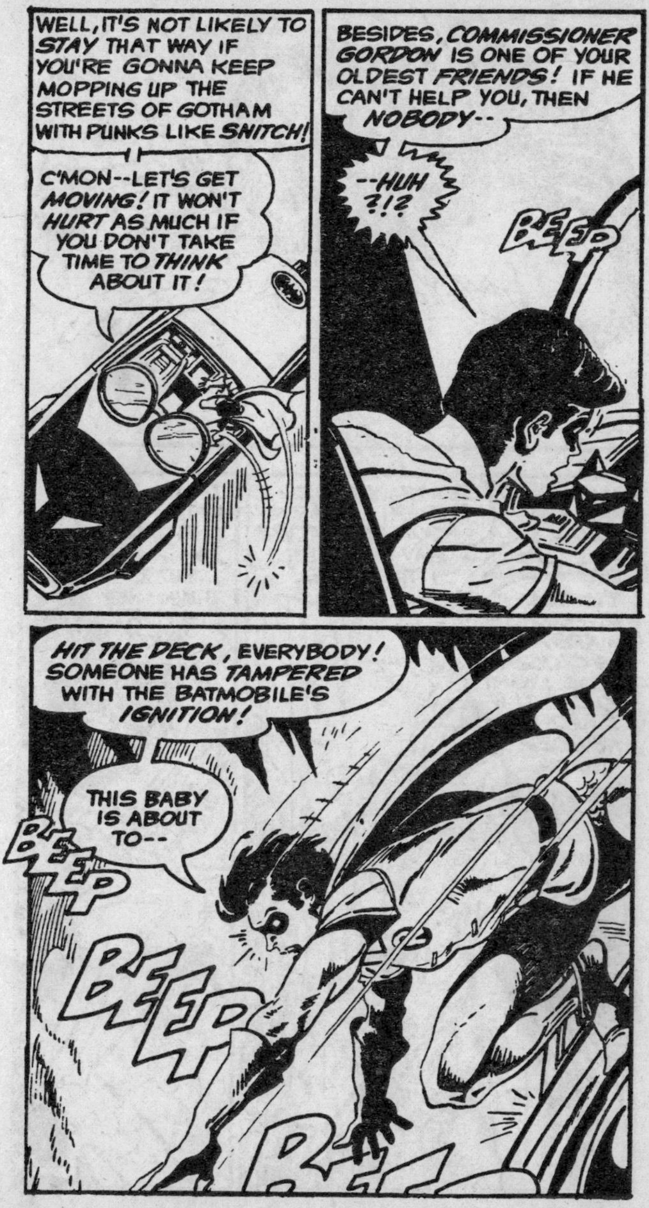
WELL, IT'S NOT LIKELY TO STAY THAT WAY IF YOU'RE GONNA KEEP MOPPING UP THE STREETS OF GOTHAM WITH PUNKS LIKE SNITCH!
C'MON--LET'S GET MOVING! IT WON'T HURT AS MUCH IF YOU DON'T TAKE TIME TO THINK ABOUT IT!
BESIDES, COMMISSIONER GORDON IS ONE OF YOUR OLDEST FRIENDS! IF HE CAN'T HELP YOU, THEN NOBODY--
--HUH ?!?
BEEP
HIT THE DECK, EVERYBODY! SOMEONE HAS TAMPERED WITH THE BATMOBILE'S IGNITION!
THIS BABY IS ABOUT TO--
BEEP
BEEP

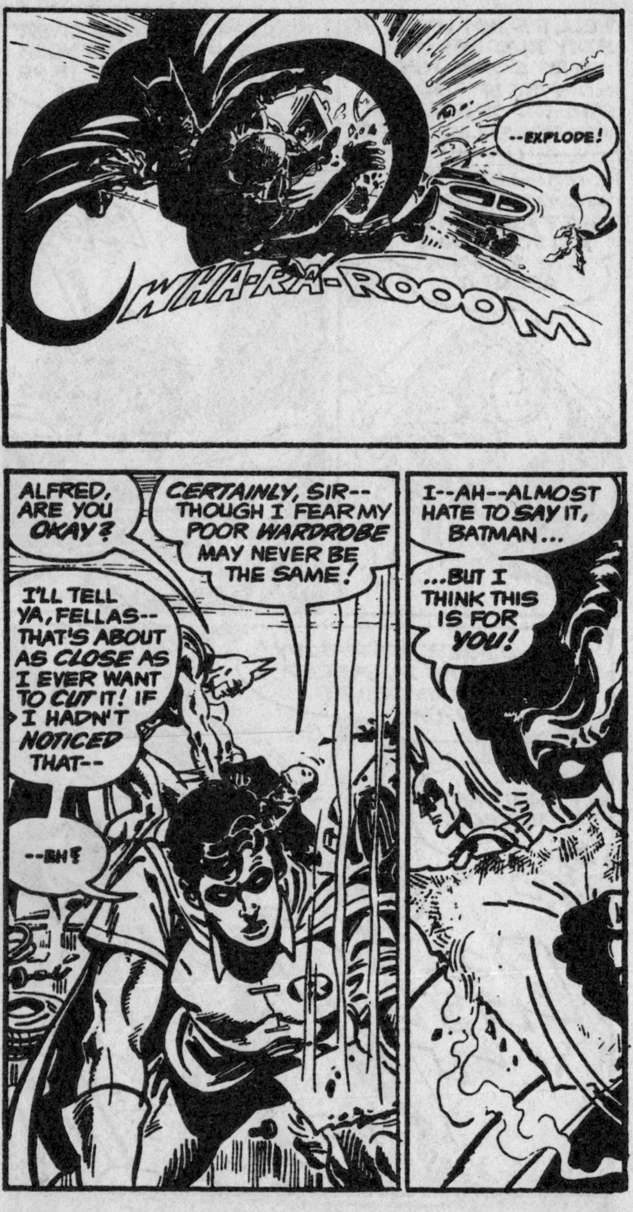
--EXPLODE!
WHA-RA-ROOOM
ALFRED, ARE YOU OKAY?
CERTAINLY, SIR-- THOUGH I FEAR MY POOR WARDROBE MAY NEVER BE THE SAME!
I'LL TELL YA, FELLAS-- THAT'S ABOUT AS CLOSE AS I EVER WANT TO CUT IT! IF I HADN'T NOTICED THAT--
--EH?
I--AH--ALMOST HATE TO SAY IT, BATMAN...
...BUT I THINK THIS IS FOR YOU!

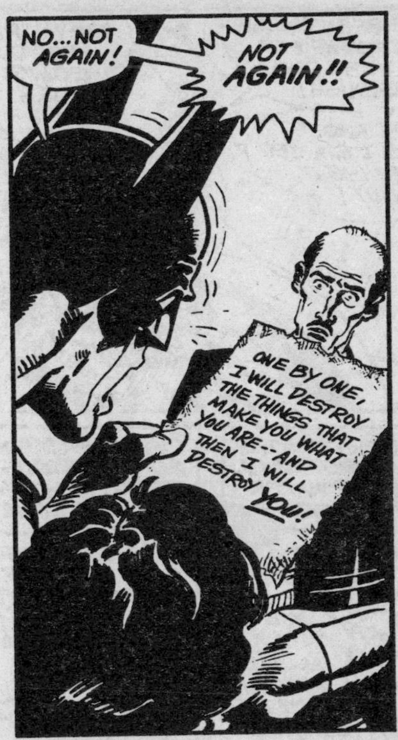
NO...NOT AGAIN!
NOT AGAIN!!
ONE BY ONE, I WILL DESTROY THE THINGS THAT MAKE YOU WHAT YOU ARE--AND THEN I WILL DESTROY YOU!

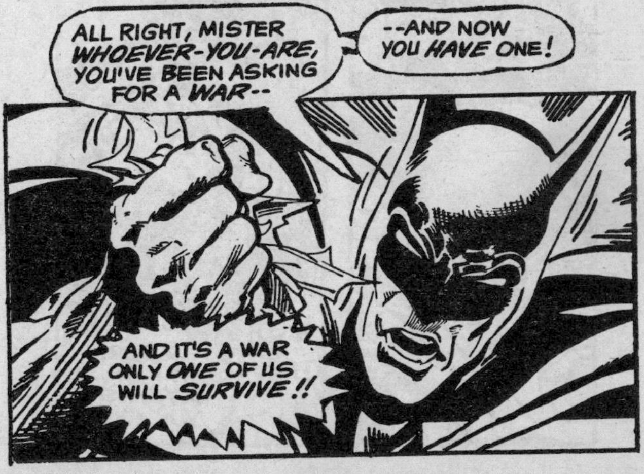
ALL RIGHT, MISTER WHOEVER-YOU-ARE, YOU'VE BEEN ASKING FOR A WAR--
--AND NOW YOU HAVE ONE!
AND IT'S A WAR ONLY ONE OF US WILL SURVIVE!!

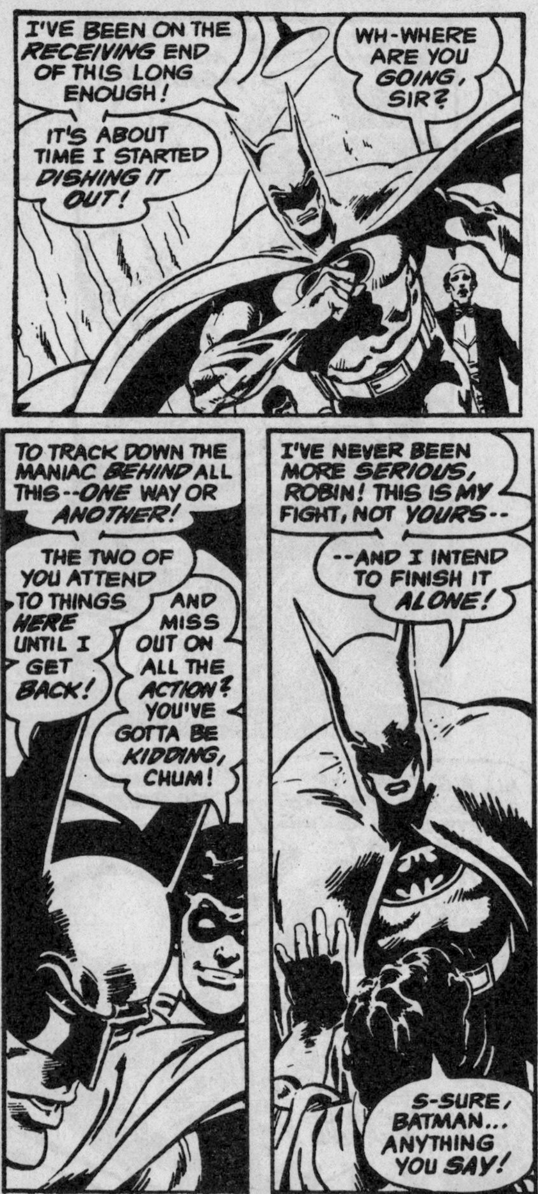
I'VE BEEN ON THE RECEIVING END OF THIS LONG ENOUGH!
IT'S ABOUT TIME I STARTED DISHING IT OUT!
WH-WHERE ARE YOU GOING, SIR?
TO TRACK DOWN THE MANIAC BEHIND ALL THIS--ONE WAY OR ANOTHER!
THE TWO OF YOU ATTEND TO THINGS HERE UNTIL I GET BACK!
AND MISS OUT ON ALL THE ACTION? YOU'VE GOTTA BE KIDDING, CHUM!
I'VE NEVER BEEN MORE SERIOUS, ROBIN! THIS IS MY FIGHT, NOT YOURS--
--AND I INTEND TO FINISH IT ALONE!
S-SURE, BATMAN... ANYTHING YOU SAY!

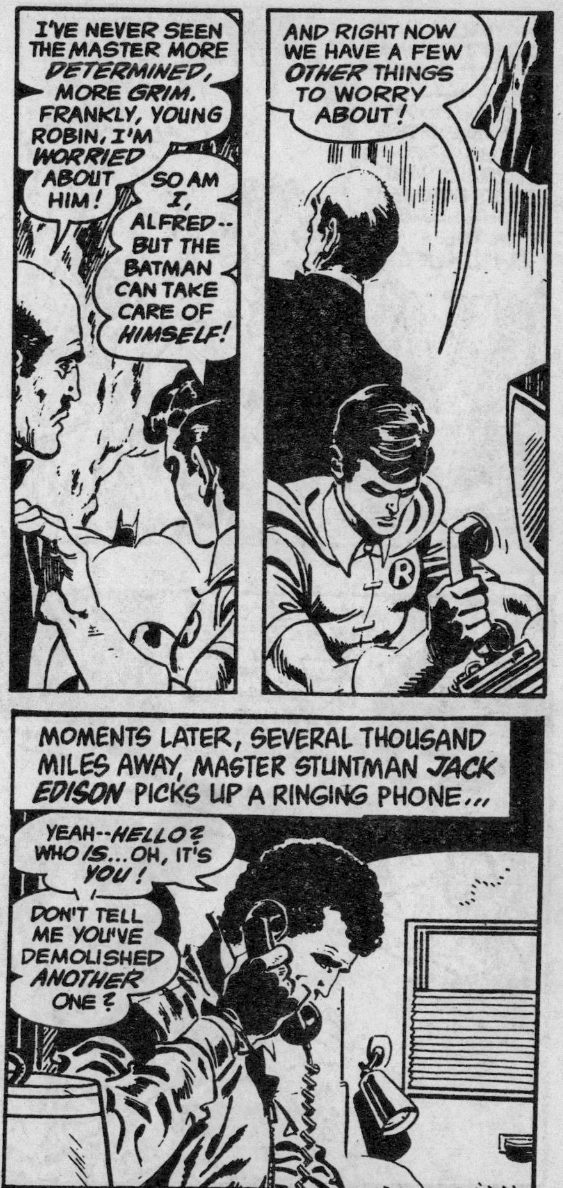
I'VE NEVER SEEN THE MASTER MORE DETERMINED, MORE GRIM. FRANKLY, YOUNG ROBIN, I'M WORRIED ABOUT HIM!
SO AM I, ALFRED--BUT THE BATMAN CAN TAKE CARE OF HIMSELF!
AND RIGHT NOW WE HAVE A FEW OTHER THINGS TO WORRY ABOUT!
MOMENTS LATER, SEVERAL THOUSAND MILES AWAY, MASTER STUNTMAN JACK EDISON PICKS UP A RINGING PHONE...
YEAH--HELLO? WHO IS...OH, IT'S YOU!
DON'T TELL ME YOU'VE DEMOLISHED ANOTHER ONE?

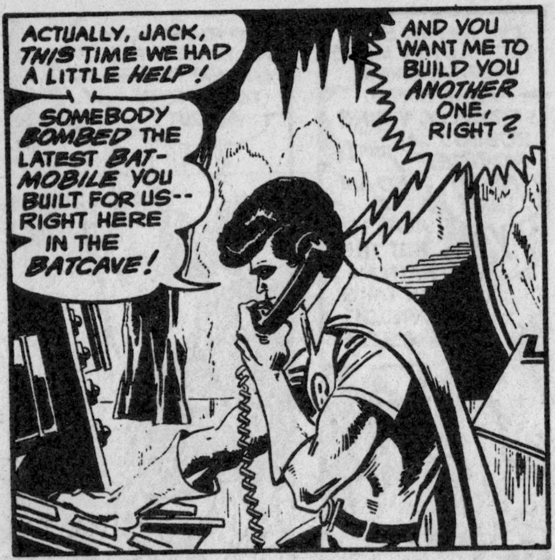
ACTUALLY, JACK, THIS TIME WE HAD A LITTLE HELP!
SOMEBODY BOMBED THE LATEST BAT-MOBILE YOU BUILT FOR US-- RIGHT HERE IN THE BATCAVE!
AND YOU WANT ME TO BUILD YOU ANOTHER ONE, RIGHT?

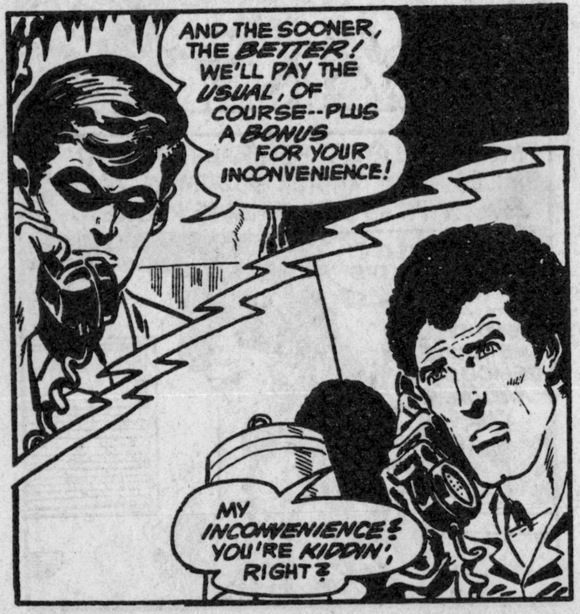
AND THE SOONER, THE BETTER! WE'LL PAY THE USUAL, OF COURSE--PLUS A BONUS FOR YOUR INCONVENIENCE!
MY INCONVENIENCE? YOU'RE KIDDIN', RIGHT?

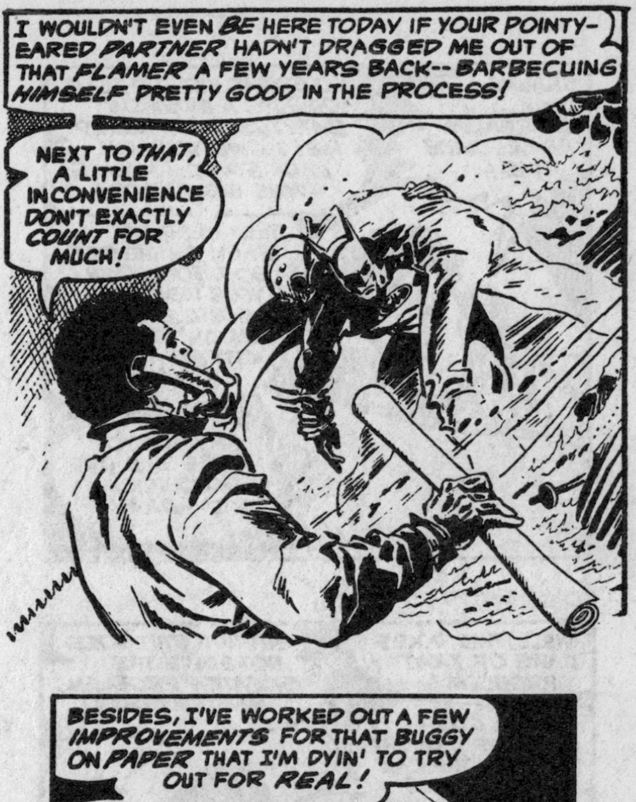
I WOULDN'T EVEN BE HERE TODAY IF YOUR POINTY-EARED PARTNER HADN'T DRAGGED ME OUT OF THAT FLAMER A FEW YEARS BACK-- BARBECUING HIMSELF PRETTY GOOD IN THE PROCESS!
NEXT TO THAT, A LITTLE INCONVENIENCE DON'T EXACTLY COUNT FOR MUCH!

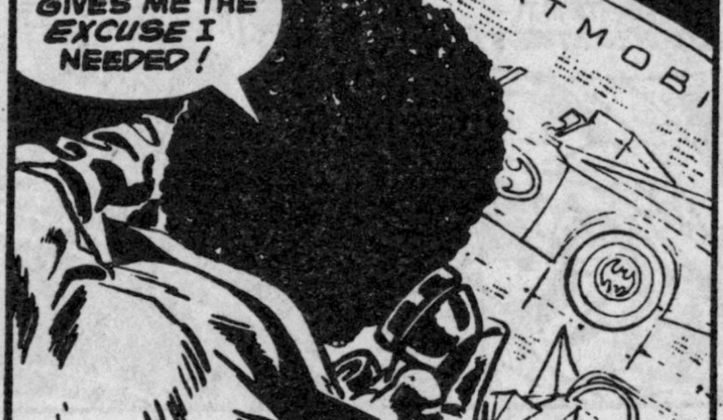
BESIDES, I'VE WORKED OUT A FEW IMPROVEMENTS FOR THAT BUGGY ON PAPER THAT I'M DYIN' TO TRY OUT FOR REAL!
THIS JUST GIVES ME THE EXCUSE I NEEDED!
BATMOBI

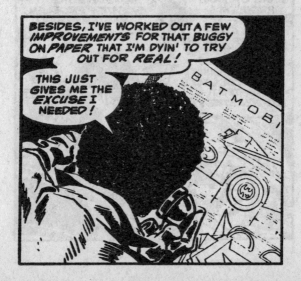

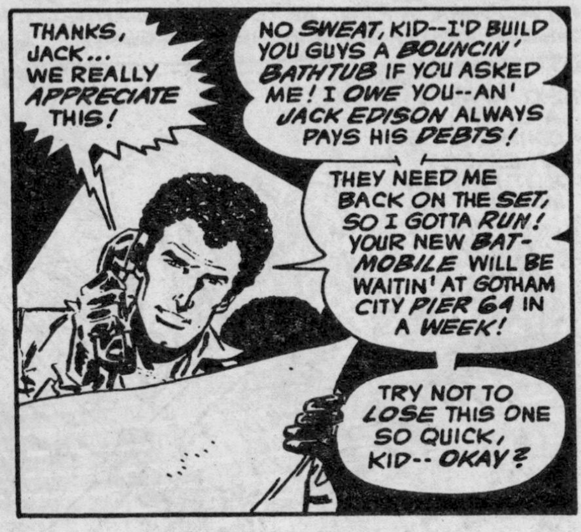
THANKS, JACK... WE REALLY APPRECIATE THIS!
NO SWEAT, KID--I'D BUILD YOU GUYS A BOUNCIN' BATHTUB IF YOU ASKED ME! I OWE YOU--AN' JACK EDISON ALWAYS PAYS HIS DEBTS!
THEY NEED ME BACK ON THE SET, SO I GOTTA RUN! YOUR NEW BAT-MOBILE WILL BE WAITIN' AT GOTHAM CITY PIER 64 IN A WEEK!
TRY NOT TO LOSE THIS ONE SO QUICK, KID-- OKAY?

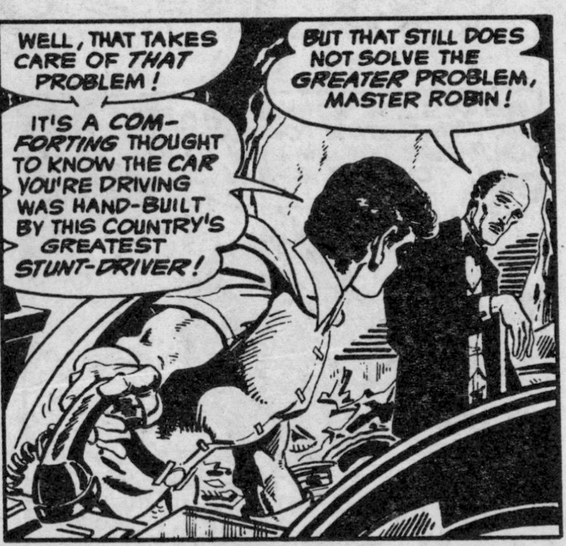
WELL, THAT TAKES CARE OF THAT PROBLEM!
IT'S A COM-FORTING THOUGHT TO KNOW THE CAR YOU'RE DRIVING WAS HAND-BUILT BY THIS COUNTRY'S GREATEST STUNT-DRIVER!
BUT THAT STILL DOES NOT SOLVE THE GREATER PROBLEM, MASTER ROBIN!

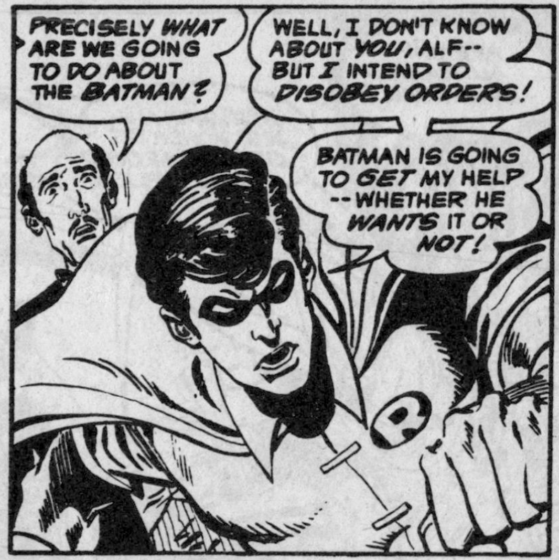
PRECISELY WHAT ARE WE GOING TO DO ABOUT THE BATMAN?
WELL, I DON'T KNOW ABOUT YOU, ALF-- BUT I INTEND TO DISOBEY ORDERS!
BATMAN IS GOING TO GET MY HELP --WHETHER HE WANTS IT OR NOT!

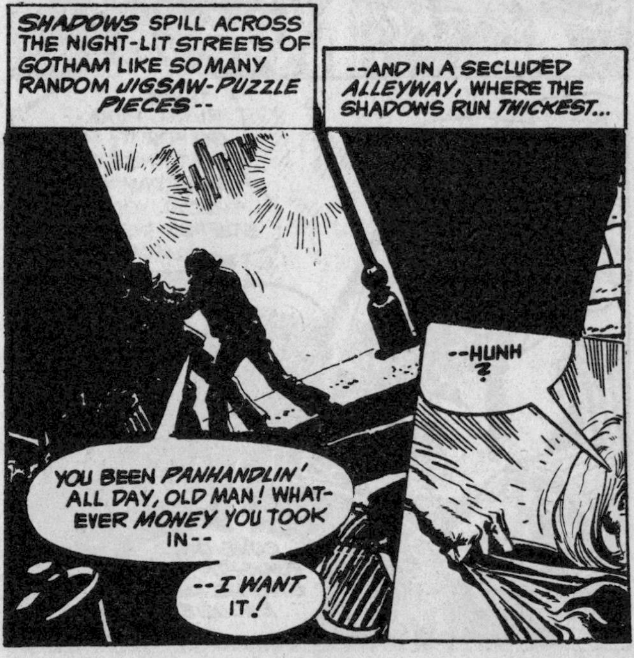
SHADOWS SPILL ACROSS THE NIGHT-LIT STREETS OF GOTHAM LIKE SO MANY RANDOM JIGSAW-PUZZLE PIECES--
--AND IN A SECLUDED ALLEYWAY, WHERE THE SHADOWS RUN THICKEST...
YOU BEEN PANHANDLIN' ALL DAY, OLD MAN! WHAT-EVER MONEY YOU TOOK IN--
--I WANT IT!
--HUNH?

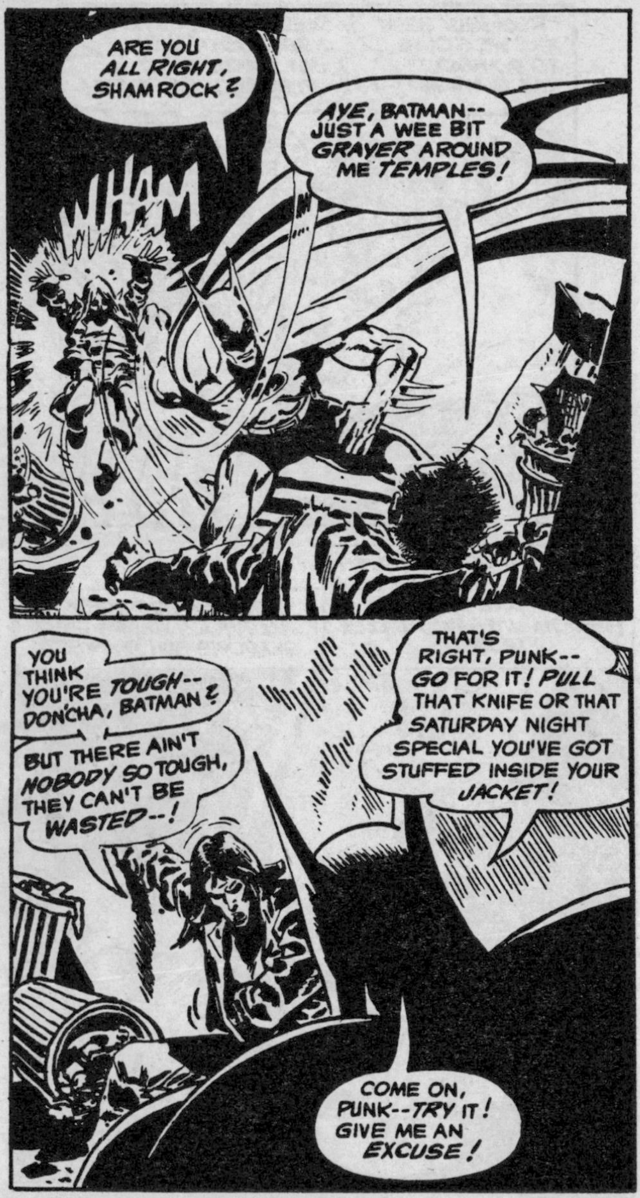
ARE YOU ALL RIGHT, SHAMROCK?
AYE, BATMAN-- JUST A WEE BIT GRAYER AROUND ME TEMPLES!
WHAM
YOU THINK YOU'RE TOUGH-- DON'CHA, BATMAN?
BUT THERE AIN'T NOBODY SO TOUGH, THEY CAN'T BE WASTED--!
THAT'S RIGHT, PUNK-- GO FOR IT! PULL THAT KNIFE OR THAT SATURDAY NIGHT SPECIAL YOU'VE GOT STUFFED INSIDE YOUR JACKET!
COME ON, PUNK--TRY IT! GIVE ME AN EXCUSE!

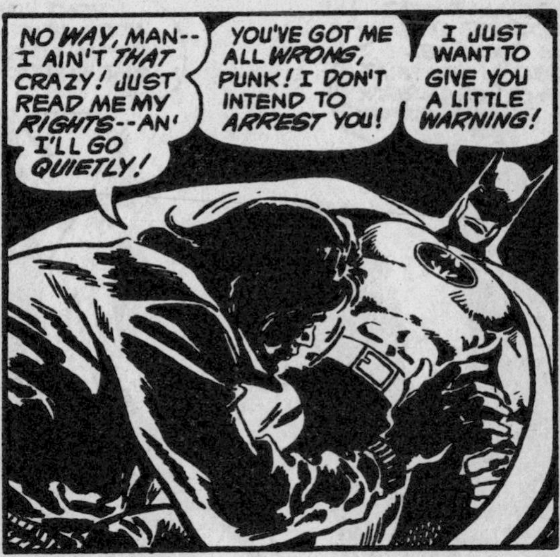
NO WAY, MAN-- I AIN'T THAT CRAZY! JUST READ ME MY RIGHTS--AN' I'LL GO QUIETLY!
YOU'VE GOT ME ALL WRONG, PUNK! I DON'T INTEND TO ARREST YOU!
I JUST WANT TO GIVE YOU A LITTLE WARNING!

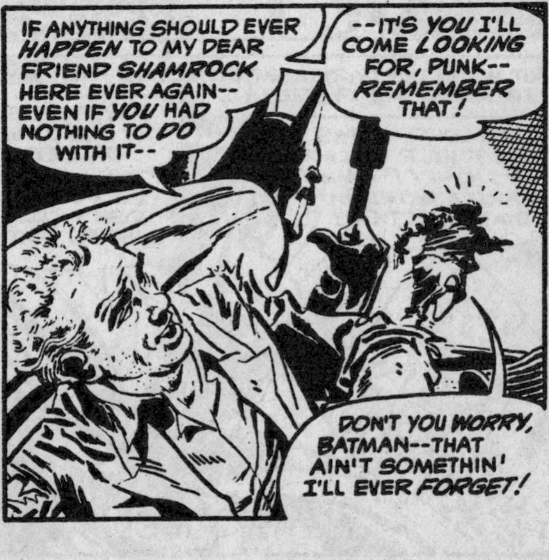
IF ANYTHING SHOULD EVER HAPPEN TO MY DEAR FRIEND SHAMROCK HERE EVER AGAIN-- EVEN IF YOU HAD NOTHING TO DO WITH IT--
--IT'S YOU I'LL COME LOOKING FOR, PUNK-- REMEMBER THAT!
DON'T YOU WORRY, BATMAN--THAT AIN'T SOMETHIN' I'LL EVER FORGET!

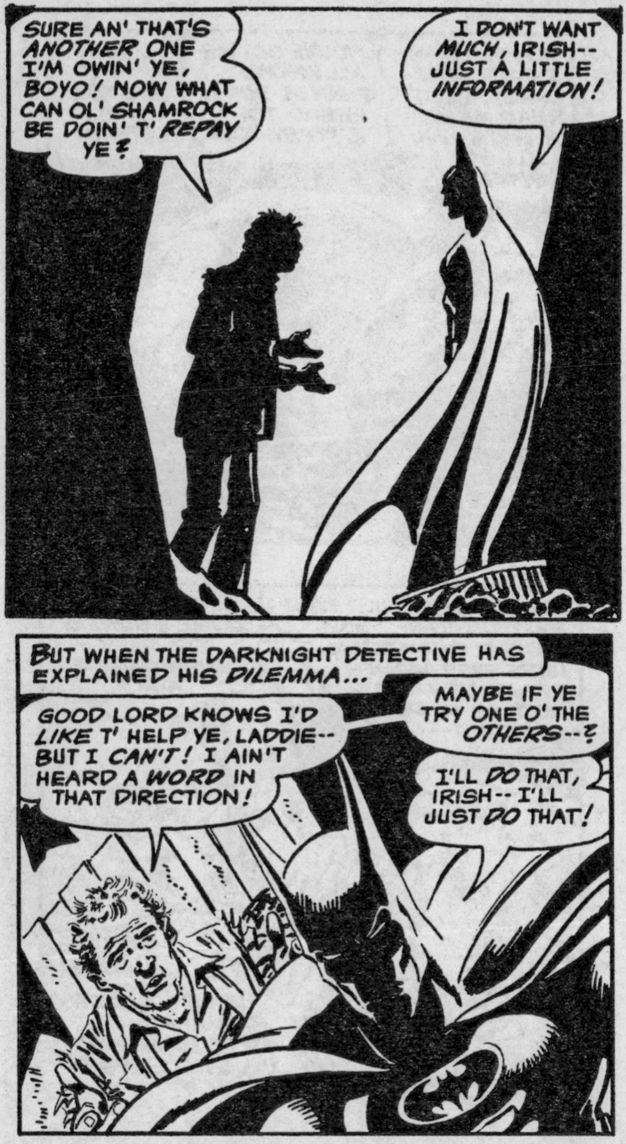
SURE AN' THAT'S ANOTHER ONE I'M OWIN' YE, BOYO! NOW WHAT CAN OL' SHAMROCK BE DOIN' T' REPAY YE?
I DON'T WANT MUCH, IRISH-- JUST A LITTLE INFORMATION!
BUT WHEN THE DARKNIGHT DETECTIVE HAS EXPLAINED HIS DILEMMA...
GOOD LORD KNOWS I'D LIKE T' HELP YE, LADDIE-- BUT I CAN'T! I AIN'T HEARD A WORD IN THAT DIRECTION!
MAYBE IF YE TRY ONE O' THE OTHERS--?
I'LL DO THAT, IRISH-- I'LL JUST DO THAT!

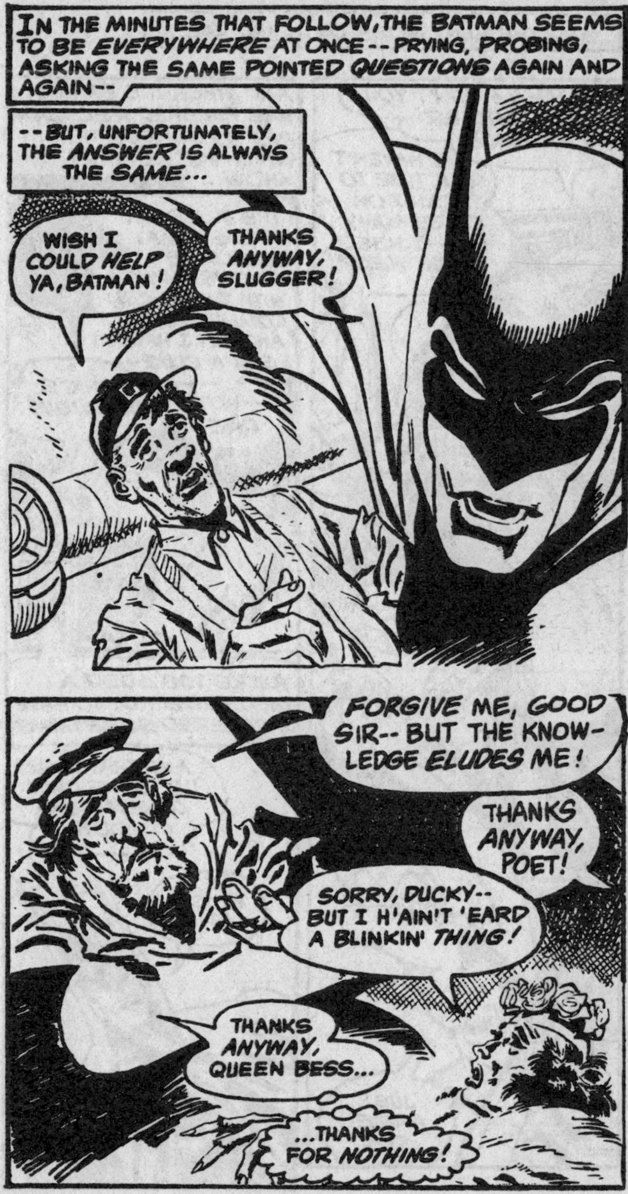
IN THE MINUTES THAT FOLLOW, THE BATMAN SEEMS TO BE EVERYWHERE AT ONCE -- PRYING, PROBING, ASKING THE SAME POINTED QUESTIONS AGAIN AND AGAIN--
--BUT, UNFORTUNATELY, THE ANSWER IS ALWAYS THE SAME...
WISH I COULD HELP YA, BATMAN!
THANKS ANYWAY, SLUGGER!
FORGIVE ME, GOOD SIR-- BUT THE KNOW-LEDGE ELUDES ME!
THANKS ANYWAY, POET!
SORRY, DUCKY-- BUT I H'AIN'T 'EARD A BLINKIN' THING!
THANKS ANYWAY, QUEEN BESS...
...THANKS FOR NOTHING!

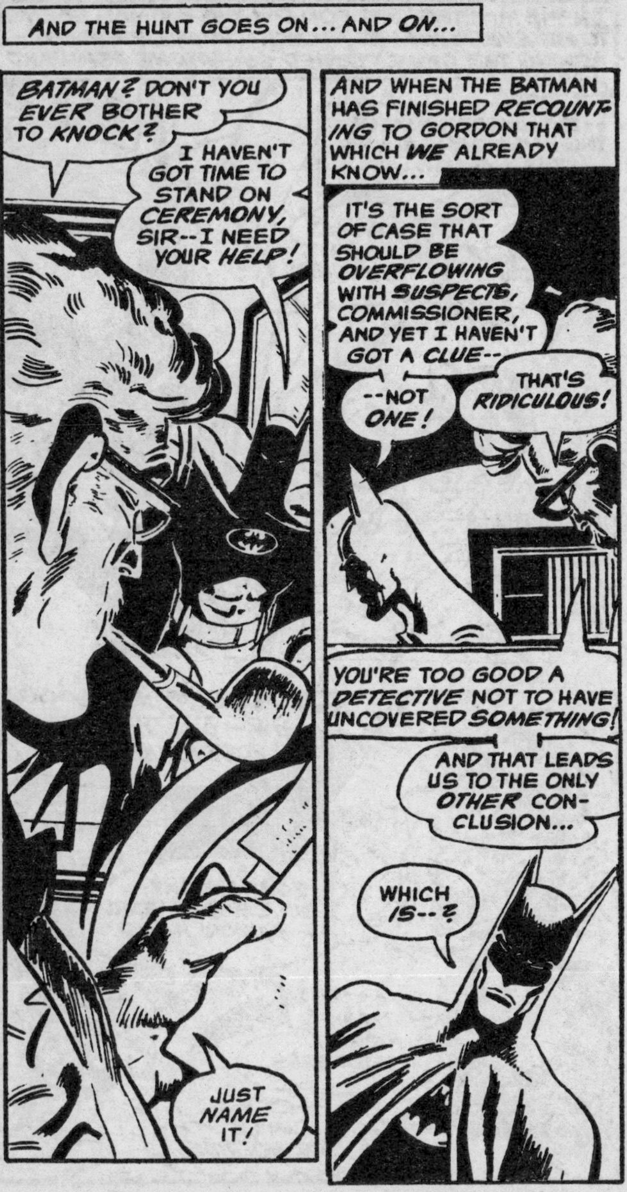
AND THE HUNT GOES ON... AND ON...
BATMAN? DON'T YOU EVER BOTHER TO KNOCK?
I HAVEN'T GOT TIME TO STAND ON CEREMONY, SIR--I NEED YOUR HELP!
JUST NAME IT!
AND WHEN THE BATMAN HAS FINISHED RECOUNTING TO GORDON THAT WHICH WE ALREADY KNOW...
IT'S THE SORT OF CASE THAT SHOULD BE OVERFLOWING WITH SUSPECTS, COMMISSIONER, AND YET I HAVEN'T GOT A CLUE--
--NOT ONE!
THAT'S RIDICULOUS!
YOU'RE TOO GOOD A DETECTIVE NOT TO HAVE UNCOVERED SOMETHING!
AND THAT LEADS US TO THE ONLY OTHER CONCLUSION...
WHICH IS--?

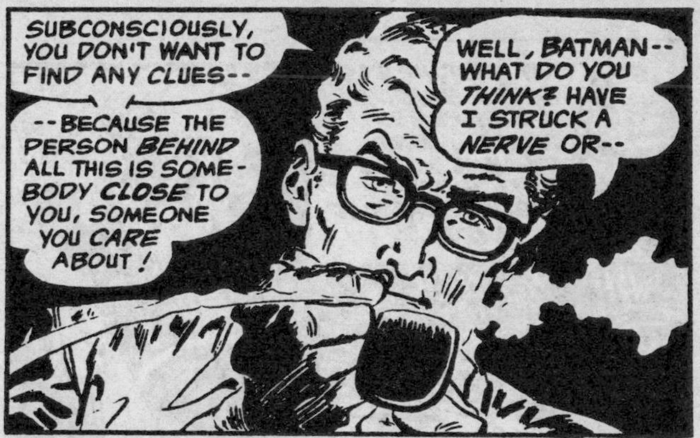
SUBCONSCIOUSLY, YOU DON'T WANT TO FIND ANY CLUES--
--BECAUSE THE PERSON BEHIND ALL THIS IS SOMEBODY CLOSE TO YOU, SOMEONE YOU CARE ABOUT!
WELL, BATMAN-- WHAT DO YOU THINK? HAVE I STRUCK A NERVE OR--

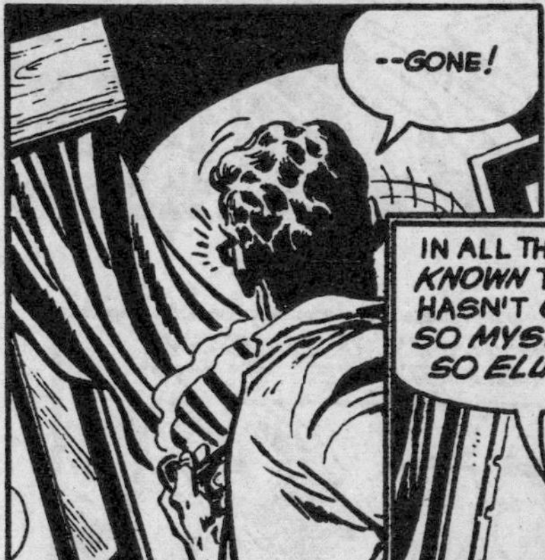
--GONE!

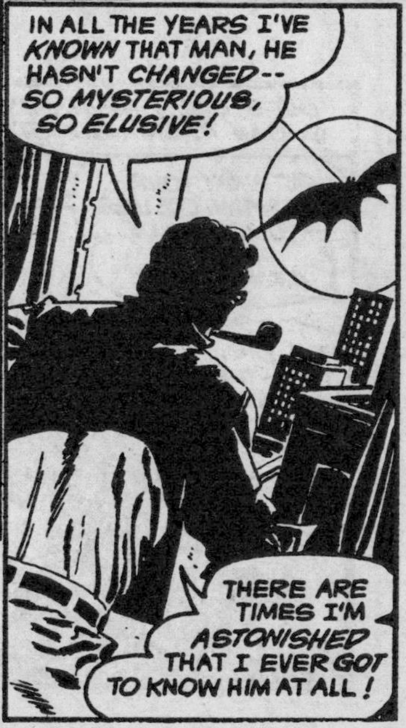
IN ALL THE YEARS I'VE KNOWN THAT MAN, HE HASN'T CHANGED-- SO MYSTERIOUS, SO ELUSIVE!
THERE ARE TIMES I'M ASTONISHED THAT I EVER GOT TO KNOW HIM AT ALL!

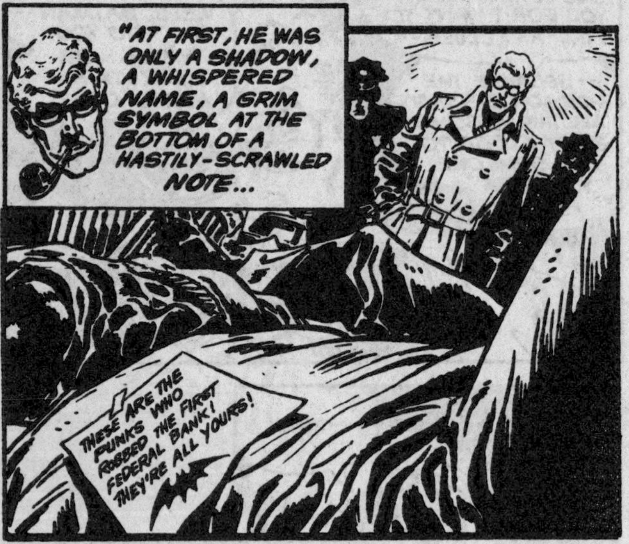
"AT FIRST, HE WAS ONLY A SHADOW, A WHISPERED NAME, A GRIM SYMBOL AT THE BOTTOM OF A HASTILY-SCRAWLED NOTE...
THESE ARE THE PUNKS WHO ROBBED THE FIRST FEDERAL BANK! THEY'RE ALL YOURS!

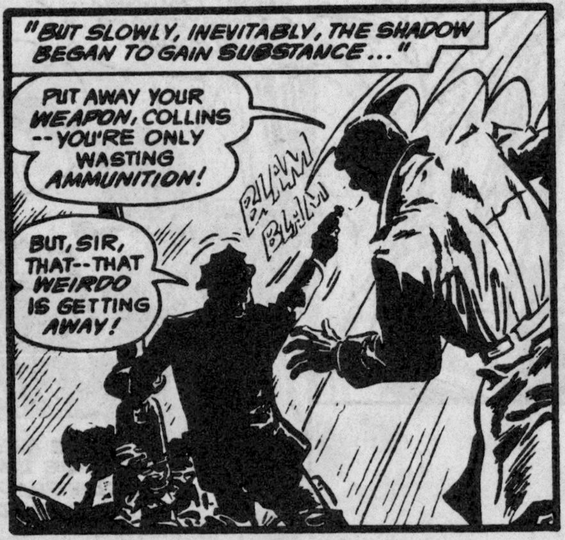
"BUT SLOWLY, INEVITABLY, THE SHADOW BEGAN TO GAIN SUBSTANCE..."
PUT AWAY YOUR WEAPON, COLLINS --YOU'RE ONLY WASTING AMMUNITION!
BUT, SIR, THAT--THAT WEIRDO IS GETTING AWAY!

I WOULDN'T WORRY TOO MUCH ABOUT THAT IF I WERE YOU, COLLINS...
I HAVE THE UNCOMFORTABLE FEELING THAT WE'LL BE HEARING FROM THAT CHARACTER AGAIN!
"I DIDN'T REALLY HAVE TO BE PSYCHIC TO MAKE THAT ASSUMPTION--AND THE DAYS AND WEEKS THAT FOLLOWED PROVED ME DEPRESSINGLY RIGHT...
PD
GP

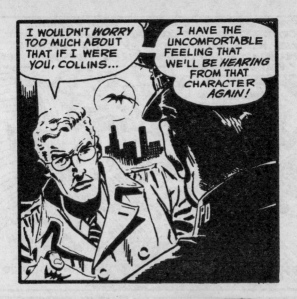

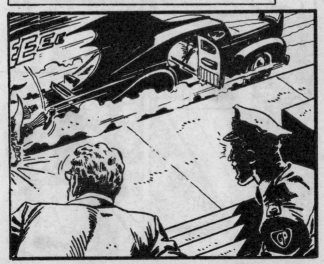

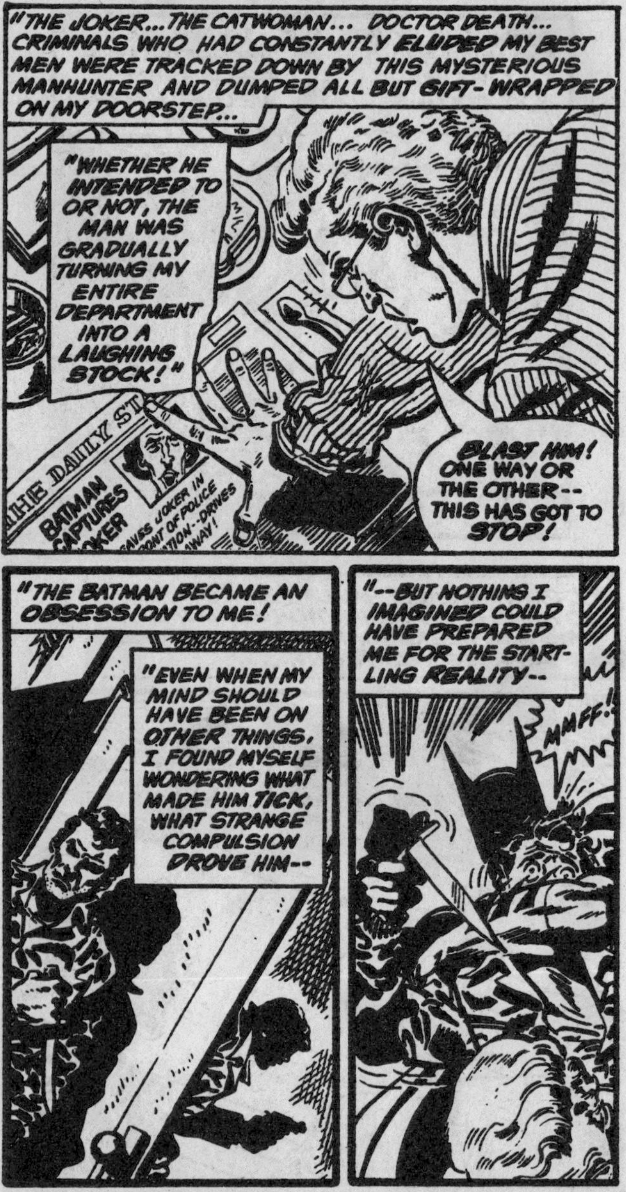
"THE JOKER...THE CATWOMAN... DOCTOR DEATH... CRIMINALS WHO HAD CONSTANTLY ELUDED MY BEST MEN WERE TRACKED DOWN BY THIS MYSTERIOUS MANHUNTER AND DUMPED ALL BUT GIFT-WRAPPED ON MY DOORSTEP...
"WHETHER HE INTENDED TO OR NOT, THE MAN WAS GRADUALLY TURNING MY ENTIRE DEPARTMENT INTO A LAUGHING STOCK!"
THE DAILY ST
BATMAN CAPTURES JOKER
BLAST HIM! ONE WAY OR THE OTHER-- THIS HAS GOT TO STOP!
"THE BATMAN BECAME AN OBSESSION TO ME!
"EVEN WHEN MY MIND SHOULD HAVE BEEN ON OTHER THINGS, I FOUND MYSELF WONDERING WHAT MADE HIM TICK, WHAT STRANGE COMPULSION DROVE HIM--
"--BUT NOTHING I IMAGINED COULD HAVE PREPARED ME FOR THE STARTLING REALITY--
MMFF!!

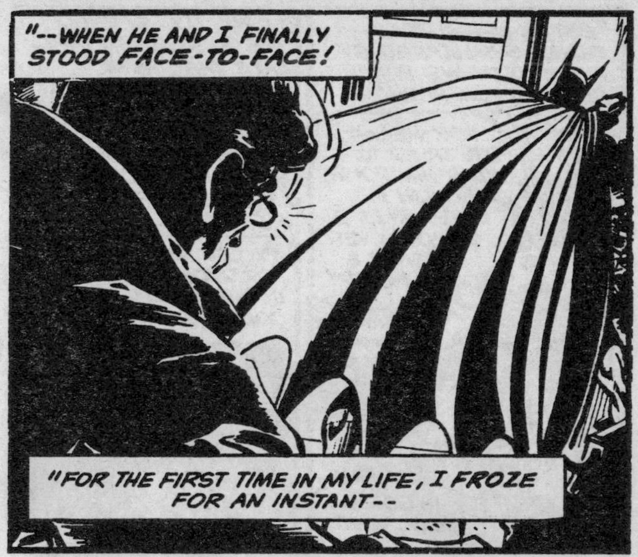
"--WHEN HE AND I FINALLY STOOD FACE-TO-FACE!
"FOR THE FIRST TIME IN MY LIFE, I FROZE FOR AN INSTANT--

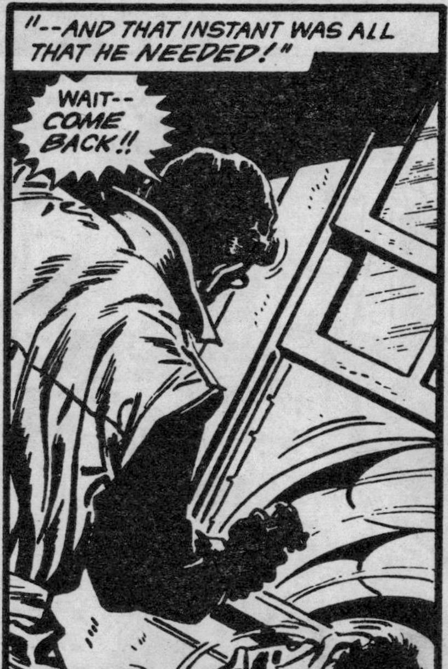
"--AND THAT INSTANT WAS ALL THAT HE NEEDED!"
WAIT-- COME BACK!!

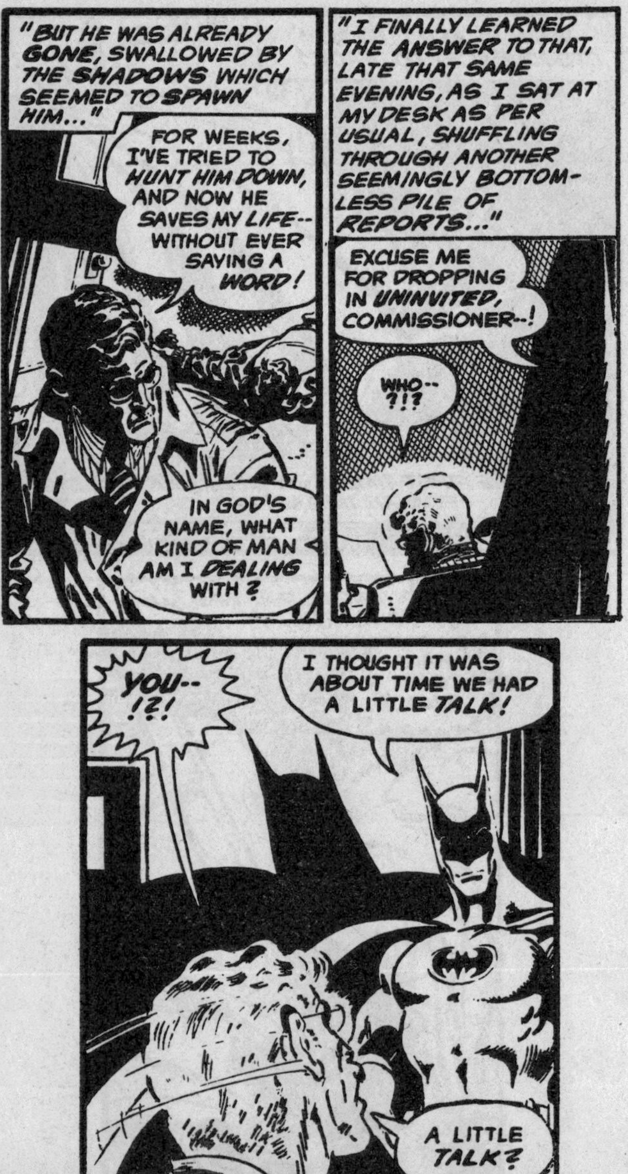

"BUT HE WAS ALREADY GONE, SWALLOWED BY THE SHADOWS WHICH SEEMED TO SPAWN HIM..."
FOR WEEKS, I'VE TRIED TO HUNT HIM DOWN, AND NOW HE SAVES MY LIFE-- WITHOUT EVER SAYING A WORD!
IN GOD'S NAME, WHAT KIND OF MAN AM I DEALING WITH?
"I FINALLY LEARNED THE ANSWER TO THAT, LATE THAT SAME EVENING, AS I SAT AT MY DESK AS PER USUAL, SHUFFLING THROUGH ANOTHER SEEMINGLY BOTTOM-LESS PILE OF REPORTS..."
EXCUSE ME FOR DROPPING IN UNINVITED, COMMISSIONER--!
WHO-- ?!?
YOU-- !?!
I THOUGHT IT WAS ABOUT TIME WE HAD A LITTLE TALK!
A LITTLE TALK?

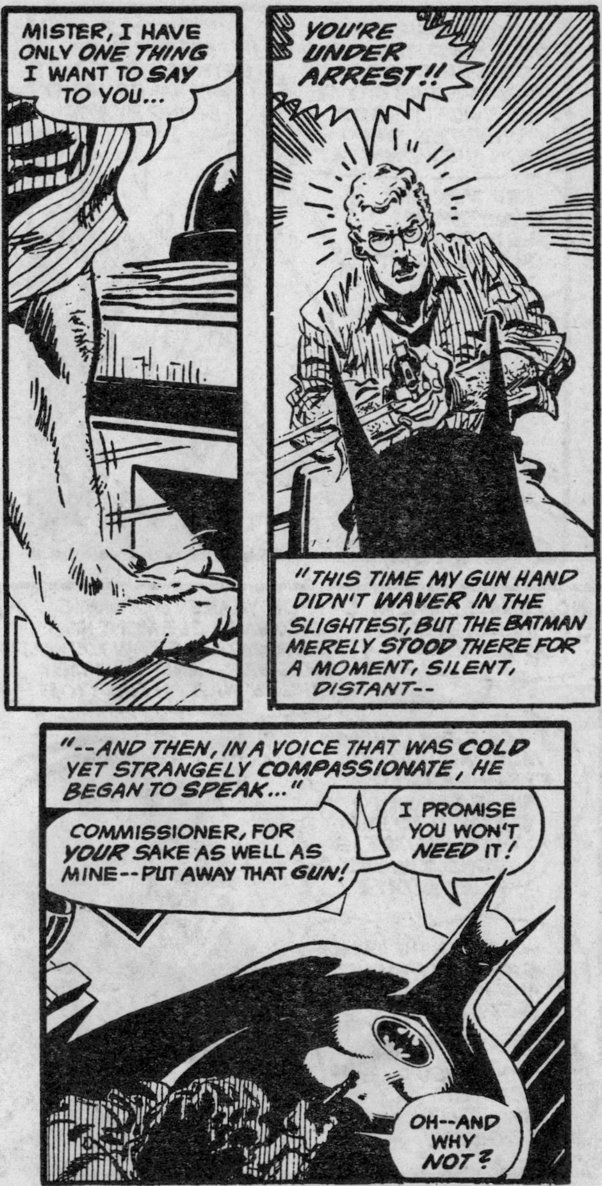
MISTER, I HAVE ONLY ONE THING I WANT TO SAY TO YOU...
YOU'RE UNDER ARREST!!
"THIS TIME MY GUN HAND DIDN'T WAVER IN THE SLIGHTEST, BUT THE BATMAN MERELY STOOD THERE FOR A MOMENT, SILENT, DISTANT--
"--AND THEN, IN A VOICE THAT WAS COLD YET STRANGELY COMPASSIONATE, HE BEGAN TO SPEAK..."
COMMISSIONER, FOR YOUR SAKE AS WELL AS MINE--PUT AWAY THAT GUN!
I PROMISE YOU WON'T NEED IT!
OH--AND WHY NOT?

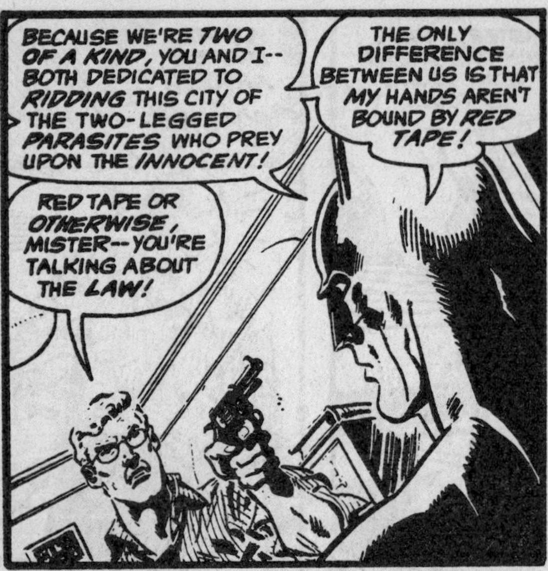
BECAUSE WE'RE TWO OF A KIND, YOU AND I--BOTH DEDICATED TO RIDDING THIS CITY OF THE TWO-LEGGED PARASITES WHO PREY UPON THE INNOCENT!
THE ONLY DIFFERENCE BETWEEN US IS THAT MY HANDS AREN'T BOUND BY RED TAPE!
RED TAPE OR OTHERWISE, MISTER--YOU'RE TALKING ABOUT THE LAW!

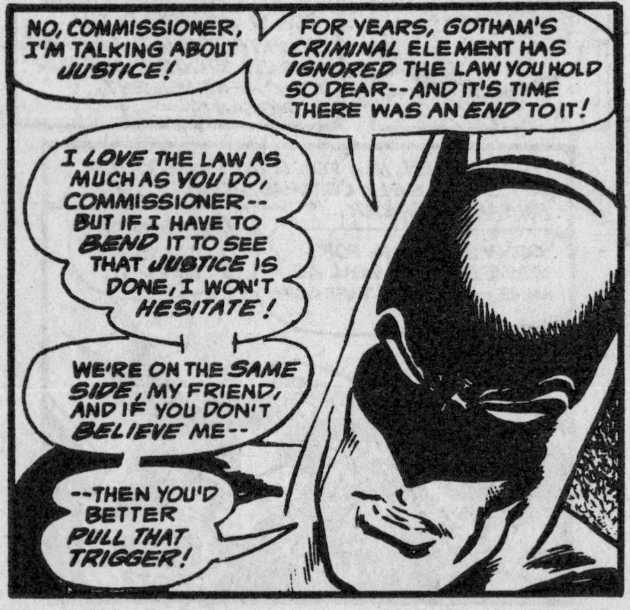
NO, COMMISSIONER, I'M TALKING ABOUT JUSTICE!
FOR YEARS, GOTHAM'S CRIMINAL ELEMENT HAS IGNORED THE LAW YOU HOLD SO DEAR--AND IT'S TIME THERE WAS AN END TO IT!
I LOVE THE LAW AS MUCH AS YOU DO, COMMISSIONER--BUT IF I HAVE TO BEND IT TO SEE THAT JUSTICE IS DONE, I WON'T HESITATE!
WE'RE ON THE SAME SIDE, MY FRIEND, AND IF YOU DON'T BELIEVE ME--
--THEN YOU'D BETTER PULL THAT TRIGGER!

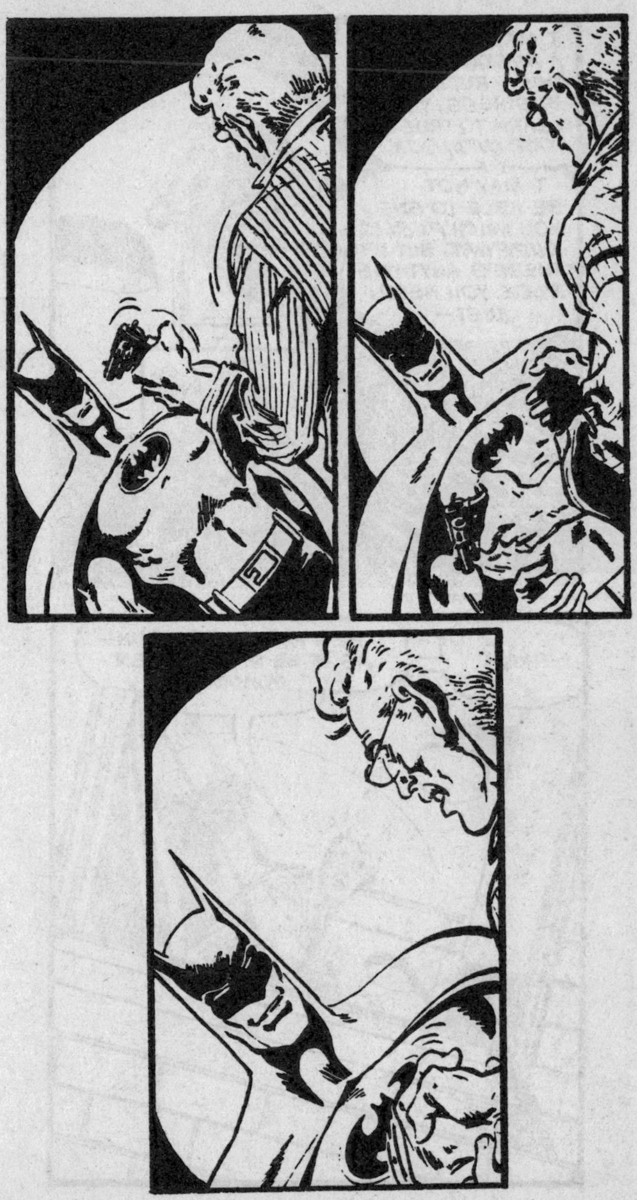

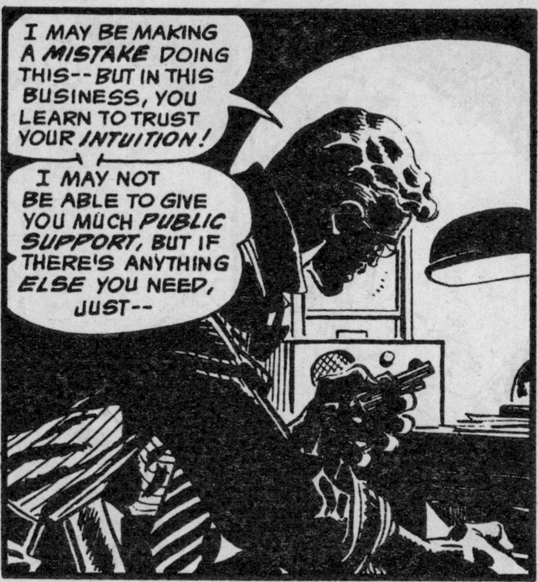
I MAY BE MAKING A MISTAKE DOING THIS--BUT IN THIS BUSINESS, YOU LEARN TO TRUST YOUR INTUITION!
I MAY NOT BE ABLE TO GIVE YOU MUCH PUBLIC SUPPORT, BUT IF THERE'S ANYTHING ELSE YOU NEED, JUST--

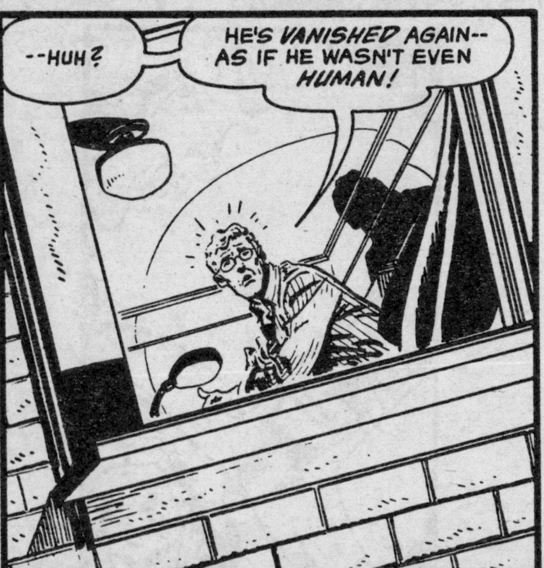
--HUH?
HE'S VANISHED AGAIN--AS IF HE WASN'T EVEN HUMAN!

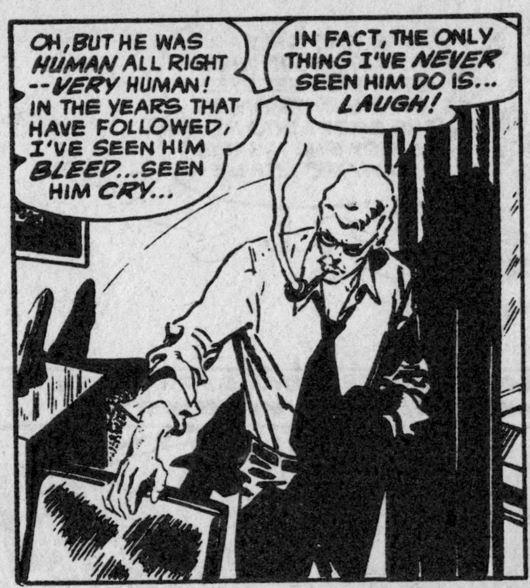
OH, BUT HE WAS HUMAN ALL RIGHT --VERY HUMAN! IN THE YEARS THAT HAVE FOLLOWED, I'VE SEEN HIM BLEED... SEEN HIM CRY...
IN FACT, THE ONLY THING I'VE NEVER SEEN HIM DO IS... LAUGH!

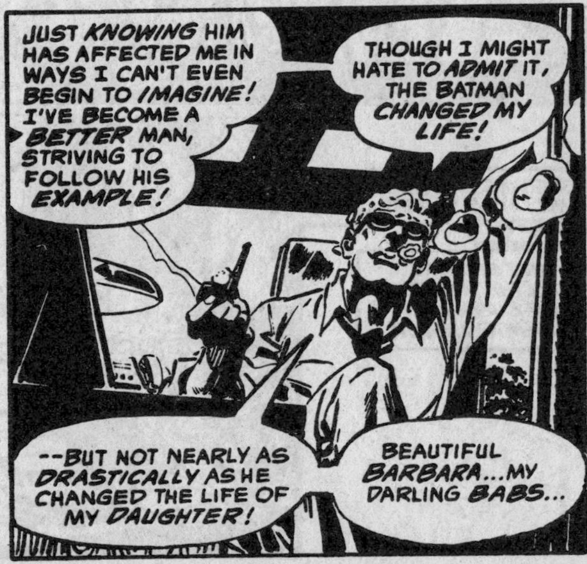
JUST KNOWING HIM HAS AFFECTED ME IN WAYS I CAN'T EVEN BEGIN TO IMAGINE! I'VE BECOME A BETTER MAN, STRIVING TO FOLLOW HIS EXAMPLE!
THOUGH I MIGHT HATE TO ADMIT IT, THE BATMAN CHANGED MY LIFE!
--BUT NOT NEARLY AS DRASTICALLY AS HE CHANGED THE LIFE OF MY DAUGHTER!
BEAUTIFUL BARBARA... MY DARLING BABS...

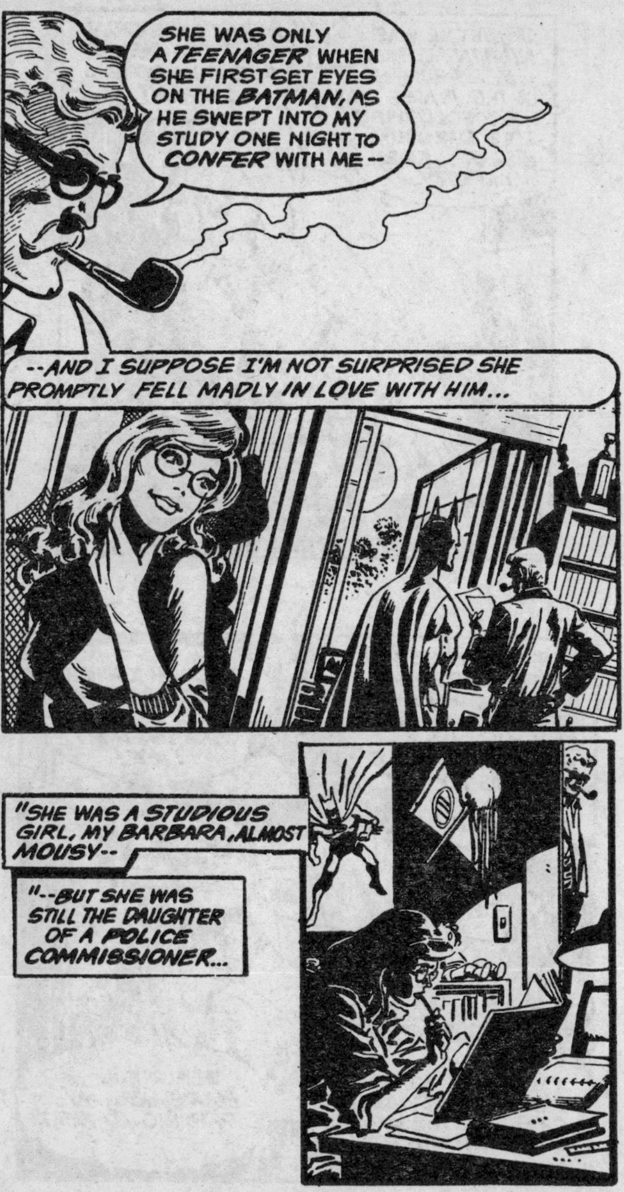

SHE WAS ONLY A TEENAGER WHEN SHE FIRST SET EYES ON THE BATMAN, AS HE SWEPT INTO MY STUDY ONE NIGHT TO CONFER WITH ME--
--AND I SUPPOSE I'M NOT SURPRISED SHE PROMPTLY FELL MADLY IN LOVE WITH HIM...
"SHE WAS A STUDIOUS GIRL, MY BARBARA, ALMOST MOUSY--
"--BUT SHE WAS STILL THE DAUGHTER OF A POLICE COMMISSIONER...

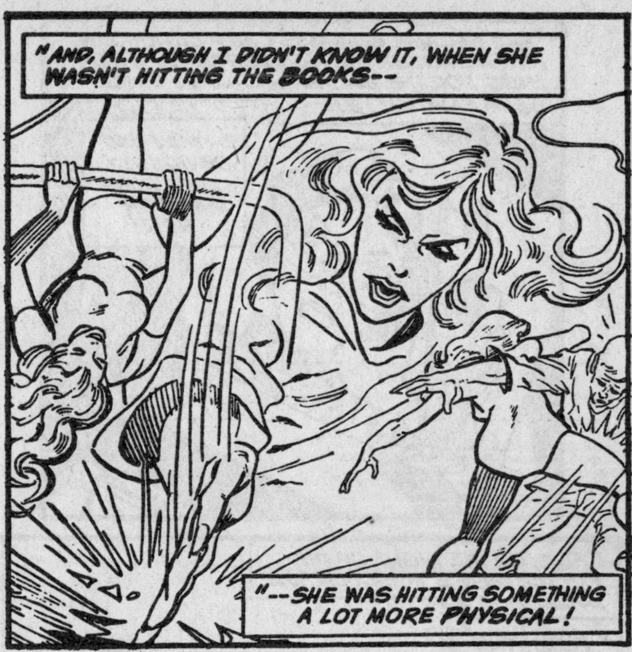
"AND, ALTHOUGH I DIDN'T KNOW IT, WHEN SHE WASN'T HITTING THE BOOKS--
"--SHE WAS HITTING SOMETHING A LOT MORE PHYSICAL!

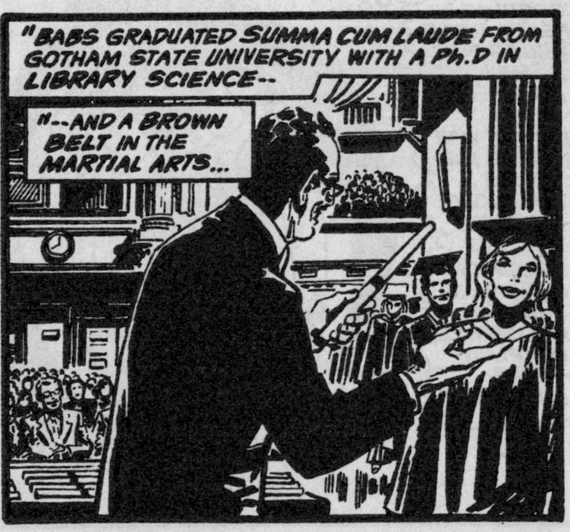
"BABS GRADUATED SUMMA CUM LAUDE FROM GOTHAM STATE UNIVERSITY WITH A Ph.D IN LIBRARY SCIENCE--
"--AND A BROWN BELT IN THE MARTIAL ARTS...

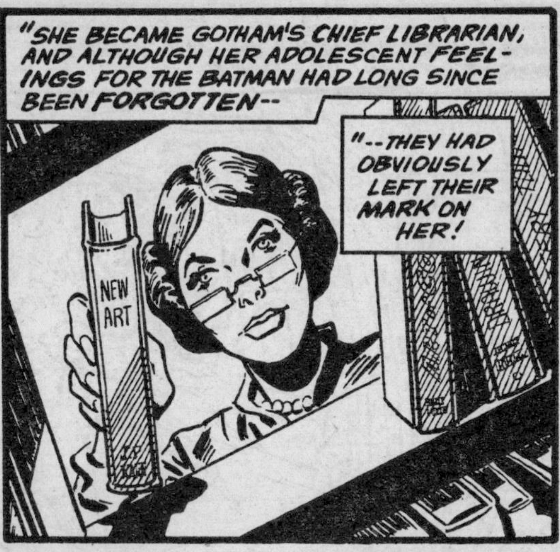
"SHE BECAME GOTHAM'S CHIEF LIBRARIAN, AND ALTHOUGH HER ADOLESCENT FEEL-INGS FOR THE BATMAN HAD LONG SINCE BEEN FORGOTTEN--
"--THEY HAD OBVIOUSLY LEFT THEIR MARK ON HER!
NEW ART

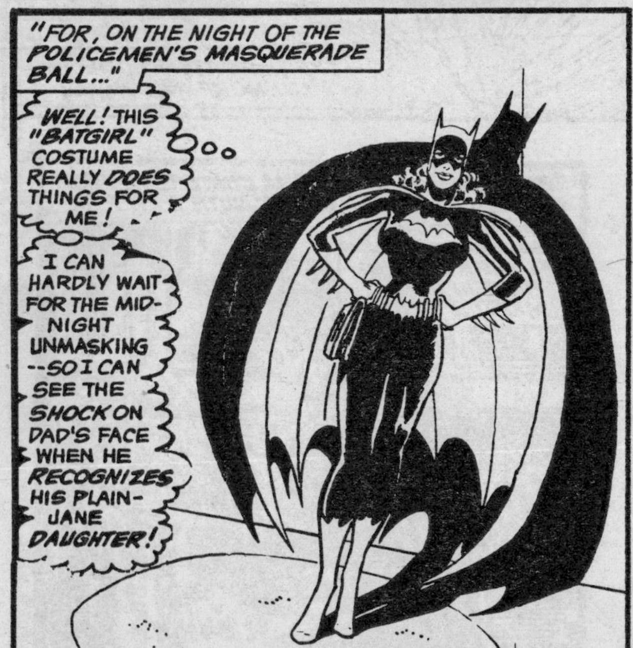
"FOR, ON THE NIGHT OF THE POLICEMEN'S MASQUERADE BALL..."
WELL! THIS "BATGIRL" COSTUME REALLY DOES THINGS FOR ME!
I CAN HARDLY WAIT FOR THE MID-NIGHT UNMASKING --SO I CAN SEE THE SHOCK ON DAD'S FACE WHEN HE RECOGNIZES HIS PLAIN-JANE DAUGHTER!

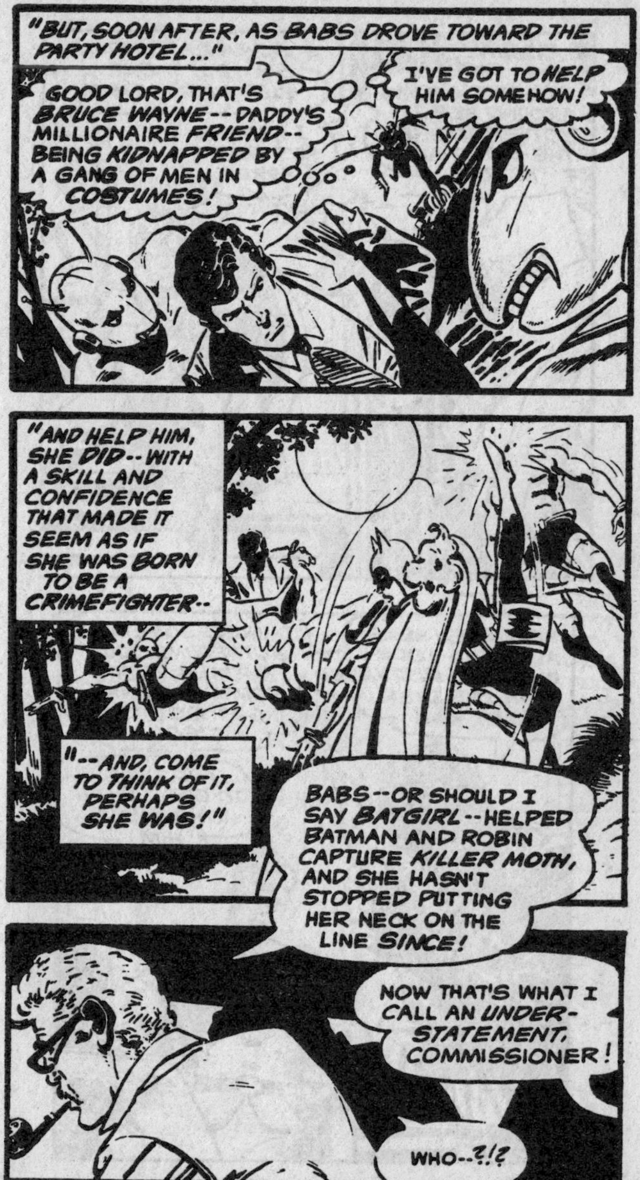

"BUT, SOON AFTER, AS BABS DROVE TOWARD THE PARTY HOTEL..."
GOOD LORD, THAT'S BRUCE WAYNE--DADDY'S MILLIONAIRE FRIEND--BEING KIDNAPPED BY A GANG OF MEN IN COSTUMES!
I'VE GOT TO HELP HIM SOMEHOW!
"AND HELP HIM, SHE DID--WITH A SKILL AND CONFIDENCE THAT MADE IT SEEM AS IF SHE WAS BORN TO BE A CRIMEFIGHTER--
"--AND, COME TO THINK OF IT, PERHAPS SHE WAS!"
BABS--OR SHOULD I SAY BATGIRL--HELPED BATMAN AND ROBIN CAPTURE KILLER MOTH, AND SHE HASN'T STOPPED PUTTING HER NECK ON THE LINE SINCE!
NOW THAT'S WHAT I CALL AN UNDER-STATEMENT, COMMISSIONER!
WHO--?!?

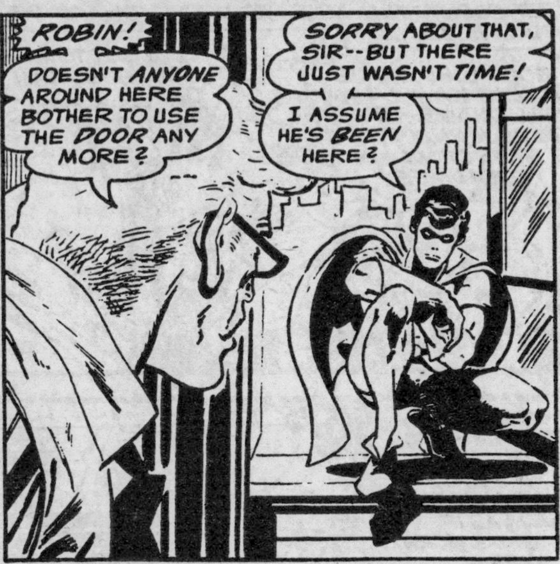
ROBIN!
DOESN'T ANYONE AROUND HERE BOTHER TO USE THE DOOR ANY MORE?
SORRY ABOUT THAT, SIR--BUT THERE JUST WASN'T TIME!
I ASSUME HE'S BEEN HERE?

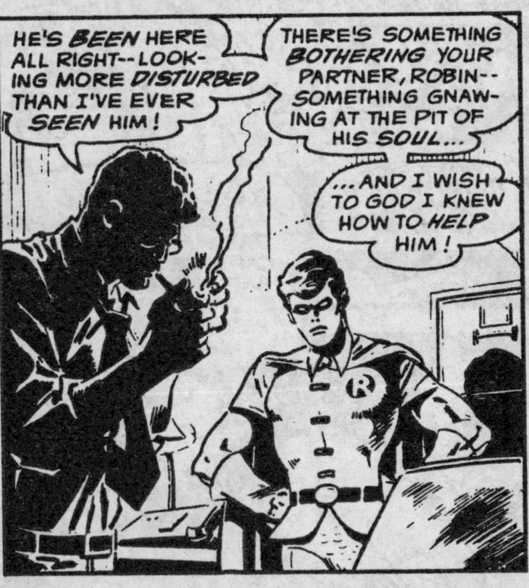
HE'S BEEN HERE ALL RIGHT--LOOKING MORE DISTURBED THAN I'VE EVER SEEN HIM!
THERE'S SOMETHING BOTHERING YOUR PARTNER, ROBIN--SOMETHING GNAWING AT THE PIT OF HIS SOUL...
...AND I WISH TO GOD I KNEW HOW TO HELP HIM!

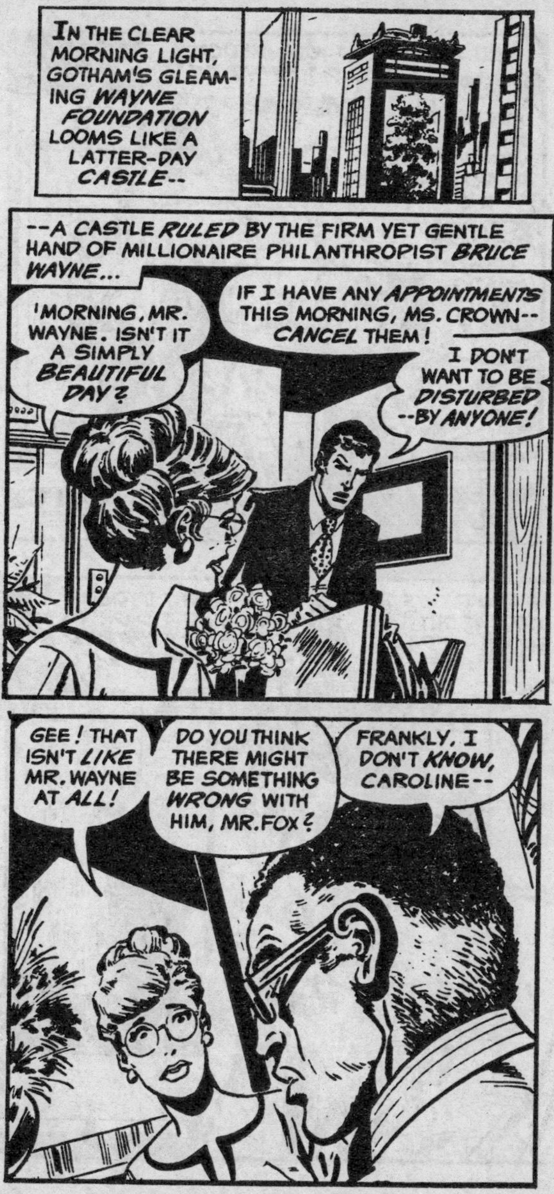
IN THE CLEAR MORNING LIGHT, GOTHAM'S GLEAMING WAYNE FOUNDATION LOOMS LIKE A LATTER-DAY CASTLE--
--A CASTLE RULED BY THE FIRM YET GENTLE HAND OF MILLIONAIRE PHILANTHROPIST BRUCE WAYNE...
'MORNING, MR. WAYNE. ISN'T IT A SIMPLY BEAUTIFUL DAY?
IF I HAVE ANY APPOINTMENTS THIS MORNING, MS. CROWN-- CANCEL THEM!
I DON'T WANT TO BE DISTURBED --BY ANYONE!
GEE! THAT ISN'T LIKE MR. WAYNE AT ALL!
DO YOU THINK THERE MIGHT BE SOMETHING WRONG WITH HIM, MR. FOX?
FRANKLY, I DON'T KNOW, CAROLINE--

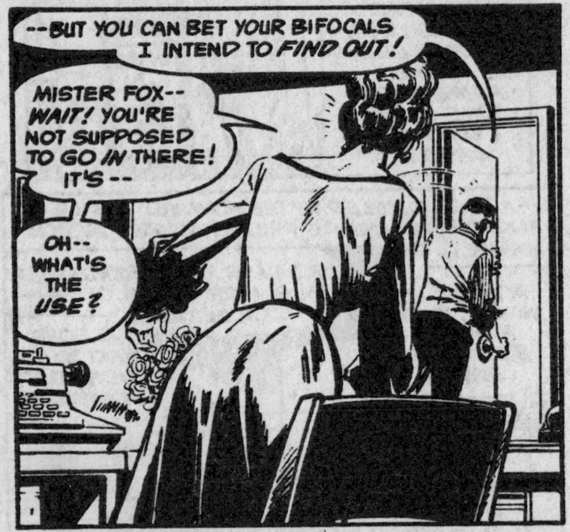
--BUT YOU CAN BET YOUR BIFOCALS I INTEND TO FIND OUT!
MISTER FOX-- WAIT! YOU'RE NOT SUPPOSED TO GO IN THERE! IT'S --
OH-- WHAT'S THE USE?

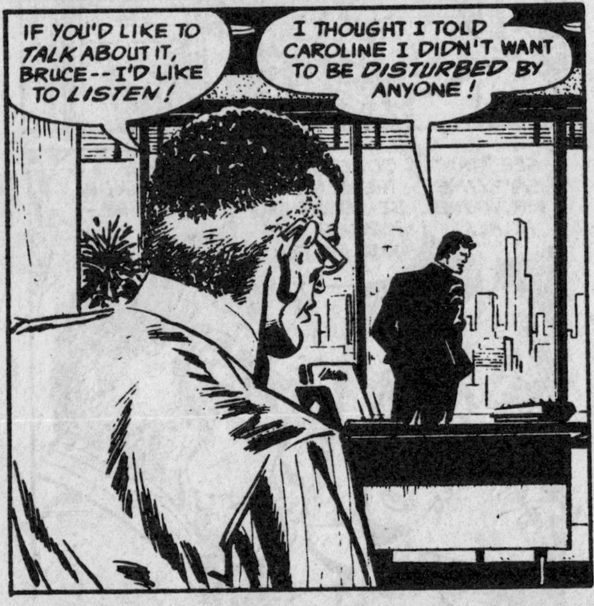
I THOUGHT I TOLD CAROLINE I DIDN'T WANT TO BE DISTURBED BY ANYONE!
IF YOU'D LIKE TO TALK ABOUT IT, BRUCE--I'D LIKE TO LISTEN!

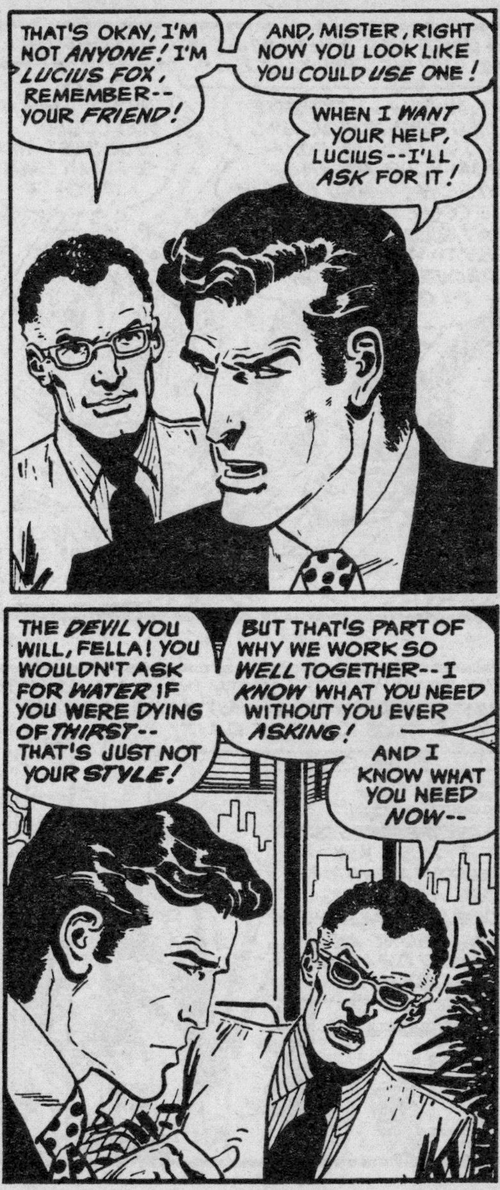
THAT'S OKAY, I'M NOT ANYONE! I'M LUCIUS FOX, REMEMBER-- YOUR FRIEND!
AND, MISTER, RIGHT NOW YOU LOOK LIKE YOU COULD USE ONE!
WHEN I WANT YOUR HELP, LUCIUS--I'LL ASK FOR IT!
THE DEVIL YOU WILL, FELLA! YOU WOULDN'T ASK FOR WATER IF YOU WERE DYING OF THIRST-- THAT'S JUST NOT YOUR STYLE!
BUT THAT'S PART OF WHY WE WORK SO WELL TOGETHER--I KNOW WHAT YOU NEED WITHOUT YOU EVER ASKING!
AND I KNOW WHAT YOU NEED NOW--

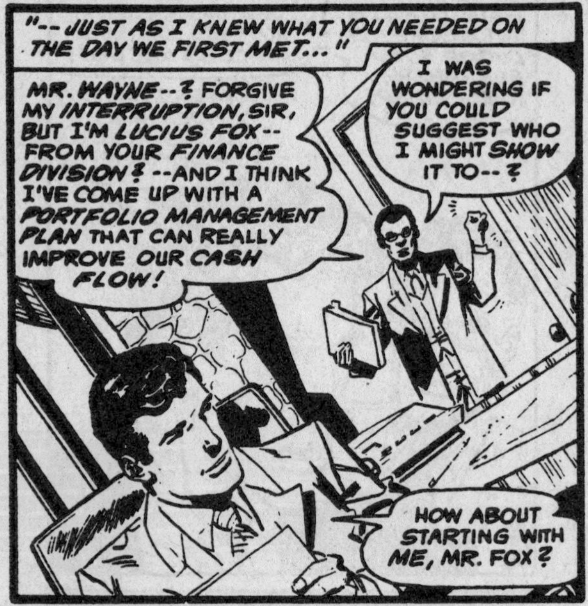
"-- JUST AS I KNEW WHAT YOU NEEDED ON THE DAY WE FIRST MET..."
MR. WAYNE--? FORGIVE MY INTERRUPTION, SIR, BUT I'M LUCIUS FOX--FROM YOUR FINANCE DIVISION! --AND I THINK I'VE COME UP WITH A PORTFOLIO MANAGEMENT PLAN THAT CAN REALLY IMPROVE OUR CASH FLOW!
I WAS WONDERING IF YOU COULD SUGGEST WHO I MIGHT SHOW IT TO--?
HOW ABOUT STARTING WITH ME, MR. FOX?

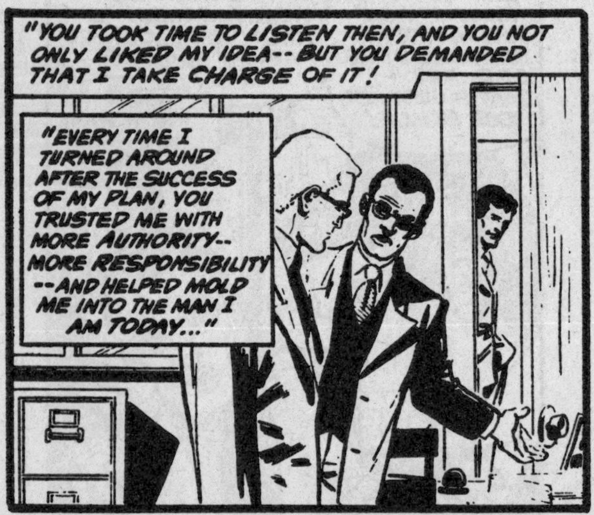
"YOU TOOK TIME TO LISTEN THEN, AND YOU NOT ONLY LIKED MY IDEA-- BUT YOU DEMANDED THAT I TAKE CHARGE OF IT!
"EVERY TIME I TURNED AROUND AFTER THE SUCCESS OF MY PLAN, YOU TRUSTED ME WITH MORE AUTHORITY--MORE RESPONSIBILITY --AND HELPED MOLD ME INTO THE MAN I AM TODAY..."

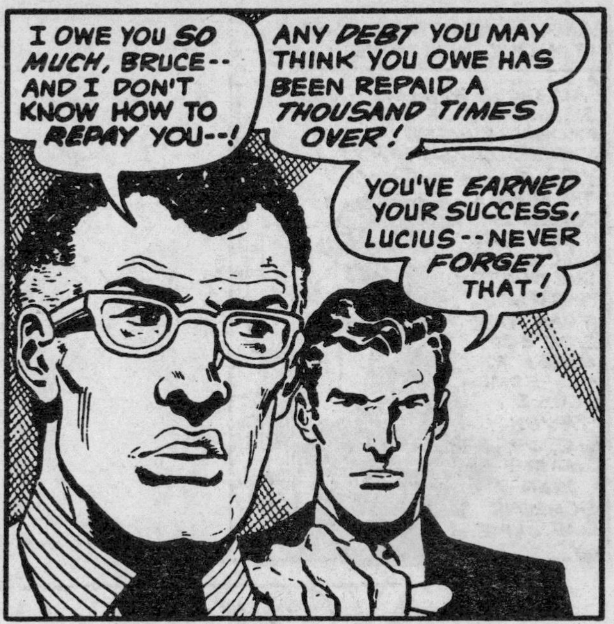
I OWE YOU SO MUCH, BRUCE--AND I DON'T KNOW HOW TO REPAY YOU--!
ANY DEBT YOU MAY THINK YOU OWE HAS BEEN REPAID A THOUSAND TIMES OVER!
YOU'VE EARNED YOUR SUCCESS, LUCIUS--NEVER FORGET THAT!

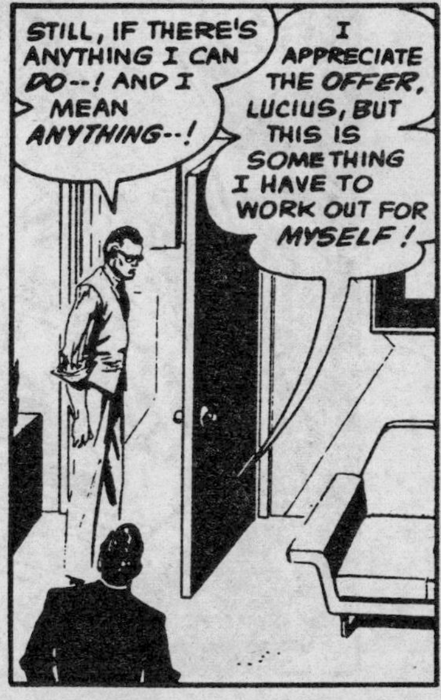
STILL, IF THERE'S ANYTHING I CAN DO--! AND I MEAN ANYTHING--!
I APPRECIATE THE OFFER, LUCIUS, BUT THIS IS SOMETHING I HAVE TO WORK OUT FOR MYSELF!

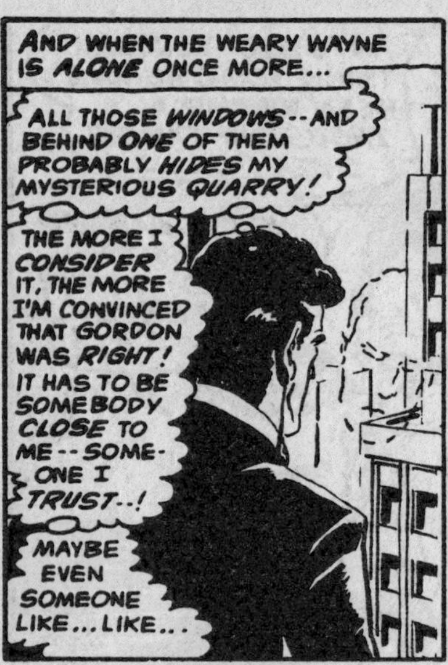
AND WHEN THE WEARY WAYNE IS ALONE ONCE MORE...
ALL THOSE WINDOWS--AND BEHIND ONE OF THEM PROBABLY HIDES MY MYSTERIOUS QUARRY!
THE MORE I CONSIDER IT, THE MORE I'M CONVINCED THAT GORDON WAS RIGHT! IT HAS TO BE SOMEBODY CLOSE TO ME--SOME-ONE I TRUST--!
MAYBE EVEN SOMEONE LIKE... LIKE...

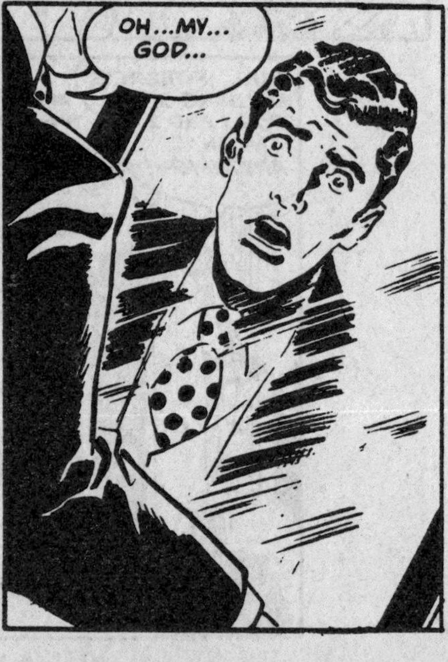
OH...MY... GOD...

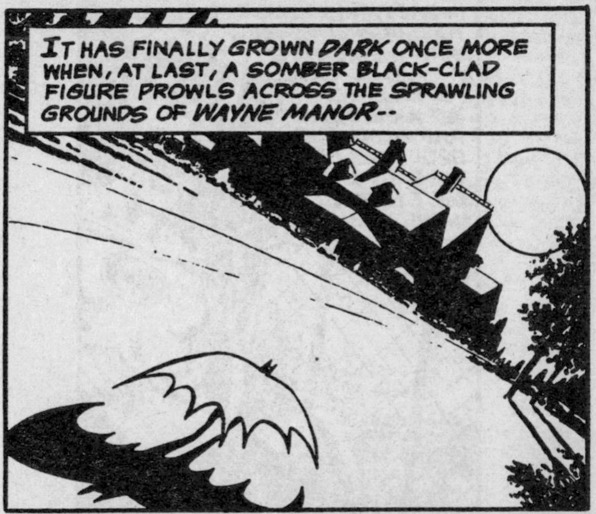
IT HAS FINALLY GROWN DARK ONCE MORE WHEN, AT LAST, A SOMBER BLACK-CLAD FIGURE PROWLS ACROSS THE SPRAWLING GROUNDS OF WAYNE MANOR--

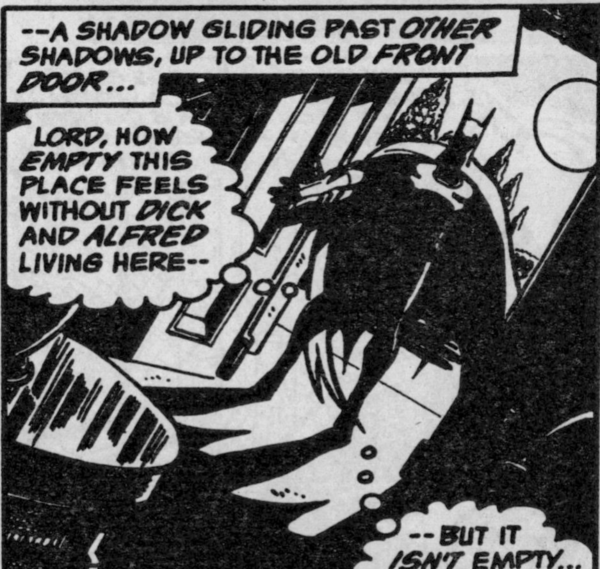
--A SHADOW GLIDING PAST OTHER SHADOWS, UP TO THE OLD FRONT DOOR...
LORD, HOW EMPTY THIS PLACE FEELS WITHOUT DICK AND ALFRED LIVING HERE--
--BUT IT ISN'T EMPTY... NOT REALLY!

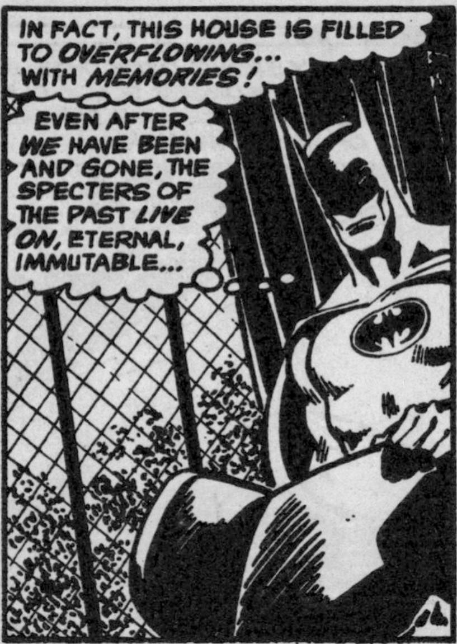
IN FACT, THIS HOUSE IS FILLED TO OVERFLOWING... WITH MEMORIES!
EVEN AFTER WE HAVE BEEN AND GONE, THE SPECTERS OF THE PAST LIVE ON, ETERNAL, IMMUTABLE...

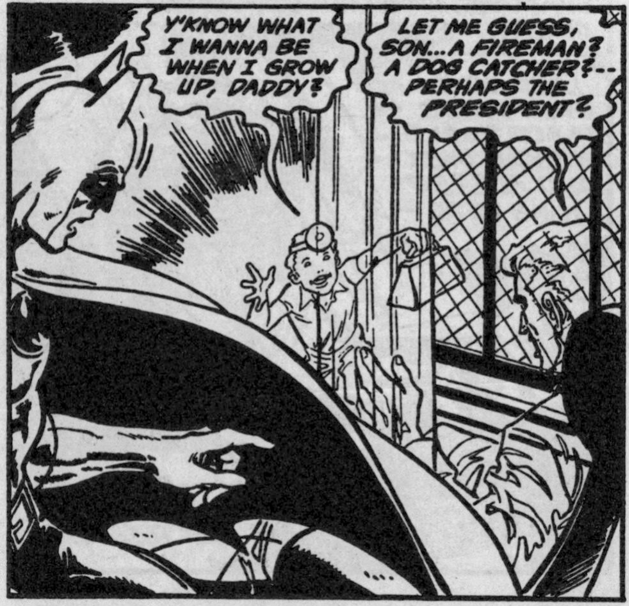
Y'KNOW WHAT I WANNA BE WHEN I GROW UP, DADDY?
LET ME GUESS, SON...A FIREMAN? A DOG CATCHER?-- PERHAPS THE PRESIDENT?

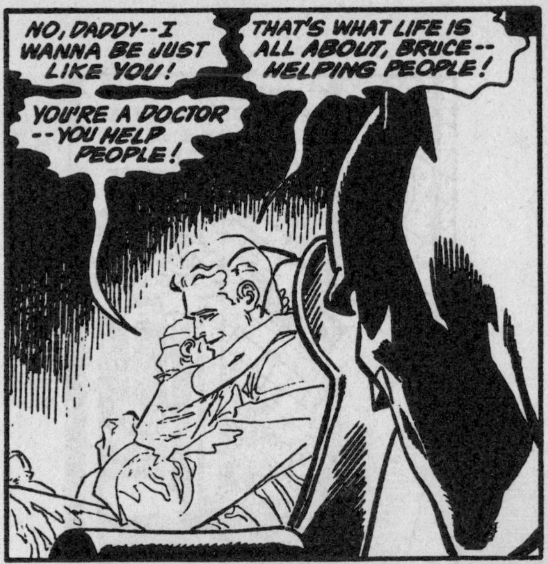
NO, DADDY--I WANNA BE JUST LIKE YOU!
YOU'RE A DOCTOR --YOU HELP PEOPLE!
THAT'S WHAT LIFE IS ALL ABOUT, BRUCE-- HELPING PEOPLE!

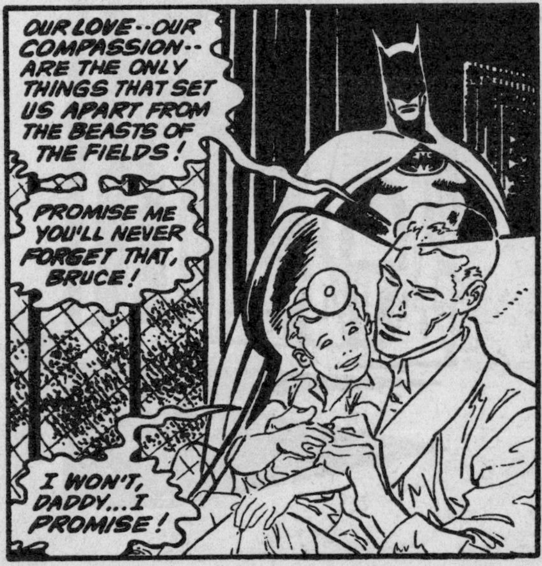
OUR LOVE--OUR COMPASSION-- ARE THE ONLY THINGS THAT SET US APART FROM THE BEASTS OF THE FIELDS!
PROMISE ME YOU'LL NEVER FORGET THAT, BRUCE!
I WON'T, DADDY...I PROMISE!

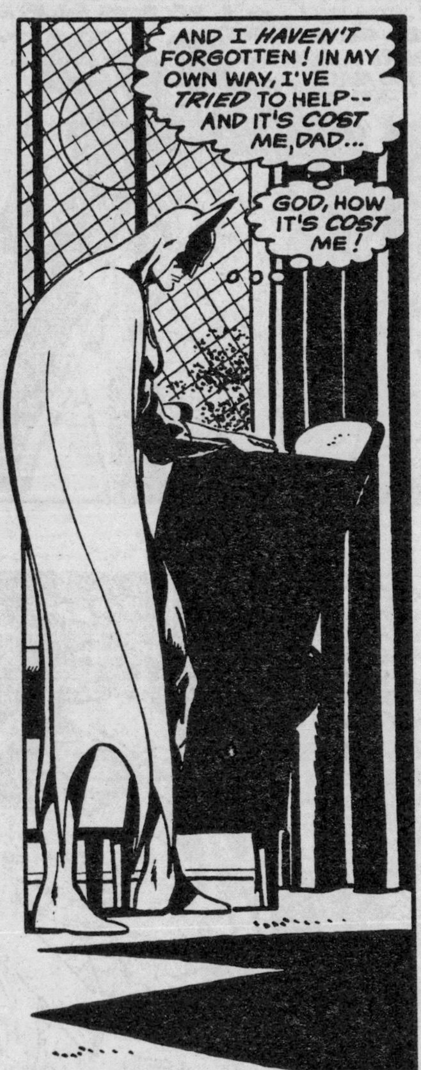
AND I HAVEN'T FORGOTTEN! IN MY OWN WAY, I'VE TRIED TO HELP-- AND IT'S COST ME, DAD...
GOD, HOW IT'S COST ME!

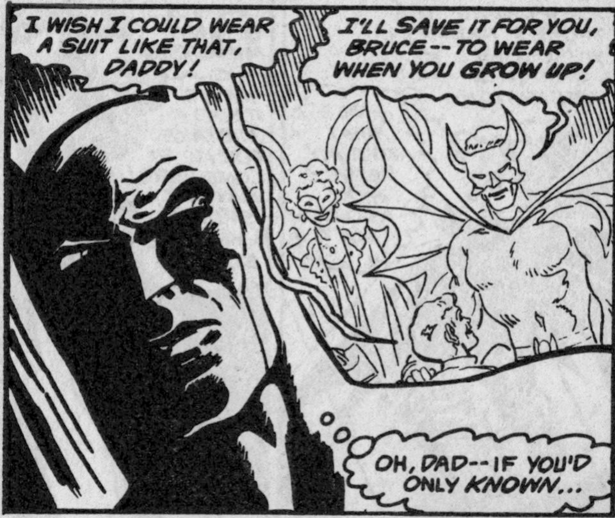
I WISH I COULD WEAR A SUIT LIKE THAT, DADDY!
I'LL SAVE IT FOR YOU, BRUCE--TO WEAR WHEN YOU GROW UP!
OH, DAD--IF YOU'D ONLY KNOWN...

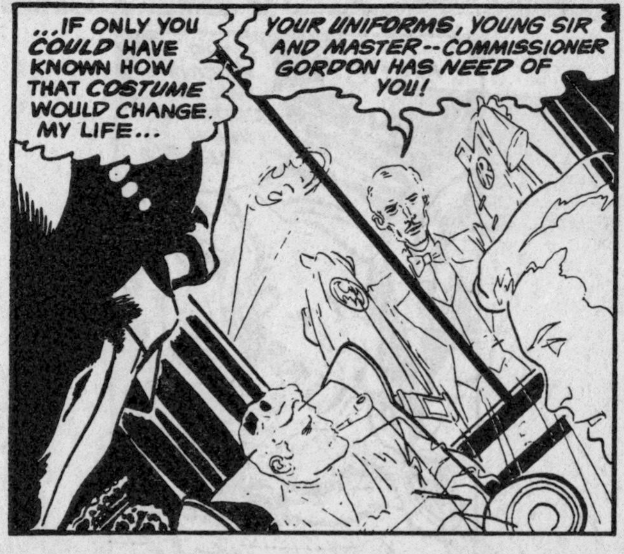
...IF ONLY YOU COULD HAVE KNOWN HOW THAT COSTUME WOULD CHANGE MY LIFE...
YOUR UNIFORMS, YOUNG SIR AND MASTER--COMMISSIONER GORDON HAS NEED OF YOU!

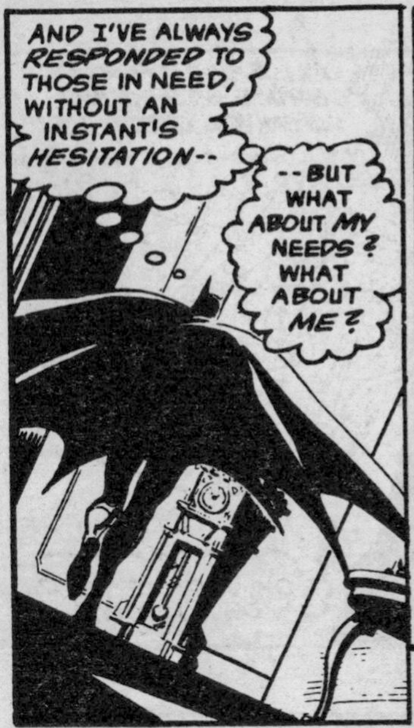
AND I'VE ALWAYS RESPONDED TO THOSE IN NEED, WITHOUT AN INSTANT'S HESITATION--
--BUT WHAT ABOUT MY NEEDS? WHAT ABOUT ME?

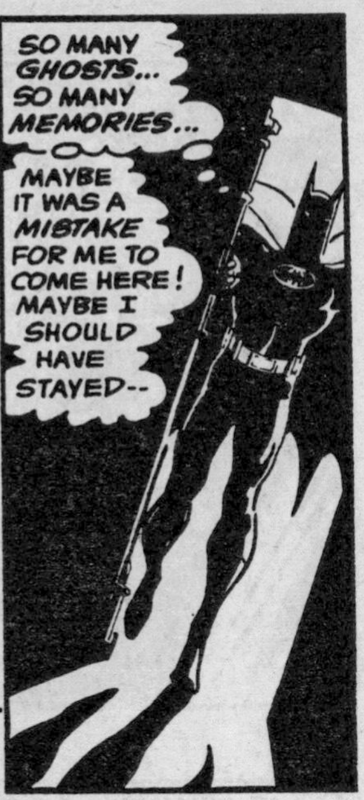
SO MANY GHOSTS... SO MANY MEMORIES...
MAYBE IT WAS A MISTAKE FOR ME TO COME HERE! MAYBE I SHOULD HAVE STAYED--

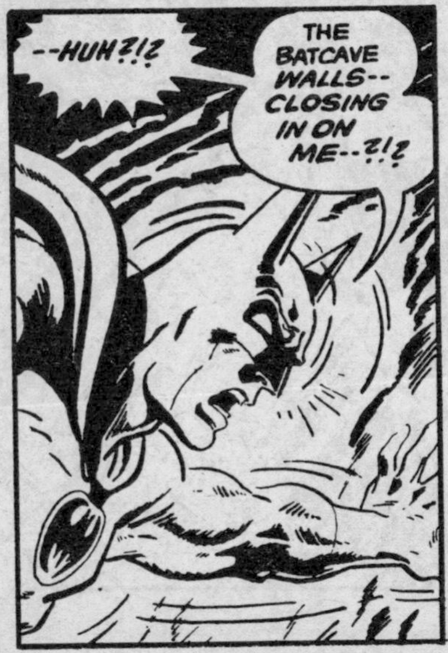
--HUH?!?
THE BATCAVE WALLS--CLOSING IN ON ME--?!?

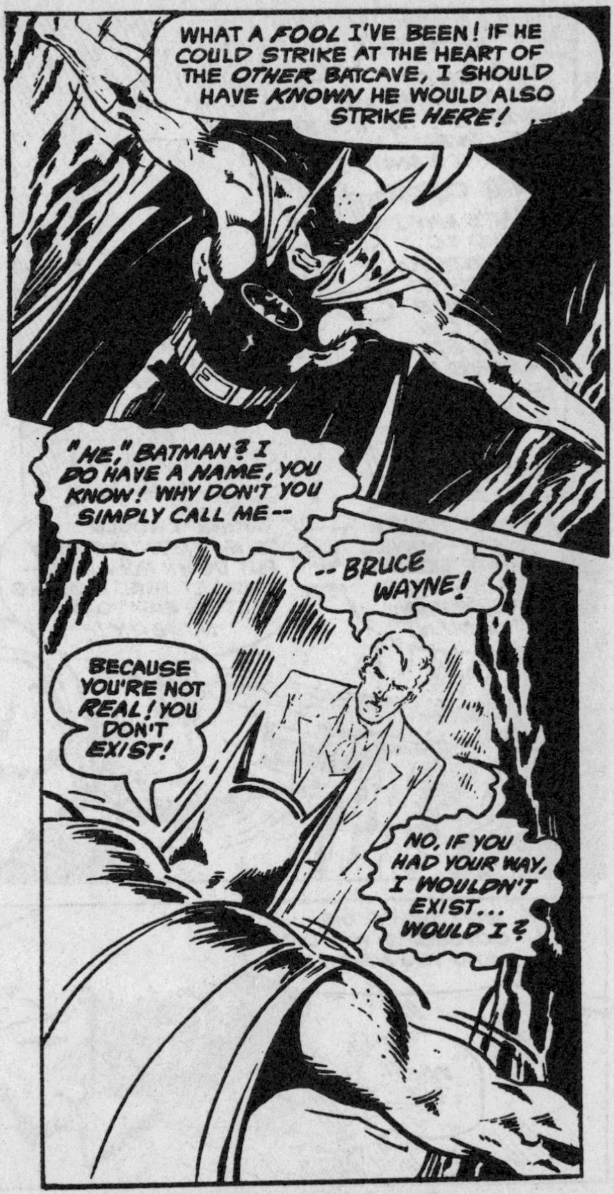
WHAT A FOOL I'VE BEEN! IF HE COULD STRIKE AT THE HEART OF THE OTHER BATCAVE, I SHOULD HAVE KNOWN HE WOULD ALSO STRIKE HERE!
"HE," BATMAN? I DO HAVE A NAME, YOU KNOW! WHY DON'T YOU SIMPLY CALL ME--
--BRUCE WAYNE!
BECAUSE YOU'RE NOT REAL! YOU DON'T EXIST!
NO, IF YOU HAD YOUR WAY, I WOULDN'T EXIST... WOULD I?

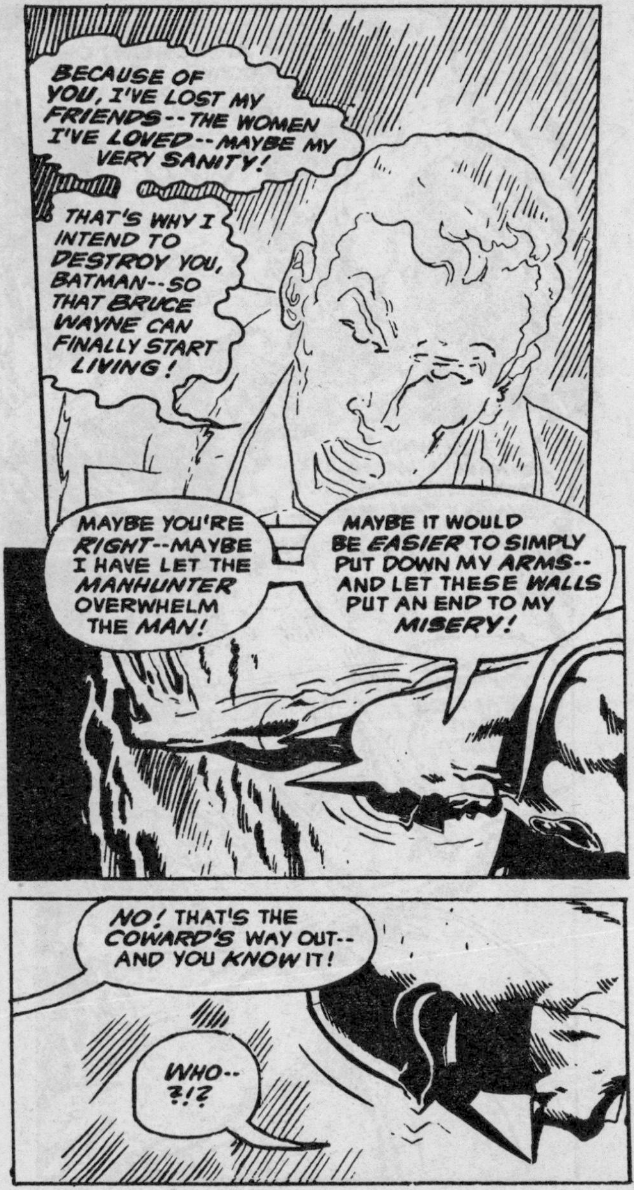
BECAUSE OF YOU, I'VE LOST MY FRIENDS--THE WOMEN I'VE LOVED--MAYBE MY VERY SANITY!
THAT'S WHY I INTEND TO DESTROY YOU, BATMAN--SO THAT BRUCE WAYNE CAN FINALLY START LIVING!
MAYBE YOU'RE RIGHT--MAYBE I HAVE LET THE MANHUNTER OVERWHELM THE MAN!
MAYBE IT WOULD BE EASIER TO SIMPLY PUT DOWN MY ARMS--AND LET THESE WALLS PUT AN END TO MY MISERY!
NO! THAT'S THE COWARD'S WAY OUT--AND YOU KNOW IT!
WHO--?!?

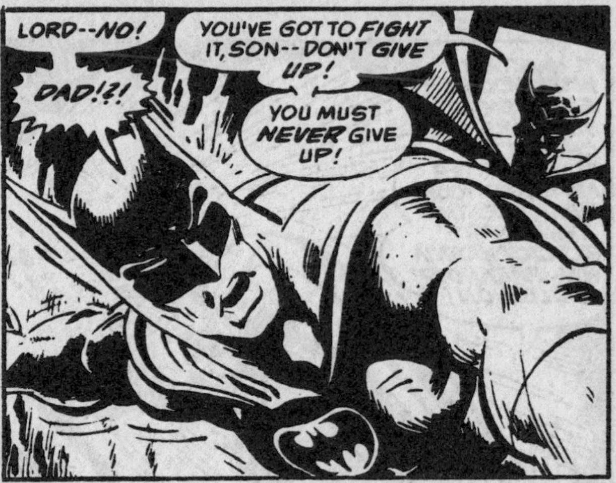
LORD--NO!
DAD!?!
YOU'VE GOT TO FIGHT IT, SON--DON'T GIVE UP!
YOU MUST NEVER GIVE UP!

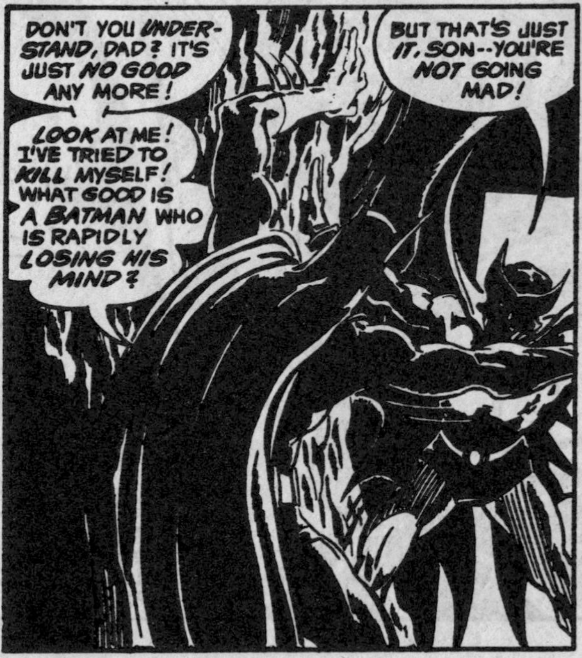
DON'T YOU UNDERSTAND, DAD? IT'S JUST NO GOOD ANY MORE!
LOOK AT ME! I'VE TRIED TO KILL MYSELF! WHAT GOOD IS A BATMAN WHO IS RAPIDLY LOSING HIS MIND?
BUT THAT'S JUST IT, SON--YOU'RE NOT GOING MAD!

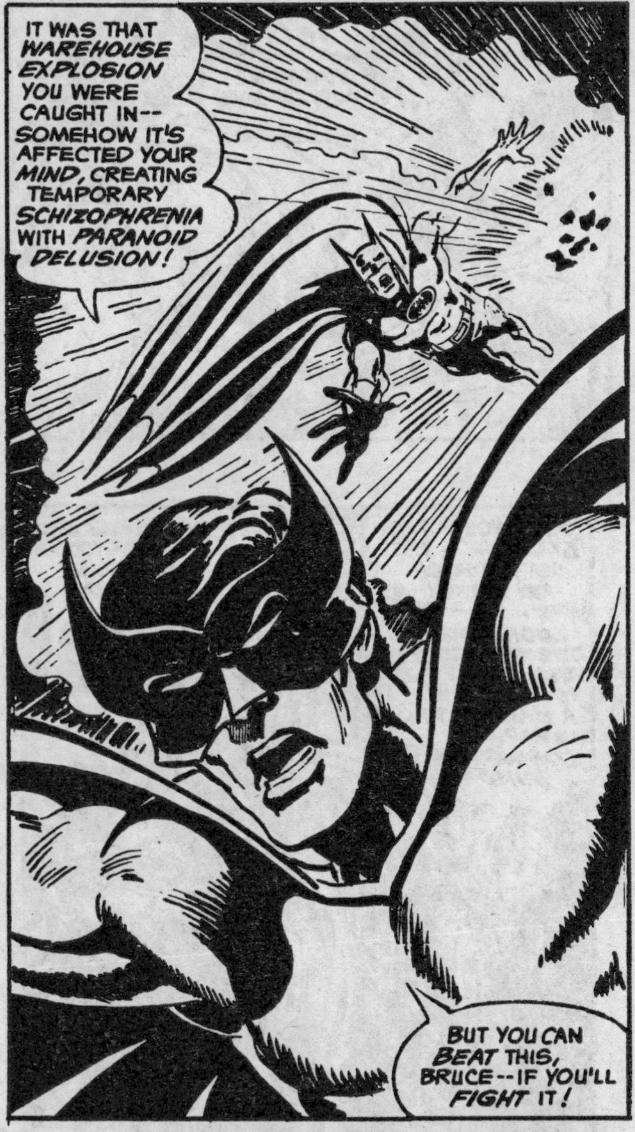
IT WAS THAT WAREHOUSE EXPLOSION YOU WERE CAUGHT IN-- SOMEHOW IT'S AFFECTED YOUR MIND, CREATING TEMPORARY SCHIZOPHRENIA WITH PARANOID DELUSION!
BUT YOU CAN BEAT THIS, BRUCE--IF YOU'LL FIGHT IT!

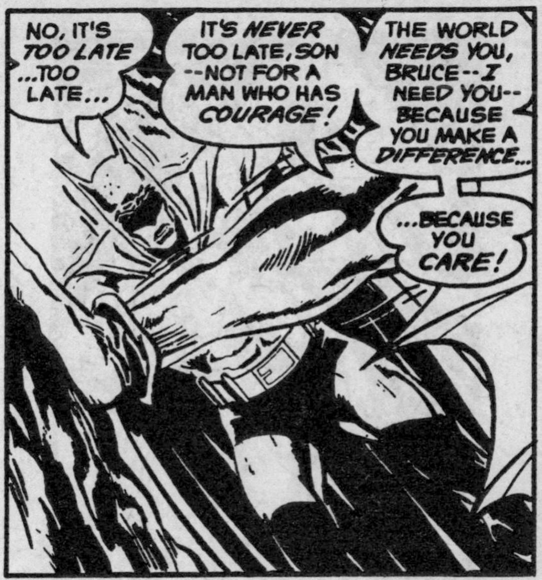
NO, IT'S TOO LATE ...TOO LATE...
IT'S NEVER TOO LATE, SON --NOT FOR A MAN WHO HAS COURAGE!
THE WORLD NEEDS YOU, BRUCE--I NEED YOU--BECAUSE YOU MAKE A DIFFERENCE...
...BECAUSE YOU CARE!

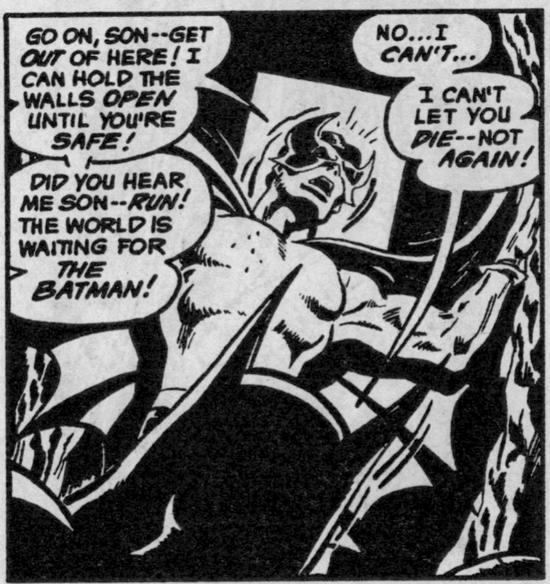
GO ON, SON--GET OUT OF HERE! I CAN HOLD THE WALLS OPEN UNTIL YOU'RE SAFE!
DID YOU HEAR ME SON--RUN! THE WORLD IS WAITING FOR THE BATMAN!
NO...I CAN'T...
I CAN'T LET YOU DIE--NOT AGAIN!

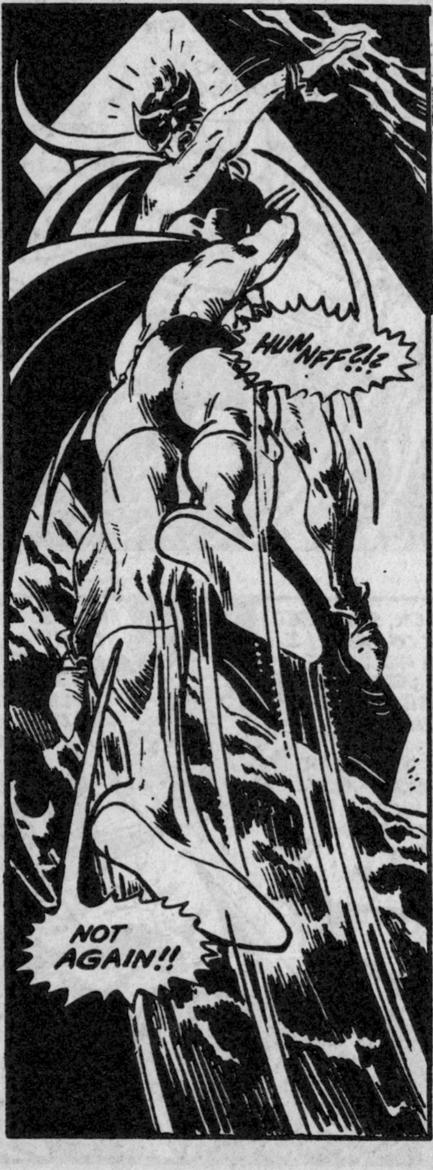
HUMNFF?!?
NOT AGAIN!!

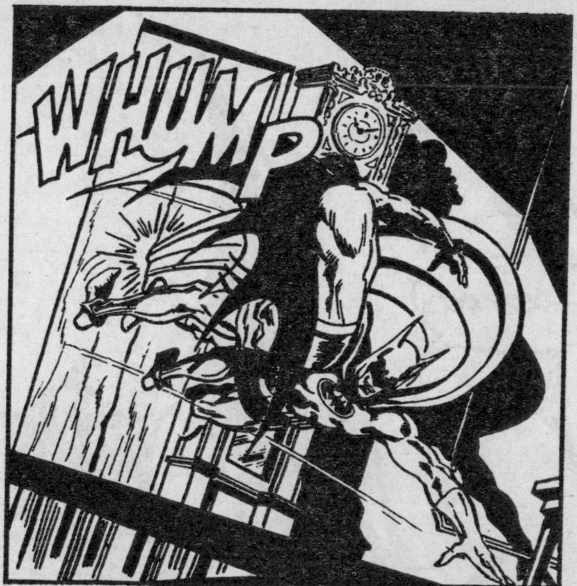
WHUMP

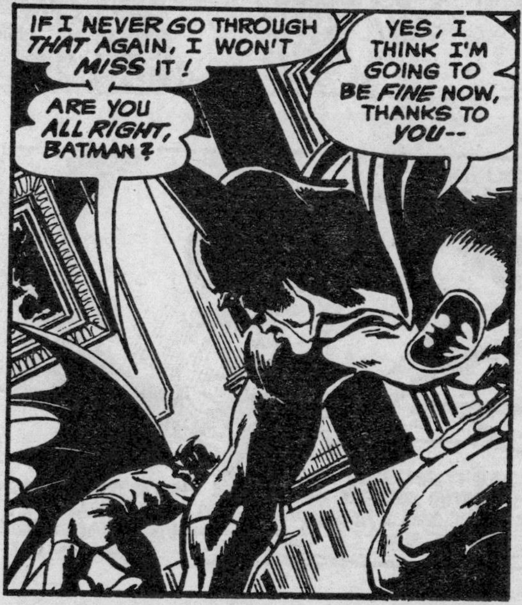
IF I NEVER GO THROUGH THAT AGAIN, I WON'T MISS IT!
ARE YOU ALL RIGHT, BATMAN?
YES, I THINK I'M GOING TO BE FINE NOW, THANKS TO YOU--

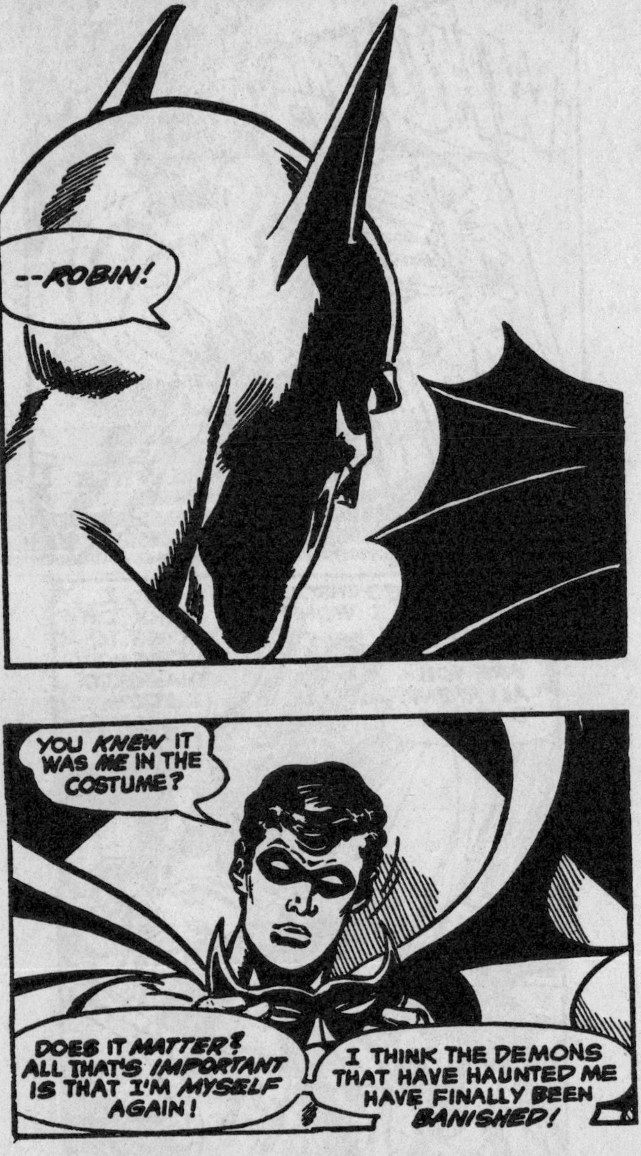
--ROBIN!
YOU KNEW IT WAS ME IN THE COSTUME?
DOES IT MATTER? ALL THAT'S IMPORTANT IS THAT I'M MYSELF AGAIN!
I THINK THE DEMONS THAT HAVE HAUNTED ME HAVE FINALLY BEEN BANISHED!

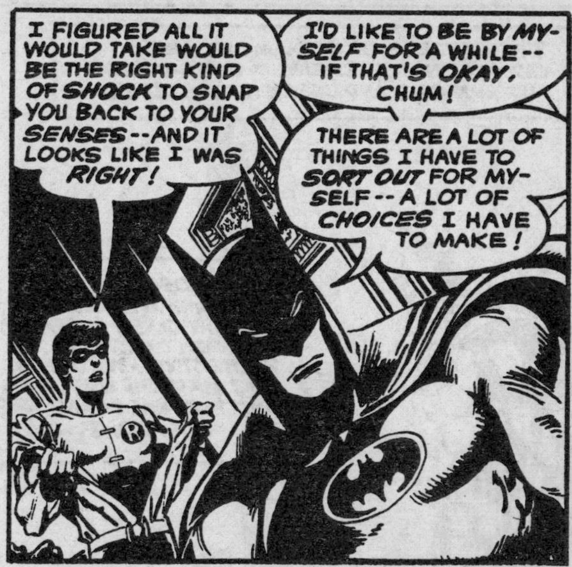
I FIGURED ALL IT WOULD TAKE WOULD BE THE RIGHT KIND OF SHOCK TO SNAP YOU BACK TO YOUR SENSES--AND IT LOOKS LIKE I WAS RIGHT!
I'D LIKE TO BE BY MYSELF FOR A WHILE--IF THAT'S OKAY, CHUM!
THERE ARE A LOT OF THINGS I HAVE TO SORT OUT FOR MYSELF--A LOT OF CHOICES I HAVE TO MAKE!

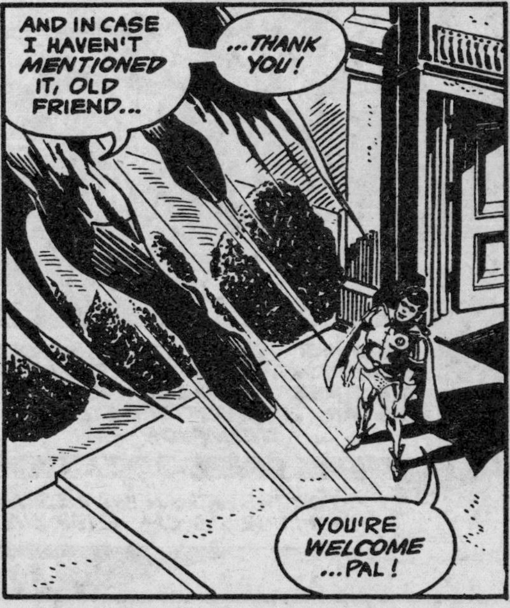
AND IN CASE I HAVEN'T MENTIONED IT, OLD FRIEND...
...THANK YOU!
YOU'RE WELCOME ...PAL!

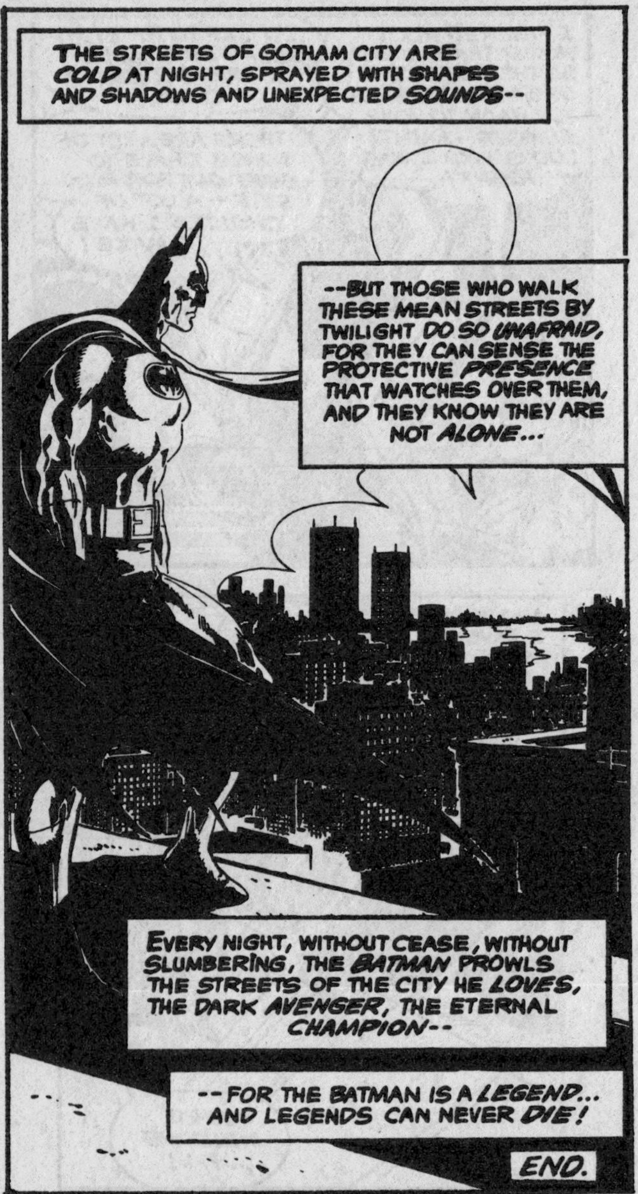
THE STREETS OF GOTHAM CITY ARE COLD AT NIGHT, SPRAYED WITH SHAPES AND SHADOWS AND UNEXPECTED SOUNDS--
--BUT THOSE WHO WALK THESE MEAN STREETS BY TWILIGHT DO SO UNAFRAID, FOR THEY CAN SENSE THE PROTECTIVE PRESENCE THAT WATCHES OVER THEM, AND THEY KNOW THEY ARE NOT ALONE...
EVERY NIGHT, WITHOUT CEASE, WITHOUT SLUMBERING, THE BATMAN PROWLS THE STREETS OF THE CITY HE LOVES, THE DARK AVENGER, THE ETERNAL CHAMPION--
--FOR THE BATMAN IS A LEGEND... AND LEGENDS CAN NEVER DIE!
END.